MW01097185

# REAL ESTATE
# IS THE
# GOLD
# IN YOUR FUTURE

## DEMPSEY J. TRAVIS

URBAN RESEARCH PRESS, INC.

840 E. 87TH ST. • CHICAGO, IL 60619

This publication is designed to provide accurate and authoritative information, not legal advice. Events and laws may change after publication.
The author and publisher specifically disclaim any liability, loss, or risk,
personal or otherwise, which is incurred as a consequence, directly or
indirectly, of the use and application of any of the contents of the work.
Before acting on any suggestion presented in this book, legal or other
professional assistance may be advisable.

Copyright © 1988 by Urban Research Press, Inc.
840 E. 87th Street, Chicago, Illinois 60619
All rights reserved
Printed in the United States of America
First Edition

**Library of Congress Cataloging-in-Publication Data**

Travis, Dempsey, 1920-
    Real estate is the gold in your future.

    Bibliography: p.
    Includes index.
    1. Real estate business.  2. Real estate
business—Case studies.  3. Real estate investment.
4. Real estate investment—Case studies.  I. Title.
HD1279.T3   1988          332.63'24          87-37177
ISBN: 0-941484-07-6

No part of this publication may be reproduced or transmitted in any
form or by any means, electronic or mechanical, including photocopy,
recording or any information storage and retrieval system, without permission in writing from the publisher.

# DEDICATION

*This book is dedicated to the late Mayor Harold Washington of Chicago, who died "riding in his saddle" at 1:30 p.m. Wednesday, November 25, 1987.*

*During his 4½ years in office, Mayor Washington pushed forward the greatest building boom in the Loop area since the big fire that all but destroyed Chicago's central business district 118 years ago.*

*Harold Washington will be remembered as a mayor of all the people of Chicago, a leader who impartially provided city services and public improvements throughout every one of Chicago's 50 political wards.*

# ACKNOWLEDGMENTS

First and foremost, I wish to express my gratitude and appreciation for the invaluable interviews given by my real estate clients. Their willingness to share their time and experiences made this work possible.

Ruby Davis, the senior researcher for my last three best-selling books has delivered again for my fourth. Thus, she validates me: a non-fiction writer whose work is not thoroughly researched and documented is not worth his salt.

Writing "Real Estate is the Gold in Your Future" would have taken a great deal longer to finish if it were not for my administrative assistant Catherine Jones, who doubles in brass as a copy editor and transcriber. She is the queen of proficiency in transcribing interviews from the cassette to the typed page.

Every writer has an editor who peeps over his or her shoulder. For this book, the person who performed that task was Dorothy Parr Riesen, who displayed both patience and skill in bringing the project to its final form.

It would be gross negligence on my part not to thank the National Association of Real Estate Board for the use of its extensive real estate library, which reportedly houses the largest collection of real estate books in America.

Incidentally, after 40 years of marriage, my wife Moselynne has resigned to the fact that I am going to spend the balance of my golden years with her as a writer-in-residence, producing at least one book a year.

# INTRODUCTION

"Real Estate is the Gold in Your Future" is a product of the author's 40 years of experience in an active and successful career as a real estate broker, real estate consultant and mortgage banker. This book is an affirmation of my conviction that any person willing to work hard and apply their God-given common sense to the task can make a fortune in real estate and, in turn, enjoy the fruits of the American dream.

The subject of real estate entrepreneurship is presented here in a unique format. Each chapter of the book is supported by an actual case study of individuals and families who have become wealthy by following my philosophy, which permeates this work.

The content and scope of coverage in this easily-read edition is not matched by any other how-to book on the market today, according to the real estate professionals who have read advance galleys. The reader will also observe that the work moves smoothly, intermixing the text with real-life business histories on how others have become successful. A comprehensive real estate glossary in the back of the book will aid readers who wish to broaden their real estate vocabulary.

"Real Estate is the Gold in Your Future" is 30 years overdue because it has been that long since my colleagues and clients started asking me to put my real estate ideas and experiences in writing. Now that it's completed, I sincerely hope I have not disappointed those who insisted that I have something to contribute. As in everything I have accomplished, I gave this effort my best.

**Dempsey J. Travis**
Chicago, Illinois

# TABLE OF CONTENTS

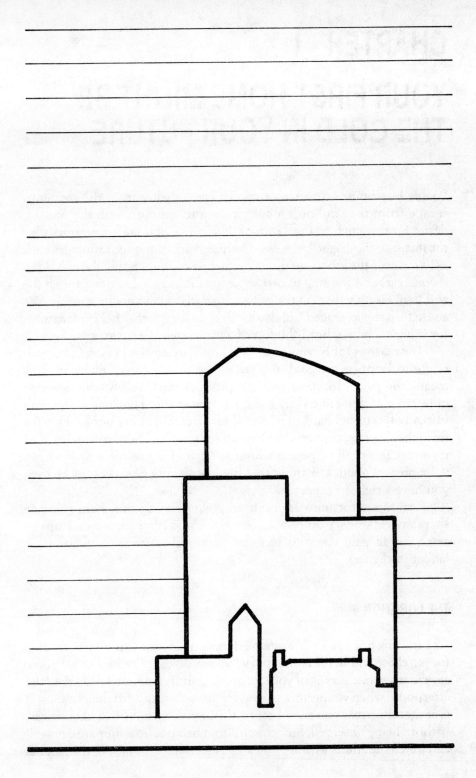

# CHAPTER I

# YOUR FIRST HOME MIGHT BE THE GOLD IN YOUR FUTURE

People buy houses for many reasons: basic shelter from the elements, escape from the landlord, a compulsion to keep up with the Smiths, desire for the amenities and economic security of home ownership, plus the image of the "right" address. There also are economic rationales such as living near the job to cut down on fuel costs, eliminating the need for a second car, and wanting to own a piece of America. Let's not forget the children. Getting them in the right school district is very important. We could fill a single-spaced laundry list 9½ feet long with other explanations for buying a home, but I think we have covered the basic ones.

The reasons for buying your first home are always personal, but real estate will not be the gold in your future if you don't buy right. This means the price, location and the product must fulfill your security objectives. If you fail to buy right, the house could become your tomb instead of a springboard to financial security. If you are not looking for financial security, then this book is not for you. You need read no further if you are among those people who are prepared to go to your graves from your present abodes or think that life has already given you more than you have a right to expect.

Real estate fortunes are built on great expectations. I am going to share my experience on how to buy right, and offer some other tips to assist you in your rise to success by using real estate as a rung on your ladder to the top.


## THE LOCATION

As a starting point, we will examine the site of a home you are considering for purchase within the context of its surroundings. The best time to take a socioeconomic survey of your future neighbors is about 3 o'clock in the afternoon, when youngsters are leaving school enroute to their homes. It is at that time that you can observe, through the windshield of your car, without being observed, how the children behave, how they are dressed, and watch the adults who are waiting to meet them. If some of the parents are in cars, the model and maintenance of their ride may give some clue of whether they have arrived socially or are just striving to make ends meet. Don't forget to check out the people who reside in the houses on both sides of the property that you are interested in buying. Who are they? What kinds of jobs do they have? How many children do they have? Are they bunking or living?

Other neighborhood telltale signs you should watch for are the alleys and back yards. Are the alleys kept broom clean? Are the backyard lawns manicured or littered with discarded objects? Is there a pride of ownership displayed throughout the neighborhood? If the answer is yes, then you are prepared to take the next step.

## THE SUBJECT PROPERTY

Does the property have curb appeal? Is it the type of house you would be proud to point out and say to your boss or best friend, "That's my place!"? Does the house conform to the general trend in the area, both in design and price? Will it be easy to sell in the event you are transferred or lose your job?

One of the worst decisions you can make is to buy a two-bedroom, one-bath 800-square-foot house in an area where the average home is 1,600 square feet with three bedrooms, two full baths, a powder room and crowned with a large, rectangular living room adjoined by a spacious dining room that will accommodate 20 seated guests, plus a large kitchen and paneled recreation room.

The two-bedroom house is definitely non-conforming. However, the house may appeal to you because you are not financially able to buy a larger place in the neighborhood. Hence, your desire to get into a good location with the right address can be an overwhelming factor in your decision to buy.

The purchase of such a small home by a young couple on a fast career track might prove to be a very smart move in the short run, smarter than buying an oversized white elephant to carry on their backs 16 hours a day and sleep with eight hours every night. And that is exactly what you do when you bite off more house than you can financially afford to digest. I have seen couples under 35 years old who are figuratively hunched over like most centenarians as a result of carrying heavy mortgages and other ancillary housing expenses on their financially-weak backs.

Being overloaded with debt is not restricted to families making $50,000 or less. During the 20 years I have served on loan committees for several lending institutions, I have seen thousands of balance sheets of individuals who earn as much as $800,000 per year, plus bonuses, yet were inflicted with a virus that caused them to spend more than they earned. The affliction usually is caused by an insatiable desire to stay ahead of the Jones' or keep up with the O'Malleys. I have been in mansions with 20 or more rooms where the owners could not afford to heat and furnish anything above the first floor, and yet, in an effort to keep up a good home front, his and her Mercedes, plus a Rolls-Royce for show, are parked in their horseshoe-shaped driveway. There is no question in my mind that those homes were tombs for the occupants.

## RATING THE CONSTRUCTION

In my 40 years of experience in the real estate business, I have never seen a cheaply built home with quality equipment. If you inspect a house and find a quality name-brand heating plant, good plumbing, 220 wiring and top-of-the-line bath fixtures, you can almost be certain that that portion of the house that is behind the dry or plastered walls is of the same quality.

On the other hand, I have seen houses riddled with poor workmanship and poor design camouflaged with superior decorating jobs and bathroom fixtures that would complement Nancy Reagan's White House. This is the type of housing fraud that the late and great jazz musician Louis Jordan had in mind when he wrote a song called: "Beware." Since the average lay real estate buyer or inexperienced real estate broker would not be able to discern such coverups, it's advisable to consult a professional real estate broker, and in some cases, a building inspector, along with an appraiser.

A reliable real estate broker will point out that the stains on the basement floor or on the lower section of the wall that look like dried milk could indicate water leakage of long duration, or a possible sewer problem. If the basement walls or floors have recently been painted, beware! A good broker would also advise you cracks are common in the foundation of older houses and in themselves may be nothing to be alarmed about. However, if the house is fairly new, the broker should warn you that the cracks could indicate a very serious problem. Moreover, if a house is 30 or more years old, and has not had a second roofing, the chances of your replacing the roof in one to three years are excellent. You should also be aware of old wiring because electrical appliances are major investments in modern homes. Before 1940, even the more luxurious homes featured only a radio, record player, clock and refrigerator. The amperage needed in the old days was usually about 30.

Today, the amperage must be at least 60 or better to meet the building codes. Therefore, in calculating the price in your offer to buy, consider the fact that new wiring could very well cost anywhere from $2,000 to $10,000, depending on the size of the house.

Old houses have old plumbing. In many instances, the homes have an iron plumbing system that may be filled with lime, which has caused the pipes to corrode over a long period of time. In turn, this reduces the water pressure, like fatty tissues in the human arteries that cause a reduction in the flow of blood to the heart and leads to eventual blockage. In some of the better-constructed old buildings, you will find copper plumbing which does not corrode and will last as long as the building stands. A quick on-site test is to flush the toilet and turn on the water in both the sink and the tub simultaneously to measure the water pressure coming through the system.

Beware of black stains on the walls near heating vents because they signal that the furnace is giving off smoke and may have to be replaced within months after you take possession of the property. Requesting copies of the utility bills for a 24-month period will give you some indication of the efficiency of the furnace as well as the insulation of the building. But heating bills won't reveal a totally accurate picture for your projected personal needs because there are many human variables to be considered. Keep in mind some people are cold-natured, others are hot in 60-degree temperatures, and for very practical reasons, some put on sweaters and long underwear and cut the thermostat down.

A recent survey compared utility bills of similar-sized homes and 5,000 apartment units occupied by various ethnic groups in different sections of a large metropolitan area. The study showed that elderly people usually like temperatures 10 to 15 degrees higher than people under 60 years of age. Heat requirements also varied among ethnic groups. Blacks, Hispanics, and Asians generally preferred higher temperatures than most northern Europeans feel are comfortable. This data underscores the many subtle factors experienced brokers deal with daily, but might be lost to amateurs in the field.

## PRICING THE HOME

Pricing a property is subject to market conditions of supply and demand, and other economic factors as availability of money and the prevailing mortgage interest rates. The percentage of Americans who own homes has been declining at a steady rate since the late 1970s after 35 years of increases. Homes are becoming less affordable because prices have risen much faster than incomes. According to the Bureau of Census, the median family income increased only 183 percent in the last 16 years, whereas the median home price rose by 249 percent.

In spite of these statistics, it's my opinion that owning a home is still an achievable dream if the buyer lowers his sights. Although pricing is not an exact science, the rule of thumb for determining the price of a particular piece of property is to study the recent sales of comparable properties in the same general area. Such a survey puts you in the right ballpark for determining the market price because you will have used the same formula that the bank appraiser and the professional realtor employed. If a house is worth $65,000 but priced at $85,000, the owner is asking for trouble.

The location of the house and its square footage is very important in determining the price. In other words, a house with 800 square feet certainly couldn't have the same value as one with 1,600 square feet if the properties are located in the same general area. You should also take into consideration the number of rooms, whether the kitchen and baths are modernized, and the age of the property. Although a property may be chronologically 90 years old, if it has been modernized, it could have an effective life extension of 50 years or more.

Many buyers overlook the fact that a professional broker will not waste time on listing a property at an unreasonably high price. Unrealistic prices makes brokering more difficult, if not impossible. Moreover, an incorrectly listed property will stay on the market for an extended period of time. Advertising and showing an overappraised property is simply not economical.

We must take into consideration the experience and the reputation of the brokers we use because he or she can be a real factor in protecting both the buyer and seller against making serious mistakes in buying or selling a home. An unsupervised neophyte salesperson can create problems for the broker, the buyer and the seller. It pays to ask real estate salespersons how long they have been in the business, and what they have sold and for whom in the past 90 days. Check out the references. I know that young salespeople like young physicians must practice on someone; I maintain that the somebody that they practice on has to be somebody else, not me.

A seasoned real estate person is aware that virtually all Americans of substantial economic means are real estate investors and homeowners, and that you, too, should be making your move in real estate. Ninety percent of Americans in the upper economic class own a home and 4 percent own an apartment or condominium, according to a recent Louis Harris & Associates poll, conducted by the National Opinion Research

Organization. Keep in mind that you cannot win a race unless you enter it.

The poll, "A Success in America: A Study of the Upper Affluent," is based on 500 interviews with people who have a net worth of $500,000, excluding primary residence, or a minimum annual income of $100,000. Although $100,000 may sound like all of the money in the world, it's not. In my business, I have seen many public school teachers with net worths that exceeded $500,000.

It's back to the old adage, it is not what you make but what you do with what you have made. Therefore, I say to the brave and stouthearted souls: Take a chance. You may discover that $100,000 is merely a small shadow on the real estate empire that is the gold in your future.

## MORTGAGING REAL ESTATE

Once you sign the contract, the real work of finding a mortgage company or bank willing to tailor a mortgage to fit your needs begins. In most instances, the real estate broker, whose fingers should be on the pulse of the mortgage market, can save you numerous calls and footsteps by simply referring you to the mortgagee or the lender known to be interested in making loans in your particular area.

As strange as it may seem, some buyers reject the opportunity of letting the broker do the work and attempt to do it themselves. These buyers usually say that somebody has promised to make them a dream mortgage just as soon as they find a house that they are interested in buying, and that their special angel will make a 95 percent loan when the prevailing market is 80 percent. The broker who permits this kind of nonsense from a buyer can lose four to six weeks before the money explorer discovers that the banking friend will not back up the promise of a fountain of money available for the asking.

If a hard-nosed buyer insists on finding the mortgage, here is an intelligent approach that is easy to follow. First, check the mortgage charts that appear in the Friday or Sunday editions of most metropolitan newspapers throughout the United States. These list all of the banks and savings and loan institutions making mortgages in a given area, and also indicate the interest spread charged for various types of buildings, plus the points needed to close the deal. By using the comparative mortgage chart, some buyers have been able to successfully set up and negotiate their own mortgage package. However, since procuring a mortgage is in the broker's court, it's to your advantage to let the broker earn his or her keep by bringing you and the mortgagee together, and in the process save a lot of money and time. The broker offers you the following services without charge.

- A broker who is in constant contact with various lenders can arrange with a lending institution to set up an appointment for a particular buyer, and get that buyer favorable treatment. This is particularly true if the broker does an extensive amount of business with a particular savings and loan association or bank and has a good track record for recommending qualified buyers.
- Although the broker is not on the bank's payroll, he or she actually functions as a bird dog and as a lifeline for the bank. Most of the loans made by banking institutions are created as a result of sales that were put together by some broker. The real estate person is the key to the equation. It's in the broker's interest to see that the deal closes. Remember, the broker does not get paid until the transaction has been completed. Be assured a broker is not going to recommend that you see an unfriendly banker.
- The broker understands the various types of mortgages that are available in the various shops. For example, the most desirable mortgage, in my opinion, is what we call a fixed-rate mortgage. A fixed-rate mortgage is one where you pay the same interest rate throughout the life of the mortgage with an option to prepay without penalty. With fixed-rate mortgages, I recommend that you get the very longest payback period possible, say 30 or 40 years. Keep in mind you have the perogative to pay off the loan as quickly as you choose. Double the payments if you can or make an extra payment each year. In other words, if every year you would make 13 payments instead of 12, you save a lot of interest.

Here's an example of the benefits:

Assume you have a 10.75 percent, 30-year fixed-rate mortgage for $80,000 and your monthly payments are $746.79. Your total payments on the principal and interest at the end of the period would be $268,842.63. However, by simply adding $1,000 to your regular monthly payment once a year, you reduce the amortization period of the mortgage from 30 years to 19 years and one month, and you save $80,169.21 in interest.

A long-term mortgage with fast acceleration privileges is a prudent buy. Some people might say, "No, I don't want a 30-year mortgage, that's too long. I am 70 years old and I don't expect to live more than 10 years." That's not the point. The point is you could very well get sick in the interim and a 10-year mortgage might work a hardship on your budget, whereas the 30-year mortgage will enable you to have a lower monthly fixed budget.

Remember, you can reduce the pay period of a mortgage without permission, but you cannot extend a mortgage without going through a lot of bureaucratic grief, and chances are you still will lose. If you keep that in mind, you will always try to get as long a period as possible to amortize the loan.

A relatively new consumer product is on the block. Called the adjustable rate mortgage, or ARM, it has a clause that enables lending institutions to increase the interest rate on the mortgage note annually, semiannually and in some cases, quarterly. The annual cap is 2 percent and the life cap of the mortgage is 6 percent. There are institutions that make adjustable mortgages on commercial property; that is, six apartment units or more that change the interest on your loan as frequently as the treasury bill or prime rate changes. There have been instances when the prime rate has changed as often as four times in two months and there was no cap because it was a commercial loan. In contrast, on residential properties, you can start off with an 8½ percent ARM loan. The 6 percent life cap on the mortgage can carry you up to 14½ percent within three years.

However, the bank cannot capriciously raise your rate because the ARM rates are tied to a financial index that moves in the direction of the treasury bills, Government National Mortgage Association (GNMA) bonds, and money market fund rates. If the index falls, the ARM rates are adjusted downward. My position on ARM mortgages is that if the lending institutions want to obligate you to take an ARM, they might as well take your leg and your head because you are theirs. ARM mortgages are dangerous because they shift the risk to the borrower from the lender. Beware!

A good product, if you can get it, is an assumable mortgage. An assumable mortgage means that the person selling the building has a mortgage on it with a high enough principal balance to meet your affordable down payment. Another plus for assumables is the fact that you don't have to pay additional points, which could be several thousand dollars, and you are probably getting a favorable interest rate inasmuch as the mortgage was made at an earlier period.

On the other hand, I can think of some individuals who assumed mortgages only to find out after the deal is closed that there was a non-assumable clause in the mortgage. This means that the mortgagee has the right to call for the payment of the entire balance at once and if it is not forthcoming, the lender could foreclose. These tragedies would not happen if some overworked lawyer had checked out the mortgage document before permitting a client to enter into the contract.

An old instrument that is frequently used is a purchase money mortgage, when the seller makes the mortgage. For example, your broker may introduce you to a seller who does not need cash immediately and agrees to let you pay $10,000 down on a $60,000 deal with the understanding that the seller will hold a $50,000 purchase money mortgage at a fixed interest rate for a period of 10, 15, or 20 years.

The purchase money mortgage is a loan made in heaven because you don't have the usual expenses found in the open market. Moreover, seller financing is quick since you can close a deal within 10 days to two weeks, or as soon as you can bring title down, as opposed to the six- to eight-week period that is usually required to close out when working through a mortgage banker or savings and loan institution.

Another financing mechanism, the wraparound mortgage, is a commercial product of the '60s. Originally used on large transactions, meaning $1 million to $10 million commercial real estate deals, it has been adopted in the residential market. The wraparound works as follows:

Assume you find a house for sale at $100,000, and you agree to pay $20,000 down. There is a mortgage on the building for $70,000. There is a $10,000 gap between your down payment and the outstanding assumable mortgage. The seller agrees to take a second mortgage, which, in effect, is wrapped around the first since you are paying two rates. The rates are probably 12 percent on the second mortgage that the seller is holding and maybe 10 percent on the first mortgage held by the lender. This kind of financing arrangement is what I call icing on the cake because there are no origination fees to be paid. Moreover, there is no waiting time involved in processing and closing the deal.

## VA LOANS: TRIPLE-A RATED

All war veterans who were honorably discharged from the military service qualify to receive a Veterans Administration (VA) mortgage certificate. Contrary to public opinion, the Veterans Administration does not make mortgages. It simply insures the mortgage. With such insurance, most lenders consider VA loans triple-A in that the lender's money is at a minimum amount of risk. Veterans Administration financing, created for returning veterans of World War II, has enabled millions of veterans to buy homes with a 0 to 5 percent down payment. Veterans can buy a house worth more than $100,000 in some geographic locations, with no cash required at all if they find a friendly seller who is willing to pay the points and closing costs.

Moreover, the Veterans Administration has what is called an alternative repayment plan, which will reduce the veteran's mortgage payments during the early years when income is low and increase gradually as the borrower becomes more financially stabilized. This Graduated Payment Mortgage (GPM) is available to all qualified veterans who choose this option, but unfortunately, most veterans are not aware that the option exists. Moreover, millions of World War II veterans have never used their VA certificates.

The Graduated Payment Mortgage is particularly useful to a first-time buyer because it calls for very small monthly payments in the early years of the loan when the buyer's earning power may be low but growing. The VA lending manual indicates that the first-year payment is even lower than on a traditional VA fixed-rate loan. The effective payment rate in the GPM program during the first year is approximately 2.7 percent below that of a VA fixed-rate loan. However, the payments increase gradually through the first five years and then level out to a fixed constant for the balance of the 30-year amortization period.

Although the GPM program decreases the buyer's monthly payments and increases the ability to qualify, it requires more cash than the regular VA loan, approximately 7 percent of the sale price as a down payment. Major incentives for a veteran or GI to purchase are the easier conditions in qualifying for the programs and lower monthly mortgage payments, sometimes approximately 23 percent less than they would be ordinarily.

In contrast to the conventional mortgage loans, VA mortgages are assumable; that is, they do not have due-on-sale clauses. As we discussed earlier, the due-on-sale clause prevents the home buyer from allowing another buyer, veteran or otherwise, to assume a loan without the written consent of the original mortgage lender.

Another advantage of the VA loan over the more conventional loan is that even when conventional loans are assumable, the lender still may have the option of approving the ownership transfer and require the new buyer to pay points or closing costs and a higher interest rate. In my opinion, a VA loan is an offer that no veteran should refuse.

## FHA LOANS

Federal Housing Administration insured loans are for any U.S. residents 18 years or older. The FHA program carries a very low down payment requirement. That is 3 percent on the first $25,000 of value and closing costs, and 5 percent on the remainder, the remainder meaning that above the first $25,000. The FHA also has a GPM that works very much like the Veterans Administration's, starting the buyer out with lower initial interest rates. Moreover, the FHA offers five different GPM plans, each with different monthly payments, so chances are that buyers with reasonably good credit can find a plan that's tailored to their needs. Again, the GPM plan requires the buyer to make a higher equity commitment than would be made under the regular program.

The FHA also has a plan that I call the family plan. It's better known as equity sharing. A buyer who is short on cash and unable to meet high monthly payments is permitted to couple up with a relative or friend in order to qualify for a mortgage. Each person will own a percentage of the house and make the mortgage payment based on their equity interest. In the event the dwelling is occupied by only one of the investors, the non-occupant is entitled to rent for a pro rata share of equity.

In the equity program, the buyers frequently are able to negotiate a loan of up to 97 percent of the value plus closing costs providing the premises are occupied by at least one of the equity participants. The occupancy feature reduces the amount of money needed to close the real estate deal.

Federal, state and city home buying programs have opened hundreds of doors that make it possible for any employed person with good credit to become a homeowner. Therefore, you should capture the present opportunities to become a property owner. Land, unlike cars and other consumable items, does not roll off an assembly line. It's not likely that we will produce any more land. Therefore, I advise you to get your piece of property today with the realization that real estate is the gold in your future.

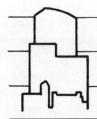

# The Diary of Roberta Diamond:
## A Homebuyer with a System*

### "My real estate investment has given me a better return than my stock portfolio."

I was born in Philadelphia in 1957. My father was a school custodian and my stepmother is a domestic. I received my bachelor's degree in communications at Temple University. I have two younger sisters and one older brother who are struggling to complete college. My family has always rented; we basically are the working poor.

I came to Chicago because I was hired by a major media outlet that had been scouting for a black person with my skills.

I didn't buy a house for several years after relocating to Chicago because I felt that I might move to New York or Los Angeles, due to the nature of the business. My initial abode in Chicago was located in the Lincoln Park area because I was told by a fellow employee that was the best place to live if I wanted to be close to the job and close to transportation. At first I didn't know Lincoln Park from Lincolnwood or South Shore from Hyde Park.

I was very comfortable in my first apartment, which was in a two-flat plus one building. It was called an English basement, or garden apartment. I paid $450 per month rent. The young white couple who owned this building had purchased it for $250,000 and continued to invest money on improvements. I watched what

---

*These case histories are documented; only the names were changed to protect the confidentiality of the real estate consultant-client relationship.

they were doing for about two years, and also noticed that property values in the Lincoln Park area were continually going up. I said to myself it was time to start looking for a place to buy for Roberta Diamond.

Before I started looking seriously, I bought a small tape recorder and a notebook that I always carried with me. Real estate people hated to see me coming because they intuitively knew I was going to ask lots of questions and record or write down their responses. Several objected to me using a tape recorder. Maybe they thought I was working as an investigator for the Federal Bureau of Investigation or the Internal Revenue department. Obviously, I wasn't working for either but I have always been very meticulous and organized in everything I do, including looking for real estate.

I knew exactly the kind of real estate I wanted to buy. I was making $53,000 a year and I was a good saver. I didn't want to buy a piece of property that would make me house poor because I still wanted to travel and do things. I sought property with the determination of a Sherlock Holmes and for an entire year wrote detailed notes on everything that I had seen.

In the pursuit of property leads, I would get the Sunday *Chicago Tribune* and *Chicago Sun-Times* on Saturday afternoon as soon as they came out and go through the real estate section, clipping everything that interested me by street and price range. I didn't want to spend more than 1½ times my annual income, although I knew that the bank qualifying ceiling was 2½ times my annual income.

Real estate agents frequently encouraged me to look at properties in price ranges as high as $125,000. I turned deaf ears to their suggestions, although my salary could support a $100,000 plus mortgage.

I seemed to run real estate men up the walls when I questioned them via telephone: What's the plumbing system like? Does the building have 220 electrical service? Does each apartment in the building have separate utilities? What is the construction—is it frame, brick or stucco? I talked to so many real estate people that I began to sound like one.

I began to act like a professional real estate agent when I bought a map of the city and a yellow magic marker and started highlighting housing patterns based upon the newspaper ads. I drove through the sections I had marked and took copious notes on areas where rehabbing was taking place.

Weather permitting, I would spend as much as 14 hours a week looking. Maybe I'd spend six hours on Saturday, six hours on Sunday and a couple of more hours whenever I could steal the time. I noticed that the housing movement was toward the north and northwest. Both appeared to be very ripe for buying and holding real property.

When I drove around, I'd make it a point to stop at the neighborhood hardware store. When a neighborhood is about to turn over, there's always a lot of business going on at the hardware store. They do a brisk business when the neighborhood is being upgraded, selling all kinds of things other than light bulbs and fuses. Hot sellers were Weber grills, backyard ornaments, and what I call cutefication items, those cute little things that yuppies and buppies love.

My tours gave me a sense of housing demographics. I am particularly concerned and careful about where I live because I am single and don't have any family here. I didn't really know anything about buying a house, and had to be extraordinarily careful about what I bought. I didn't want to buy something that would turn into a second job. I didn't want to go into a house, roll up my sleeves, and start ripping walls down, upgrading the electrical systems and replacing the plumbing and things like that. I wanted to make sure that I could live with and live in what I bought.

The day finally arrived when I found the place that sounded like exactly what I wanted in the *Chicago Reader*. The property was being sold by the owner, a Chicago fireman. He evidently had a lot of free time and money because he would buy buildings, rehab them and repeat that cycle. When I say rehab I don't mean adding a fireplace, a new sink and things like that. He basically would put up new dry walls, upgrade the electrical system, upgrade the plumbing, and then sell the places.

The fireman owned several properties in the Lakeview area, two of them next door to each other. One he maintained for himself because he had to have a city address, but he didn't actually live there. He was asking $79,900 for the two-flat that I was interested in. It had a back yard and front yard, but no garage.

On my first walk through the fireman's building, I liked it. My initial offer of $65,000 was ridiculous, and we slowly worked our way up to $74,000. The year was 1984 and the interest rates were about 12½ percent. I decided I would only put 5 percent down, and the savings and loan association made me take out a PMI mortgage insurance. It had to reinsure 15 percent and limit their exposure to an 80 percent mortgage.

I could have made a larger down payment but I didn't want to tie my money up in a building. I sleep better when I have a healthy bank account. I didn't see the advantage of putting the money in a building if I could have $10,000 in the bank and get a fairly decent interest rate on a CD or Money Market Fund. Moreover, I knew I could afford the monthly payments and I do have some stocks and some municipal bonds. But by and large, the bulk of my money is in a bank account. I am from the old school, a conservative investor.

At this point, the author and Roberta Diamond part company because I don't believe in high leverage in purchasing a home unless it is absolutely necessary. Having money in a bank account that is paying 6½ percent interest while you are paying 12 percent to a mortgage lender is counterproductive, to say the least. Ms. Diamond continues:

In the three years that I have had the house, I had a two-car garage built, with an electrical eye installed. I paid $700 for a sun deck over the back porch, hiring a carpenter who charged $15 an hour. He goes out, buys the lumber, brings the receipt back and I pay him for the lumber and for his labor. I had the walls painted and the floor stripped. Polyurethane on the floors makes them shine like mirrors. There is no wax and no worry.

In the past three years, I have noticed there's a lot of rehabbing going on in my area. A house across the street from me sold for $279,000 last spring. The high price of that house lit a bulb in my head. I pulled out my city map and started tracking how people were moving from Lincoln Park to Lakeview. It occurred to me that my neighborhood was becoming too expensive for me to think about buying another building. Therefore, I concluded that it was time to sell. When I bought my building, the average building in the area was selling for $100,000. The same properties are selling for $190,000 to $250,000 in 1987. Moreover, I noticed in the paper that a frame building in my block was being advertised for sale. It was a burned-out frame and they were asking $125,000 for it.

I immediately decided to put my property up for sale. I advertised it for $164,000, which is more than twice what I paid for it three years earlier. The first day the ad appeared, I received a call on my answering machine from a real estate agent who left a message that I was listing my house too low. In spite of what she says, I'm going ahead and selling it for $164,000 because, as I said, the neighborhood is getting too expensive and it is also getting too congested. I expect to make $80,000 plus in profit and move to Oak Park.

I'm tired of the Lakeview lifestyle, so I'm looking for a nice house out in the 'burbs. I have my eye on a Victorian building that I particularly like that I can pick up for $123,000. It has four bedrooms, a two-car garage, woodburning fireplace. It has already been cutified and I will have plenty of space where I can entertain people, in addition to room for privacy. The 700-square-foot apartment in which I'm presently living is too small for a lady who plans to get married some day, and have at least two children and a dog.

Real estate is the way to go. I have invested more money in the stock market than in real estate and received less return. My smaller real estate investment made more money.

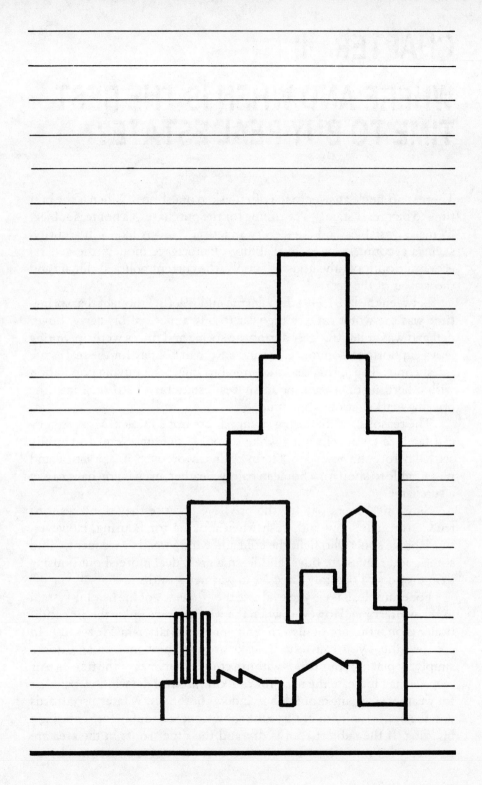

# CHAPTER II

# WHERE AND WHEN IS THE BEST TIME TO BUY REAL ESTATE?

There is no single answer to the often-asked question, "When is the best time to buy real estate?" The timing for the purchase of a home is subject to many variables and some very practical reasons like: job security, savings account balance, availability of mortgage money, the general economic outlook, the housing supply, the current political climate and the season of the year.

Between the late 1940s through the mid-1960s, I thought that spring-time was the worst time of the year to buy a piece of property. Buyer demand was at its strongest during the spring and prices were up. Spring was a euphoric season for sellers and a Roman holiday for the real estate salespeople. The spring season seemed to inject the buying population with a herd instinct, causing many real estate buyers to rush into the housing market at the same time.

The reasons for the spring stampede are not complex. Most American families favor relocating while school is out, and want to be fully settled before the new school term begins. Moreover, it is practical and pleasurable to shop for a home in balmy weather, even if you have to pay a surcharge.

Sunshine buyers pay for the privilege because they don't want to trudge through snow and slush when looking for housing. However, those brave souls who fight the cold and windy weather frequently find some good real estate buys, and learn a great deal more about housing than they could possibly discover in warmer months.

For example, it is easy to evaluate the efficiency of the heating system in the wintertime. However, when the windows are up or the air conditioner is on, you cannot discern temperature variation inside a house. In cold weather, you can test air leaks around the windows and doors simply by placing your hands within a couple of inches of the frames. Air seepage may indicate the need for caulking around the window pane, or for weather stripping around the windows or the sill. Winter also affords you the opportunity to observe the snow-covered roof before entering a building. If the subject roof is dry and the other roofs in the area are covered with snow, it is an indication that the roof is poorly insulated.

Remember, winter is a buyer's market; discouraged owners are more receptive to offers that may vary between 5 percent to 10 percent or more below their original asking price. In contrast, the seller's market arrives with the spring and summer seasons when homes look their best, surrounded by green grass and leafy trees.

In recent years, the buying season has not been determined as much by the weather as it has by the fluctuating of mortgage interest rates. The lowering of mortgage interest rates lifts the home hunter's heart on the coldest day, while rapidly escalating mortgage rates create a dearth of buyers even in the warmer months. The seller and buyer are caught between a rock and a hard place because the seller cannot move out and the buyer cannot move in.

On the other hand, when the interest rates are falling, many buyers will say, "I don't think I should buy now. The mortgage interest rates have dropped so rapidly within the past two months that I think I might be able to get a loan for 1 percent or maybe 2 percent less if I wait another month or so!"

Many buyers are procrastinators, a trait most of us share to some degree. I've known some extreme real estate naysayers—and many of those among my generation and older are still waiting for real estate prices to roll back to the Depression level of 1934 when two-flat brick buildings sold for $1,500.00 and six flats for $5,000.00.

A classic example of what can happen to indecisive homebuyers is revealed in research by Ronald Krum, et. al., of the University of Chicago. They focused on the retention of housing price appreciation gains in the home equity of 2,106 households between 1970 and 1977. The study revealed that these households had an average value increase from $18,759 in 1970 to $37,606 by 1977. Clearly, those who were in

## Average Housing Values for Continuous Owners

|      | Home Value | Remaining Mortgage Principal | Mortgage Payment |
|------|------------|------------------------------|------------------|
| 1977 | $37,606    | $6,554                       | $1,071           |
| 1976 | 30,727     | 6,713                        | 868              |
| 1975 | 28,492     |                              |                  |
| 1974 | 25,882     |                              |                  |
| 1973 | 23,570     |                              |                  |
| 1972 | 21,185     | 6,252                        | 956              |
| 1971 | 19,768     | 6,102                        | 747              |
| 1970 | 18,759     | 6,220                        | 725              |

the market but did not buy homes during that period failed to garner the benefits of the 85 percent increment in housing values. The increase in housing values reflected the extent of nominal residential price appreciation over eight years and corresponds to a 26 percent increase in hard dollars and cents above the increase in overall price levels during this period.

Note on the preceding chart that the remaining mortgage principal increased only 5.4 percent, from $6,220 in 1970 to only $6,554 in 1977. During that time, home equity increased 123.7 percent, from $12,539 in 1970 to $28,052 in 1977. Of the $18,847 average increase in home values over the period, $15,513 or 82 percent, was retained in home equity.

The study was silent on the additional benefits that the homeowners received in federal income tax subsidies for mortgage interest payments. The annual interest paid by the subject mortgagors, averaging 8.5 percent, was sheltered. Moreover, an additional federal income tax shelter came to the homeowners in the form of a real estate tax writeoff between 1970 and 1977.

There is some additional good news. Those who failed to capture the housing opportunities of the 1970s have another chance, according to a survey released by the National Association of Realtors September 22, 1987. The report, titled "Demand for Housing and Home Financing into the 21st Century," predicts the average single-family home that sold for $84,600 in 1985 or for $95,000 in 1987 will appreciate 6.5 percent per year to the year 2000. The resulting resale value of about $217,000 will convert into a 128 percent gain for homeowners who are able and willing to ride the crest.

*Changing Times Magazine* took a poll of banks, savings and loan associations, mortgage banking firms and mutual savings bank executives. Most advised buying now because they expect prices to rise or remain close to the present level. Potential buyers who can qualify for a mortgage loan may make out better by purchasing a home now rather than by waiting for interest rates to fall. Dropping interest rates usually kick off a new wave in real estate demand, causing an increase in housing prices. Moreover, by delaying the purchase of a home, one loses the tax advantage or the tax benefits that the government bestows on homeowners.

Remember, housing prices may go up or down, but homeowners as a powerful political voting block have caused Congress to remain steadfast in tax rules that favor them.

I maintain that anytime is a good time to buy real estate if you have a nose for smelling out a hot community on the rise. Some of the signs that

I suggest you sniff for are 1) proximity to a neighborhood that is currently being gentrified by urban pioneers; 2) a predominantly owner-occupied area; 3) politically strong institutional areas such as those surrounding Columbia University in New York, Temple University in Philadelphia, University of California in Berkeley and Capitol Hill in Washington. Comparably hot areas in Chicago include Loyola University, Northwestern University, Northwestern Memorial Hospital, the hospitals and clinics at the University of Chicago and the University of Illinois, University of Chicago, DePaul University, University of Illinois-Circle Campus, Michael Reese Hospital and Medical Center, and Presbyterian St. Luke's Medical Center.

Thousands of building complexes have been developed near, and in some instances, by major institutions located in the metropolitan areas around the country. The Watergate development in Washington is just a stone's throw from Capitol Hill and from the John F. Kennedy Center for the Performing Arts.

In the late 1960s and early 1970s, the only areas in Washington that attracted middle- and upper middle-income urban gentrification pioneers were Georgetown and Capitol Hill. Today, they are moving into every section of the District of Columbia, while the poor have been pushed beyond district lines into Prince George's County, Maryland.

Today, the District of Columbia's housing market is so hot and the prices are so high that first-time and moveup buyers are forced to flock to real estate developments outside the city limits of Washington that they had spurned in the recent past. The attraction is the low prices of $70,000 to $80,000 for a townhouse in projects such as Ryan Homes' Newington Heights and Newington Commons, and the bargain-priced $279,000 single-family homes in Fairfield Homes' Crosspointe Project.

The Newington Heights 310-unit townhouse community is adjacent to the Lorton Reformatory, a 58-year-old prison facility that has had its share of escapees. The concern for security among these semiurbanite pioneers was overridden by their desire to move up and be somewhat close to the District of Columbia while enjoying the lifestyle of a rural setting. In Chicago, people living in public housing fought against having a prison halfway house located near their homes. When I was a boy, my father used to say, "Hard times would make a cat eat pepper." The adage rings true in a hot real estate market where high prices make people act in an uncommon fashion.

On the other hand, middle-class housing such as Chicago's South Commons, Lake Meadows and Prairie Shores developments are in the front door of the Michael Reese Hospital and Medical Center. That institution has grown from a one-building, 60-bed hospital to 1,008 beds and 28 buildings on 47 contiguous acres of land near the city's lakefront. Property owners in that area are a signal that homebuyers in any urban community who are searching for hot real estate don't have to look farther than the areas surrounding expanding residential building complexes or major institutions. If the buyer is competing in the market against large developers and if the risk is more than most individuals can tackle, then limited partnerships, syndications and joint ventures are the answers.

For example, a once-blighted area on the south side of Chicago has become known as the Gap because, like a missing front tooth, it left a hole in the landscape. Untouched for almost two decades, the rectangularly shaped 20-block Gap is sandwiched between two new major developments. It is bordered on the east by the Lake Meadows development, which was sponsored by the New York Life Insurance Company on land acquired under the Blighted Areas Redevelopment Act of 1947, and on the west by the Illinois Institute of Technology. In 1940, the Illinois Institute of Technology owned five old buildings of the 19th Century vintage and approximately seven acres of land. In 1987, the IIT campus covers 120 acres that have been improved with 50 imposing glass, brick and steel buildings with deceptively simple exteriors and spacious, flexible interiors.

The Gap has benefitted from the environment created by both the Lake Meadows housing development and the Illinois Institute of Technology. Many properties in the area that were figuratively abandoned 10 years ago are being rehabilitated, and selling for prices ranging from $75,000 to $350,000. The beneficiaries of the rising prices were the black and white urban pioneers who smelled the meat a' cooking in a hot neighborhood on the make.

Gap-like reclamations have also been spearheaded in the Southern section of the country by home-grown carpetbaggers. For example, in Savannah, Ga., the downtown Historical District has changed from a downtrodden to a very affluent and middle-upper class location. The same spirit of gentrification has spilled over into the adjacent Victoria District of Savannah. Prices of some of the vintage houses have escalated 1,000 percent.

Of course, Atlanta has succumbed to the revitalization germ. Its citizens have restored the Inman Park area, Virginia Highlands and Ansley Park. In the last decade and a half, under the leadership of Mayors Maynard Jackson and Andrew Young, downtown Atlanta has bloomed with highrise office buildings and hotels like flowers in the springtime.

Downtown offices, hotels, and other commercial developments have created a demand for land that includes hot public housing sites across America. Low-income areas that were written off four decades ago by the downtown business establishment have come full circle; today's central city areas are ripe for real estate redevelopment. In Chicago, project sites that may be classified as red hot are Cabrini-Green, Hilliard Homes, Horner Homes, Ickes, and the Chicago Housing Authority's Lakefront Property Developments, which include six properties on the lakefront site.

The six buildings are on choice locations facing Lake Michigan. All but one have been vacated and boarded up for the past two years. To facilitate the people removal, the tenants were told that the buildings would be rehabilitated and that they would have the opportunity of first refusal for moving back in.

On November 24, 1987, a story appeared on the front page of the *Chicago Tribune* outlining a proposal conceived by Ferd Kramer, a prominent Chicago real estate developer, and backed by the Illinois Housing Development Authority. The scheme would demolish the Lakefront Property Development, and thus set a precedent for moving the Chicago underclass from their highrise lakefront apartments and other prime locations throughout the city.

The November 24, 1987, edition of the *Chicago Tribune* said:

Ferd Kramer, A. D. VanMeter, the chairman of the state housing development authority, and other proponents of the North Kenwood-Oakwood Redevelopment Plan including representatives from the University of Chicago, Amoco Corp., and the architectural firm of Skidmore, Owings and Merrill are expected to seek its approval when they meet with James A. Baugh, HUD's top public housing official in Washington, D.C., on Tuesday, November 24, 1987.

The plan, if successful, would involve demolishing four of the six 16-story highrise lakefront properties and converting two into senior citizen housing. It contains no specific proposal for replacing more than 870 family units that would be lost. As a result, the proposal has received a cold reception from Gertrude Jordan, the top U.S. Department of Housing and Urban Development (HUD) official in Chicago.

The late Mayor Harold Washington initially opposed the Kramer proposal. The mayor at first stated that the city would not renege on its commitment to renovate the lakefront highrise CHA buildings and allow the former tenants to return. However, when subsequently pressed on the matter, the mayor said he would have "no quarrel" with Kramer's proposal if public housing units in the highrises were "replicated" within Kramer's proposed renewal zone.

Kramer indicates that he does not know what position Acting Mayor Eugene Sawyer will take. "We have not met with the new mayor yet and we don't plan to until we get the CHA backing for our proposal," Kramer said.

Kramer is quoted in the Dec. 14, 1987 *Chicago Tribune* as saying that a way will be found to replace the highrise public housing units that he proposes to demolish, but added that not all of the replacement units should be concentrated inside the proposed development area.

Getting the stamp of approval of the plan by the Chicago Housing Authority Board will be the first step to get the proposal off the ground. Unless Ferd Kramer and his plan's backers can convince the board of its merit, it is not likely that they will be able to obtain the required endorsements from the city of Chicago and the U.S. Department of Housing and Urban Development (HUD), the mortgagee for the six highrises.

HUD's position is an open book because during the last months of Nixon administration, plans were laid to get HUD out of the housing the housing business. The Nixon plan has been implemented during the Reagan administration, and it's commonly known among HUD watchers that the department would like to sell at least one-third of its Chicago inventory.

It is my prediction that Lakefront Development Properties and Cabrini-Green, along with other hot properties that have been mentioned in this chapter, will follow the route of the infamous Pruitt-Igoe housing development in St. Louis by 1990 or sooner. The two St. Louis housing projects were built in 1954 and 1955 at a cost of $36 million on adjacent sites that totalled 57.5 acres and contained 33 11-story buildings that housed 10,000 residents. In 1972, during Mr. Nixon's term, the St. Louis Housing Authority, with HUD's blessings, demolished by dynamite three of the buildings. The other buildings were leveled to the ground in 1976.

With precedent for demolishing public housing set in St. Louis, the future of public housing in Chicago, and specifically for the lakefront properties and Cabrini-Green, has already been written. That Mayor Washington also saw the handwriting on the wall for low-income housing became evident at a press conference a week before he suffered a fatal heart attack on November 25, 1987. He said: "The U.S. Congress defeated the first housing bill in 40 years. We must make sure next year we put the people in Congress and in the White House that will make this a priority issue."

Cabrini-Green and the other hot public housing properties on the Near North, Near West and Near South sides are within walking distance from downtown Chicago, known as the Loop. The Loop is enjoying its largest building boom since the period following the Chicago fire of 1871, which practically destroyed the entire business district. These public housing properties are red hot and an endangered species because of their proximity to the Loop and to middle-middle, upper-middle and lower-upper income locations such as Chicago's River North, the Gold Coast on the lakefront, the Dearborn Park complex, the Illinois Institute of Technology, Mercy Hospital and Medical Center, River City and Presidential Towers.

Presidential Towers, just a short walk west of Chicago's central downtown business district, include four highrise buildings that contain 2,700 luxury apartments. The towers are signposts of a city in the early process of regentrifying itself. A census study in 1985 revealed that for the first time since 1950, Chicago's approximately 3 million population showed a small increase. The net overall increase of 2,000 was undergirded by a rise of 7,000 in the downtown populace. This minute turnaround is attributed directly to the young white affluent professionals who have opted for the urban lifestyle near the theaters, night clubs and trendy restaurants, and such cultural landmarks as the Chicago Historical Society, Orchestra Hall, the Art Institute, the Field Museum of Natural History, and the Museum of Science and Industry.

More than 15,000 residential units have been built in downtown Chicago since 1980 to accommodate the influx of members from the yuppie and buppie generations, in addition to the empty nesters who have given up the big houses in suburbia to be closer to work and the brighter lights. City planners foresee an additional increase in the downtown population of 48,000 by 1990.

"In a sense, we are redefining the function of the central city," said Elizabeth Hollander, Chicago director of planning. "It was always the center for banking, government, education, and health care, but that is becoming even more the case. And now we are adding housing, too, which puts people back on the streets and gives us the possibility of a city that is open 18 hours a day."

Six billion dollars have been pumped into downtown developments by investors, creating what Louis Masotti, an urban affairs professor at Northwestern University, refers to as the Chicago "Super Loop (downtown)." The tentacles of downtown Chicago are reaching out in all directions to satisfy its hunger for land.

Just south of Masotti's Super Loop, public housing projects located between 2000 and 2900 on South State Street, Clark Street, and Dearborn Street are in the middle of an early 21st-century expansion corridor that is on the drawing board of architects and city planners of major institutions, both public and private. Moreover, public, private and government-subsidized housing on the Near West side between Roosevelt Road and Madison Street and west to Western Avenue is in the path of a new Chicago Stadium sports complex and of the expansion of several major medical complexes.

On the Near North side of Chicago, the Cabrini-Green public housing project has been a hot real estate site in the eyes of many real estate developers for at least 25 years. The upper-middle class Carl Sandburg Village is located within a 10-minute leisurely walk from the highly publicized project. Hence, every scheme imaginable for displacing the black underclass occupants and gentrifying the area has been considered, including conversion of the complex to upper-middle class condominiums, or demolition if conversion is not feasible. Displacement of Cabrini-Green residents would have been out of the question had Mayor Harold Washington lived.

Real estate headhunters and developers locally and nationally should keep in mind that, though street and institutional names and politics will differ in each city, the game of sniffing out red-hot property deals is always the same.

Metropolitan properties that have been heavily supported by urban renewal and housing and urban redevelopment monies and subsidies are prime targets for hot housing opportunities. Society Hill in Philadelphia is a classic example of an area where urban renewal programs were used to recycle a community. The success of Society Hill infected Queens Village in South Philadelphia, which has been so gentrified that I did not recognize it or its people when I visited there in the fall of 1987. This also applied to the Whitman Section of Philadelphia. These are typical of areas written off in the late 1940s and early '50s that have been revitalized and gentrified in the '70s and '80s. The owner occupants who refused to take crumbs for their properties and run are living in Fat City now.

The gentrification process in New York is not unlike Philadelphia's because a survey by Rutgers University Center for Urban Policy Research revealed that 30 percent of the occupants living in recycled vacant commercial and industrial loft buildings in SoHo, Greenwich Village and other Lower Manhattan sections moved into these apartments and condominiums from addresses outside of the city. Three-quarters of them are college graduates, 80 percent of whom are from 20 to 40 years of age. Young urban gentrification pioneers much like those who live in the SoHo District bought the turn-of-the-century brownstones in Black and Spanish Harlem in the middle 1960s and through the early '70s for prices that ranged from $16,000 to $40,000. The same houses in today's market have values that graduate from $75,000 to $500,000.

Census tabulation lends both quantitative and qualitative support to the street-level observation of gentrification. An analysis of the 1980 New York census tract shows that several of the city's communities have been transformed by gentrification. Counted among them are Brooklyn Heights and nearby areas in Brooklyn, in addition to Greenwich Village in Manhattan. The census tract data make it possible to nail down the gentrifiction process in the other New York neighborhoods. It has been noted that the largest infiltration of urban pioneers in New York settled in a square mile area between 70th and 90th Streets across the island of Manhattan between the Hudson River and the East River. Data further support the notion that the urban pioneers are predominantly young white professionals on a fast career track, prime candidates for making megadollars in the future.

Areas of New York City that seem to have been passed over by the demographers and urbanologists have been invaded by the urban gentrifiers in search of red-hot neighborhoods in the Bronx, Flatbush, Flatlands, Green Point and Williamsburg. The movement started there in the latter half of the 1970s has continued into the 1980s.

The less-publicized sections of New York that have been recycled and gentrified are Chelsey, the Upper West side, and the East side of Manhattan, along with Park Slope, Boerum Hill and other neighborhoods with easy access to lower Manhattan and Wall Street. The 1980 census data reveal that in almost every census tract in these rediscovered neighborhoods, at least 50 percent of the residents age 25 or over have four years or more of college, as compared with a citywide proportion of 17 percent. The comparisons between the 1960 and the 1980 census data demonstrate unequivocally that urban pioneering has penetrated New York.

Gentrification pioneers have landed within the past generation in many locations throughout Chicago. One of the first major beachheads was established after the Korean War when the late Arthur Rubloff made the bold decision in the early 1960s to construct the $97 million Carl Sandburg Village complex on the Near North side, in what was a sleazy hole-in-the-soles area. Sandburg Village has attracted more than 8,000 middle- and upper middle-income people in search of good housing. The presence of the Sandburg complex generated a hot property market in the neighboring Lincoln Park and Lakeview areas and has spread as far as 6000 North into the Edgewater area. Rehabilitation followed in Old Town, New Town, Ravenswood, DePaul, and the Triangle, all on the Near North side of Chicago.

On Chicago's South side, the University of Chicago took drastic steps in 1952 to reinforce a gentrification beachhead it had established in 1892 off the shores of Lake Michigan. It launched an intensive campaign to prevent the area surrounding the university from becoming de-gentrified. This institution was deeply concerned with maintaining a compatible environment for its faculty and students. By the early 1950s, this meant fighting for its own salvation in the city of Chicago as well as for the preservation of racial integrity in the area, and creating a controlled integrated environment. The other option for the university was to stand by and watch East Hyde Park become an extension of the black ghetto to its west.

The most potent factor in enabling the University of Chicago to roll back the black belt was the use of its power and political clout in getting the Chicago City Council to approve a Hyde Park-Kenwood urban renewal plan that gave it unprecedented police power over housing in the area in 1958. The guts of the urban renewal police power permitted the university community to go to sleep nights with the assurance that it would not awaken in the jaws of the black community moments before it was to be digested.

In retrospect, I see the University of Chicago's circling of the wagons as urban pioneering in reverse. The plan was deadly, but not as deadly as Custer's last stand because it has borne fruit that has benefited the entire city. A burst of housing and commercial construction and rehabilitation in Hyde Park added new luster and vibrance to one of Chicago's old neighborhoods, and is presently the home of some of the city's leading citizens, blacks and whites. The University of Chicago's neighborhood retention plan has been adopted by many urban institutions.

The late mayors Washington and Kelly lived in the Hyde Park-Kenwood community, which envelops the University of Chicago. Along with political and educational leaders, such architectural talents as George Fred Keck and William Keck, and New York developers like Webb and Knapp were attracted by the vitality of this community.

The demand for real estate in the area has made Hyde Park-Kenwood a seller's market where the average price of houses has gone up 30 percent in the last four years. Homes that sold for $25,000 to $60,000 in the late 1950s and early 1960s are now selling for $100,000 to $1 million. The urban pioneers who purchased Hyde Park-Kenwood property in the late 1950s and early '60s clearly understand what I mean when I say real estate is the gold in your future.

The demand for housing in Hyde Park-Kenwood has led many incoming faculty members to settle in the Jackson Park Highlands, a mile or so south of the university. Highlands real estate owners have had the benefit of escalating real estate values over the past decade. Nineteen eighty-eight presidential candidate Rev. Jesse Louis Jackson lives there. Prices have risen 400 percent in the area since I sold him his home in the Highlands approximately 15 years ago.

Further along the South Side of Chicago, in the Chatham, Park Manor, and the East and West Avalon areas, other anchors are stabilizing the community and attracting more urban pioneers to their integrated neighborhoods. The centerpieces that have spearheaded the renovation and expansion are the Jackson Park Hospital with its $80 million program on South Stony Island Avenue, and the new Regal Theater in the same area, in addition to the new buildings of the Seaway National Bank, the Soft Sheen Products Company, and the block-long modern office structures housing the Independence Banking complex. These hallmarks of progress and strong stability for inner city neighborhoods reinforce the escalating values of houses and apartment buildings in their general areas.

Throughout this chapter, we have shown that there are many opportunities to buy real estate and make money without trying. There are people throughout the country who have purchased real estate and made thousands of dollars without having the foggiest notion of what happened except that they sold the building, and received three times more money than they paid for it. These people were lucky and they still believe in the tooth fairy.

On the other hand, there are those who understand the mathematics and economics of real estate and still buy wrong because they don't understand the importance of location. After all, the best-constructed hotel in the middle of the Sahara desert is worthless because there is no demand for rooms. The exception to that rule came in the late 1940s when some mobsters decided to build a gambling casino and hotel in the western section of a Nevada desert now known as Las Vegas.

Today, thousands of people drive south on Michigan Boulevard, King Drive, or north on South Indiana Avenue in Chicago, and all they see are vacant lots, buildings on sites that will soon be vacant lots, and buildings that reflect a severe case of deferred maintenance. An economic veil prevents most real estate explorers from recognizing the value of these locations and the opportunities they afford. Many times the present owners of these properties are too old to dream. Here are opportunities for young visionary real estate buyers to rekindle the dreams of the aged and move forward.

The importance of the Michigan Avenue, Dr. Martin Luther King Jr. Drive, and the Indiana Avenue locations were underscored within the past two years when Chicago's Metropolitan Mutual Assurance Company spent millions of dollars remodeling its facilities at 44th and King Drive. The Illinois Service Federal Savings and Loan Association did the same thing on 46th and King Drive a decade earlier. And Supreme Life Insurance Company has remained in its 35th and King Drive location for 66 years. Yet, people who say they are looking for hot properties have watched buildings near those institutions crumble from neglect or deadly attacks by bulldozers. Most of us have eyes but we don't see, and many of us think that Texas oil is greasy water. Moreover, most people go to their final real estate resting place walking over opportunities every step of the way.

The question at this point is what ultimately happens to some of our lost real estate opportunities. The answer is they are stolen by brick thieves. Thieves don't just take things from the interior of the abandoned structures. They steal brick by brick, many times in the broad open daylight when anyone can see. It has been estimated by Mel Hopkins, a Chicago demolition director, that between 50 to 100 buildings were stolen by brick thieves in 1986. There is a market for old Chicago bricks because they are solid and of the best quality to be found any place in the market today.

In 1987, the yuppie market in Texas was paying as much as 30 cents a brick for the Chicago product because the demand there is so high, while today most new bricks sell for under 20 cents a copy. This is the prime example that proves there are money making opportunities in Chicago real estate right down to the last brick.


## TIPS TO REMEMBER IN BUYING REAL ESTATE

□ Invest only in those properties that you or your consultants understand.
□ The best real estate bargains are not usually mortgageable because of code violations and/or lack of maintenance. Such deals can be made only for cash, so you must be in a position to raise the necessary money in a few days. The owner of one or two mortgage-free buildings is in an excellent position to raise equity money for such bargains. If a deal is properly structured, you can subsequently mortgage out, that is, get all of your money back and still own the property.
□ There are three keys to appreciation in real estate: location, location, and location. Find an area settled for more than five years where a large percentage of the homes are financed with conventional mortgage loans. Those homeowners have a lot of equity tied up in their property and there is a definite relationship between high equity and stability.

Also, look at the properties within a mile in each direction of the subject real estate.

□ Buy a house that needs paint and you will start making money with the first improvements you put in it. This is a choice method of manufacturing money, more commonly known as creating equity.

□ Many people buy other people's paint, and pay dearly for it. I like to look at a building the same as I look at a lady, unpainted. Then I know that what I see is what I get. There is no morning-after surprise.

□ Good grade schools and high schools make good neighborhoods. Check out nearby schools before you buy.

□ Always buy as near as possible to politically clout-heavy public or private institutions. When you do, you buy more than real estate. You buy the hidden influence of the institution and you buy stability.

# Clarence Stackhouse:
## The Realty Deal Maker*

*"I have always known I was destined to be successful. There has never been any doubt in my mind."*

After graduating from the University of Michigan at age 22 in 1972, Clarence Stackhouse came to Chicago and enrolled in Northwestern University Law School. He dropped out of law school in 1974 and started a used furniture business on the southeast side of Chicago near the Robert Taylor public housing project.

He had learned the used furniture trade working for a second generation American-owned firm in Youngstown, Ohio, while he attended high school. The middle-aged owner of the business took a liking to young Stackhouse because of his aggressiveness, spirit and no-nonsense personality. The wealthy businessman gave young Clarence a book titled "Think and Grow Rich." The book was dog-eared because it had been read and reread many times by the old gentleman, and there were penciled notes throughout about buying real estate. The subject of getting wealthy fascinated the young man so much that he poured over its contents as though it were poetry.

Clarence Stackhouse thought that he, like Irwin Jacobs, could grow rich in the second hand furniture business. He remained in the trade for

---

*These case studies are documented; only the names were changed to protect the confidentiality of the real estate consultant-client relationship.

4½ years before reaching the realization that his business was on the brink of failing. He recalls the following:

In the winter of 1978, I was at rock bottom. My furniture store was not producing enough money for me to pay the rent or barely keep my skin and bones together.

I was sitting in my living room one Sunday morning staring at the wall and thinking seriously. I said to myself, 'Wow, what is this thing that we call life? There has to be more to it than just being born, going to grammar school and high school. Some of us go to college, and then after graduating, get a corporate job. Then we struggle against all odds to reach the upper echelon of corporate life. In the interim, we get married, have kids, strive to buy a home in suburbia, and send our kids to college. In the final act, I will have nothing to look forward to except retiring and dying without having really ever lived.' I decided there has to be more to life than that.

And I recall shouting to the top of my lungs that Sunday morning: 'God! If that's all there is to this thing that we call life, stop my world right now! I want to get off!'

At the moment I asked God to end my journey, I heard the voice of the Rev. Dr. Johnnie Colemon, founder and minister of Christ Universal Temple, on the radio. She sounded as if she was speaking directly to me. I don't recall everything that she said, but she punched me in the middle of my stomach with the following statements: 'You are responsible for where you are. You have no one to blame but yourself. Get up off the floor and stop feeling sorry for yourself.'

With the sound of Rev. Colemon's words in my ears, I wiped the tears from my eyes and snapped to attention because I knew something good was about to happen to me. I knew I was going to become rich, but I didn't know exactly how. I went to Rev. Colemon's church the following Sunday and, needless to say, I've been going there ever since. It was in that church that I got my thoughts together. I clearly knew where I was going. I had put my goals on paper, and I was using Rev. Johnnie Colemon's road map to success as my guiding light.

The Rev. Johnnie Colemon changed my life. I got a different perspective about myself. I finally fully realized that I was responsible for my own position in this world. The Rev. Colemon taught me in one lesson that I had the power within me to become all that I wanted to be. And that it was never, never intended for God's child to be poor or to be a failure. She sermonizes that we are all destined to be successful. Unfortunately, most of us never get the message.

On Sunday, May 20, 1979, I marched right out of Christ Universal Temple and into a real estate office on South Halsted Street and applied for a job as a salesman. I was so hyped up and filled with inspiration from Rev. Colemon's sermon that my inner spirit must have penetrated the psyche of the owner of the realty company because he hired me right on the spot.

I had only been working for the real estate company a couple of months when the owner told me, 'You will never get rich off of making commissions. That's just pocket change. You make money in the real estate business from owning property, fixing it up and selling it. That's where the real money is generated.'

Well, it took me 5½ years to realize what the owner of the realty company had said. I continued to go merrily out and get property listings, bring them back to the office, and give them to the secretary, who placed them in the real estate for sale section of the *Chicago Sun-Times* and *Tribune*.

On many occasions, four or five days after I had given the ad information to the secretary, I would look for my ad in the papers and it wouldn't be there. I would go to the sales manager and ask him what happened to my ad. He would say, 'Oh Clarence, the office decided to buy that property. And the office will pay you your regular 3 percent commission.'

That was fine with me because I was after a quick buck and listing property was an easy way to make it. I did not have to be bothered with the buyer-seller hassle.

The buying and selling philosophy that the realty owner had shared with Stackhouse when he started working for the company initially did not penetrate the salesman's mind. For example, many times Clarence would list a property, and before the ink could dry on the listing contract, the owners of the realty firm would buy it. If Clarence listed a property for $20,000, they'd probably negotiate the seller into accepting an offer for maybe $12,000 to $15,000. They would fix up the property, and in a couple of months put it on the market for perhaps $40,000 to $50,000.

The realty firm's owners would make approximately $30,000 net profit on the deals, but Clarence received only $1,300 as a listing fee. There was nothing illegal with what the firm's owners were doing. It was Stackhouse who was continuously reading off the wrong page until:

One night, I worked until after 12 a.m. getting listings. I was tired but happy about my success when I had to stop for a red light. In that split second, the voice of Rev. Johnnie Colemon echoed in my ears like a fire alarm. It said, 'You are responsible for where you are. You have no one to blame but yourself if you are not rich.'

I instantly realized that I had been walking over golden opportunities and that I had to change my way of thinking. The very next day I started a program in which I would buy real estate for my own portfolio.

The first thing I did was to develop a system for acquiring property. Instead of sitting back and waiting for the phone to ring with a prospective seller on the other end of the line like most salespeople do, I started writing letters. I would target my letters to the mid-central south side of Chicago because that's where most of the older properties were located. I had observed that in the older neighborhoods there was a common denominator. The oldtimers that once lived in these buildings had moved further south as they prospered, yet they still owned the buildings. The buildings were beginning to give them problems. The tenants were giving them problems. The high gas and water bills were giving them problems. In most instances, they were about ready to give the buildings up. However, there were many senior citizens who were reluctant to sell their properties because they had either fallen in love with the old building or were troubled by the thought of their old tenants being uprooted.

One of the best methods that I found for finding these old property owners was through a tax subscription service. Each year the service would send me an updated list of property taxpayers in a specific area. After getting the tax list in hand, I worked out a letter that I still use, and which I think is one of my best. It simply said:

Dear Mrs. Emmett McDonald:
5800 S. Washington Park Ave.
Chicago, Illinois 60615

My parents are retiring December 31, and I am moving them here to Chicago to be near me. I am looking for a building like the one that you own at 78th and Lowe. If you're interested in selling this building, please contact me as soon as possible. My parents will need a place to live as soon as they arrive.

Sincerely,
Clarence Stackhouse.

I recognize that I was not exactly telling the truth. However, that letter proved to be a very, very effective marketing tool. Other salesmen in the office would ask me why I didn't do this or that to get real estate listings. Well, I would always reply, I am doing something that's working for me and it has proven to be successful. I see no reason to change.

Another reason for me to buy older properties was that I found that their average price was $15,000. I usually could handle them with $3,000 down and get an 8 percent mortgage.

There were some instances when I bought two-flat brick buildings as well as single-family homes for as little as $15,000 with $2,000 down. Sometimes they're a little bit more or less, but the average price was $15,000.

Following my program of buying old buildings and fixing them up, by early 1985 I had acquired 16 buildings. They were producing a positive cash flow, and enabling me to pay for a downtown condo and a Mercedes Benz. It was at this point that I decided that I would retire.

I left the employment of the real estate company on November 10, 1985, at age 36. I realized that most people worked to age 65 and beyond to get enough money to drive around in nice cars, live in nice homes, and since I had achieved that, I felt that I was now financially free. All my bills were paid up except the notes on my three cars. I have a 1985 Rolls-Royce and a 1986 Porsche Targa 911 Coretta. I also own a classic Porsche 914, which I store in my garage and drive roughly about 1,000 miles a year. It's obvious that I really like cars.

Financially free, I flew back and forth to Europe. I was there for Thanksgiving, went back again for Christmas. In January, I would go to Acapulco or fly over to the sunny coast of Spain. I became bored. I got tired of feeling unproductive and rootless. It did not matter how much I traveled, my mind was hungry for some meaningful activities. My phone never rang. I had nothing to do with business because my tenants called my maintenance men with their complaints.

So after almost a year of doing nothing, I decided to open up an office. I didn't want an office in a walk-in commercial location, so I purchased a condo in Hyde Park from my brother who had moved to California. It was perfect for a small office. At least it would give me some place to go and give me a bona fide reason for not sitting around the house and looking at Lake Michigan.

Now I at least had contact with some breathing humanity and my tenants could either bring the rents or mail them to my new office, rather than send them to my home address or my post office box.

After several months, I decided I better get someone to answer the telephone. It was not my intention to have a lot of people working for me. I just wanted to be an investor, buy and sell real estate, and keep those properties that produced good net cash flow.

One of my prerequisites was to never pay more than $15,000 for a bungalow or two-flat or put more than $3,000 down. In addition, the property must be able to earn my $3,000 down payment back within 12 months.

In order to make the property attractive for a renter or buyer, I put additional monies into cosmetics and installed individual heating systems in each unit. The tenants would pay all of the utility bills except the water bills.

Clarence Stackhouse is not a typical real estate broker. Therefore, I thought it would be interesting to share some of his buying and selling techniques. In my opinion, he walks from time to time on a very thin line between legal and illegal, ethical and unethical. He is an extremely bright young man, but in my years I have seen a large number of bright young men in the real estate business go to prison because, as my mother says, "They got too smart for their britches."

Stackhouse is certainly operating in violation of agency laws when he purchases a piece of real estate for himself under the disguise of selling it to somebody else. It's obvious that you cannot fairly represent the owner of real estate and negotiate at arm's length if you are representing yourself in the same transaction. In other words, an agent must not have an individual interest in a transaction unless the client is informed of the agent's involvement. The agent always must make full disclosure on all matters pertaining to the subject of the agency.

Clarence Stackhouse was not violating the law when he purchased a building in the 6600 block on Champlain Avenue for $15,000, financed it with a $12,000 mortgage and signed a note for roughly $152 a month. The owner knew that Stackhouse was buying it for himself. The owner had been renting the building for $200 per month, which was below market rent, whereas Stackhouse rented the building under the Section 8 program for $895 a month. You don't have to be a genius to recognize that this is what you call manufacturing money.

Stackhouse made the following observations:

Ninety-five percent of my buildings have been converted to individual heat and hot water. That to me is where you make your money.

On 65th and Bishop, I bought a two-flat for $15,000, paid $3,000 down, fixed it up and then had it refinanced for $48,000. Then I turned around and sold it on contract for $62,000 with $5,000 down. I have sold a half a million dollars worth of buildings that way in 1987-buildings that I bought cheap for $15,000, and had them refinanced.

The agency agreement was definitely violated in the above case because no owner of sound mind would sell a building for $15,000 that could qualify for a $48,000 mortgage.

Stackhouse has his own definition of refinancing. To him, refinancing means selling the building to a friend who can qualify for the mortgage, and who will then deed the property back to Stackhouse. He uses his friends to qualify for the mortgages, and after the closing of the deal, gives them $2,000 to $3,000 in consideration for deeding the property back to him. Stackhouse furnishes the down payment and other ancillary expenses.

It is not illegal to assume a mortgage if there is nothing in the document that prohibits it. However, making a business out of those types of transactions is very shady, to say the least. Moreover, persons involved in such transactions could be convicted of fraud under federal statutes because of misrepresentation on the application in reference to occupancy, etc.

Clarence Stackhouse describes his real estate coup d'etat as follows:

In March of 1986, I noticed an ad in the paper that was being run by the real estate company where I was formerly employed. The selling agent named in the ad was one of the firm's oldest employees. Frank Lanski was selling three buildings, a two-flat at 68th and Normal which was listed for $22,500 with $2,500 down; a four-flat at 58th and Morgan which was listed at $28,000 with $2,000 down; and another one at 72nd and Stewart for $25,000 with $2,500 down. Then there was a fourth one on East 89th Place for $17,000 with $2,000 down. This salesman never thought that property in a black-occupied area had any value.

Frank Lanski suffered with what I call the Halsted Street

mentality. He always thought that black property should be dirt cheap. To make a long story short, when I walked into the office to buy the property, I heard one of the guys say, 'Oh, old Clarence is coming back to ask for his job.' They were in for a surprise.

I bought all four of those buildings with cash, then went directly to the owner who had listed the property and purchased another five properties that he had planned to list with Frank. The package of properties was worth about $375,000. I had cosmetic jobs performed on all of the properties and then had them financed under both FHA and VA, using surrogate buyers. I subsequently sold them under contract to legitimate buyers. These properties were very attractive to home-starved buyers who had bad credit and could not qualify under any lending program. The price of homeownership was 50 percent to 100 percent higher than they would have paid if they had been able to buy directly, but I created an opportunity for them where none existed.

I know what I'm doing is not ethical, but I don't think it's illegal. I was paying 10 percent on the FHA and VA mortgages, and the contract buyers were paying me 14 percent to 15 percent on the contract. Therefore, I was getting it both ways. I'd increase the principal balance in addition to earning an interest premium.

I have only made a few mistakes or bad investments since leaving the second-hand furniture business. I bought a really nice house out in Bolingbrook. It was one of those ranch homes with five bedrooms, two baths and in a nice part of town. The owners, relatives of one of my employees, were divorcing and were just going to let the building go back. It cost me approximately $2,800 to make the mortgage current and pay the assumption fee. The monthly payments on the mortgage are $805. I had planned to get the interest rate reduced from 12.5 percent. However, in the interim, I rented the house to a lady on Section 8. The government pays me $700 on her behalf. The tenant pays $50, which is 25 percent of her income. I am losing money on that transaction every month that I stay in it.

There's only one other deal where I made a mistake. I bought a very large home for myself on the far southeast side, with the intent of fixing it up as a summer home. I have overimproved it to the tune of $150,000. The house has enormous square footage but it's in the wrong location. I violated the three principles of real estate, location, location, location, and I am going to have to take a financial bath in red ink to get rid of it.

The author sincerely hopes that Clarence Stackhouse changes his method of doing business and adheres to the true teachings of Rev. Johnnie Colemon. She has never advocated that anyone exploit his brother or sister to get ahead.

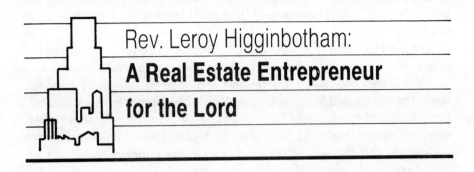

# Rev. Leroy Higginbotham:
## A Real Estate Entrepreneur
## for the Lord

*"I was ordained to become rich
selling and buying real estate."*

Leroy Higginbotham was born November 8, 1951 in Chicago, where he attended public elementary school. By the time he entered high school he had become so unruly that his parents had him transferred to Hales Franciscan Catholic High School in the hope that the school would be able to deal with his behavioral problem. It took less than three months for the sisters to admit that they couldn't handle the mean-spirited teenager, and he was transferred again. He entered an expensive private school downtown called Edmoor Academy. Edmoor was somewhat like the old Central YMCA High School on LaSalle Street, where the pupils were permitted to work at their own pace until they either graduated or dropped out. Leroy dropped out.

Leroy Higginbotham is by any standards a very handsome man. His looks and physique caused older women to become attracted to him before he had reached his 15th birthday. The unsolicited female attention gave the young man an overblown opinion of himself, which led him to believe that he could get over by adapting to the habits of the street. He followed the road of a lowlife until October 1970, a few days before his 19th birthday. That was the evening he stopped to hear a corner preacher addressing a crowd about how the highway to hell was paved with good intentions.

Although the preacher's sermon was threadbare, Higginbotham responded and attended a prayer meeting in a small northside store front

*These case histories are documented; only the names were changed to protect the confidentiality of the real estate consultant-client relationship.

church on the next Wednesday. The Holy Spirit reached inside of the youth that night, and he was ready to mend his ways and give his heart to the Lord.

Young Higginbotham immediately became an active church member and within six months was called to the ministry. The handsome teenager was appointed assistant minister and served in that capacity until the senior pastor passed in the spring of 1980. The largely female congregation elected Higginbotham pastor of the small church, whose membership was fewer than 100. The church structure was in a deteriorating condition, and the young preacher wanted to improve the lot of his membership. He launched a community drive that included large church dinners, raffles and various other means for raising funds and enlarging the membership. After several months, Higginbotham recognized that the eating programs were not going any place, and tried something he thought would have a bigger impact.

Rev. Higginbotham recalls reading an article in *Essence* magazine in which tycoon Arthur Rubloff said that there was big money to be made in the real estate industry for anyone who was smart and willing to work hard. Higginbotham knew that he possessed both prerequisites: he was street smart, and already committed to working a 24-hour day for the Lord. Determined to enter the real estate field, he gave up his full-time day job as a plumber's helper and doubled his efforts for the Lord. Higginbotham told the head deaconess of the church:

> We have a small congregation. As the leader, I'm going to have to do something to get some funds. I want to remodel our church, and the only way I can do that is to get some money. If the Lord gives me the green light, I'm going to get into the real estate business.

Higginbotham saw the green light and took his first step toward a real estate business by investing $400 in a Robert Allen "No Money Down" seminar. The Allen school dealt with buying foreclosed properties, and after three hours in the seminar, Higginbotham realized that the only person in that room who was going to make any real money was Robert Allen, the instructor.

Higginbotham also believed that he was among the few sharpies in the class who would be able to pick up enough information from Allen to put the real estate puzzle together and make it work. On the other hand, the young preacher felt that 50 percent of the information that Robert Allen was dispensing was not applicable to him, so after the class, he attempted to persuade the instructor to give him half of his money back.

Allen, who is by no means a shortstop in the brains department, refused to give him a refund, and instead invited the preacher to come out to Utah to a convention, promising that he wouldn't have to pay any additional fees for attending the sessions.

In the interim, Higginbotham met Abraham Fursenfield, touted as the foreclosure king of Chicago. Fursenfield was traveling down a totally different road from Allen's; he found enrichment through foreclosures. Allen had introduced the reverend to the foreclosure methods and Fursenfield guided him to the best sources for finding foreclosures. Higginbotham decided that he would meld the two systems. Through trial and error and with some additional reading, he became convinced that his strategy would work for anyone who had the mental glue to put the pieces together.

Higginbotham's text for getting off the ground in the real estate business was found in the Chicago Law Bulletin, which was brought to his attention by Fursenfield. The bulletin listed all properties being foreclosed on in Cook County, Illinois. With the list in hand, Higginbotham began approaching people who owned houses marked for foreclosure, assuring them that he could bail them out by paying off their delinquent mortgage and giving them a small stipend. Surely this was better than being dumped in the streets without funds, Higginbotham argued, but at first people turned a deaf ear to his sales pitch.

The good reverend finally hit pay dirt when a lady called him and reminded him that when he was by her house several months earlier, he had warned her that her house was to be sold at a sheriff's sale. She confided, "I have been trying to redeem my property, but I can't get a loan any place. I want you to come back out here and talk with me."

The lady's property is located in Harvey, Illinois. Higginbotham learned that she had gotten in some trouble with the law and served some time in jail. She hadn't kept up her mortgage note during her prison term, and her niece, who had promised to make the payment, blew the money away having a good time. Higginbotham said:

> I told the woman that she still had six months to redeem her home. If she could come up with $10,000, she could get her house back. The lady told me she was not working, and was drawing unemployment compensation. She said, 'There is no way I can do it.'
> I started to say, 'Well, I'll tell you what,' but she interrupted. 'I have a piece of land in Tennessee. If I can get down there, that's all I want because my mother left me a house and a stretch of land,' she sighed.

I asked her how much would it cost to get to Tennessee. She replied, 'I can move everything down there for a couple of thousand dollars.'

I said, 'I'll give you $2,000 if you sign a quit claim deed over to me giving me the right to go in and redeem the property.'

She agreed that that was better than being thrown out of her house. I redeemed the house for $10,000, gave her $1,200 and told her that when she was ready to move, I'd give her another $1,200 to get to Tennessee. I also gave her 60 days to stay in the house rent-free after I had secured the redemption.

Although Higginbotham succeeded in putting that deal together, he didn't feel comfortable working by himself. He went back to Fursenfield and asked him what they could work out in terms of a partnership. Fursenfield offered a 50-50 arrangement. He said that if the reverend put up the money, he would show him how to get the buildings. "I am a neophyte," the preacher thought. "Fursenfield's idea sounds like a good opportunity to work with an expert."

Fursenfield kept his end of the deal and gave Higginbotham an extensive list of buildings that had been put in the hopper for foreclosure. The reverend had already learned the theory of the canvassing procedure in Allen's and Fursenfield's classes, and was ready to start working the field.

In the field, Higginbotham would leave his card with a message attached indicating he could be helpful in assisting the property owner during every step in the foreclosure proceeding. He alerted them that a summons was going to be served by the sheriff's office and suggested that if they wanted to talk, they could contact him.

After going through this scenario for several weeks, it dawned on Higginbotham that he didn't need Fursenfield. He realized that it was not such a good deal to put up all the money and do all the work for a 50-50 split.

Higginbotham terminated his deal with Fursenfield and turned to his mother, confessing his ambition to get into real estate. His mother owned several six-flat buildings, in addition to a condominium, and responded, "Well listen. I am retired. Your dad is retired. He doesn't want to do anything with his money, but I want to do something with mine. I have $250,000 idling in several bank accounts."

Higginbotham made the same 50-50 proposition to his mother that Fursenfield had made to him. The only difference was that while he would do the work, she would furnish the money. Higginbotham also had some money he had saved while working as a plumber's helper.

The longer the preacher worked out in the field, talking to people, soliciting properties and making deals, the clearer it became that the lessons he had learned from Allen and Fursenfield actually had merit *if* you applied the Rubloff principle of working hard and smart.

The preacher decided to take a new turn to the real estate business. In addition to working on foreclosed property listings, he started bidding for HUD-owned properties. He worked at placing bids on government-owned real estate for about two months. His initial bids on two properties didn't win anything. He wasn't even close. The next month, he bid on five pieces of property and still didn't get anything, but was told that he came close to being the winner. The following month, he bid on 10 pieces of HUD property, figuring he would probably get one. As luck would have it, he actually won five, two he had bid in his name and three in his mother's name.

Things were really rolling for the preacher and his mother. They had paid $7,000 to HUD for a four-bedroom frame home, and $7,600 for a five-bedroom frame, both on the west side. Within six months, they refurbished the four-bedroom house and sold it for $43,000, and they subsequently sold the five-bedroom for $34,000.

The minister knocked $10,000 off the price of the second property because he wanted to get out of the northwest side. The travel time involved in driving clients from one side of town to the other became counterproductive. Rev. Higginbotham and his mother kept the other three pieces of real estate in their own portfolio and rented them out for $550 a month. In a year and a half, they recouped all of their front money. From that point, whatever he made in selling the three houses would be clear profit.

The reverend found one commonality in at least 50 percent of the HUD-owned "as-is" properties: they needed new furnaces. He made the cost of heating the rented properties a tenant responsibility. The preacher and his mother paid only for taxes and water.

In 1986, the Higginbothams added more than a dozen small buildings to their stable of properties. Today those properties are earning them net rents in excess of $40,000 a year after taxes and all other expenses.

Leroy and his mother had become entrepreneurs for the Lord, giving to their church 10 percent of their gross profit from every real estate deal.

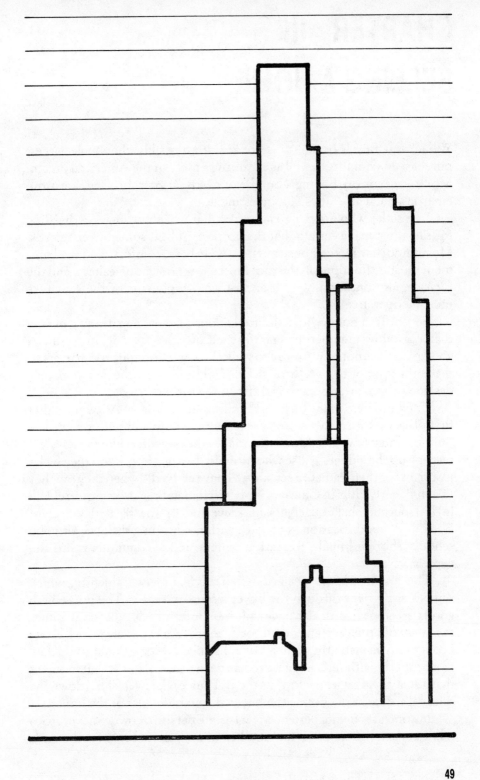

# CHAPTER III
# SELLING A HOME

When you buy a home, you are making possibly the single largest purchase in your life, as well as acquiring a piece of the American dream. Moreover, you are buying a bundle of needs: shelter, privacy, location, environmental amenities and investment.

The seller who expects to get top dollar when putting up a dwelling for sale must make certain that the property fulfills some buyer's needs. Most importantly, the house must provide basic comforts and the basement must be floodproof, the roof must show no signs of leakage, and the furnace, air conditioning unit and other components of the structure must be operative.

Secondly, a home with a desirable floor plan has a marketing plus in that it provides members of a family their own private laughing room. A good plan does not require you to walk through the dining room to get to the bathroom, or to pass through a bedroom to reach the den. A poorly designed room arrangement is difficult to market.

The third item in the buyer's bundle of needs is location, which takes first place on the resale list because it defines status and self-esteem. The building must have an address that makes the buyer feel like the family is moving up the ladder. Those who move up to a neighborhood they feel is just right for them radiate a sense of, "I have arrived," when they say they live in Beverly Hills in Chicago, Nob Hill in San Francisco, Squirrel Hill in Pittsburgh, Shaker Heights in Cleveland or the Back Bay area of Boston. A good location is usually within breathing distance of good schools, shopping malls, recreation centers, and of commuter trains and expressways.

The fourth bundle of needs is an environmental amenity, which sends a sizzle right through the buyer's sensory center. The house with good curb appeal must also have a pleasant interior odor that contributes to a sense of home and an overall good feeling. An experienced real estate broker knows instantly when a buyer has become emotionally attached to a property, although not a word has been uttered. It is at that moment that a smart real estate person lets the ambiance take over, shuts down the sales talk and simply points the buyer through the rest of the house.

In contrast, an inexperienced real estate person or owner never stops talking. As a matter of fact, a number of real estate brokers who have worked for me during my 40 plus years in the business could have made millions if they had known when to stay silent. Just one inappropriate statement can break the spell and the honeymoon is over for the potential buyer, the real estate salesman and that house.

Buyers fall in love with the houses much like people fall in love with each other; there is that first, sometimes subconscious, attraction. The specific magnetism is frequently inexplicable. Many buyers are attracted to the seller's furnishings, although they are not part of the real estate deal. On the other hand, the house interior may reflect a lifestyle the buyer wants to assume. Buyers buy furniture that they know will not be in the house when they move in, and they pay for clothes in the seller's closets that they will never wear. Buyers even pay to live near people they will never visit. Though difficult to understand, the clothes the seller is wearing many times influences the marketability of the product. Therefore, when a price is being negotiated, many non-realty factors are subliminally cranked into the equation to help the buyer determine how much he is willing to pay. As a real estate broker and consultant with a minor in psychology, I am simply reporting, not explaining, these phenomena.

Although the real estate broker is the agent for the seller, the broker must take an objective posture and examine his client's property through the eyes of a buyer. Like a buyer, the broker inspects in depth the external and internal environmental amenities of the subject property and comparable properties to determine exactly where to place a house on the scale of real estate values. In the tradition of a retail store, the seller's property is ranked among a variety of products in the realtor's picture book to get the purchaser's attention.

Some buyers are attracted by the style of the house, be it ranch, Georgian or Colonial; the position the structure occupies on the lot, such as at the rear, front or center of the grounds; the condition of the landscaping surrounding the house; and the general appearance of the neighborhood. Depending on personal taste, internal amenities translate into walk-in closets, waste disposals, the size and layout of the kitchen, built-in features such as cabinets and storage space, eat-in area, dishwasher, microwave oven, walk-in pantry, broom closet and the presence or absence of a formal dining room. Ceramic tile around the kitchen sink and the bathtubs are basic items that if missing or damaged impede marketability.

The question a real estate agent must ask and answer is how the client's property measures up in the market place. If it does not meet area standards, and the seller refuses to adjust the asking price downward, the agent has no choice but to walk away. On the other hand, you adjust the price upward if the house has amenities that are not typical for the area. These might be imported chandeliers, a log-burning fireplace, or an extra-large lot with a side drive.

Marketing data confirm that in northern climates fireplaces play a key role in the closing of real estate transactions. Many buyers are bewitched by dreams of a wine cellar stocked with aged wines, and fireplaces in the library and living room. A fireplace provides a pleasant aroma, warmth, and the thoughts of romance or possibly the opportunity of rekindling an old love before the fire goes out. I have sold homes with fireplaces to single buyers who confide that they were looking forward to a Ms. or Mr. Right with whom to share warm thoughts as they watch the logs burn down to simmering red ashes.

We must keep in mind that second-time home buyers don't just simply buy a house on their last tour of duty. They buy an experience.

Having money to invest fulfills the fifth prerequisite in the bundle of needs, a yardstick for measuring self-actualization. People invest money in homes for many reasons. Typically, houses are purchased as basic shelter for the family, but there is a substantial percentage of people who buy houses as they would acquire cars. Their house represents another badge of prestige proclaiming the new owners have financially surpassed the Joneses and the Thornburgs.

Then there are the bottom-line people who buy houses as a stepping stone for getting ahead. They see a house as an investment that they can cash in within five to 10 years and move on up the economic ladder to a larger house or apartment building. Moreover, bottom liners recognize that housing prices have consistently increased faster than inflation. They know that the yield from an investment in housing has outperformed most alternative investments, including stocks, bonds, or the popular money market funds.

When you are considering the purchase of a house, keep in mind the five bundles of needs. Also ask yourself if the house has all the necessary ingredients for an easy resale. If your answer is in the negative, then that is not the house for you although it is located in the right neighborhood.

It is the real estate agent's job in the initial interview to uncover whether the buyers have sufficient funds. Once that has been determined, the agent must discover the drive that motivates the buyers. Failure to perform this professional service frequently results in wasting everybody's time, including the buyer's, the seller's and the agent's. I usually visit with the buyer on the phone as a prescreening process, and if additional consideration is warranted, extend an invitation for him or her to visit with me in my office where we determine whether the products I have on the shelf meet their needs. It is the real estate agent's challenge in the initial visit to get as much information as possible without stepping on the buyer's last nerve.

It is surprising that even after a preliminary interview, some people who show up to buy a $150,000 house may earn $25,000 annually or less, in addition to having bad credit. They either are not aware, or ignore, that real estate agents find credit ghosts quickly through computer services that furnish all the information we need to know about a buyer within five minutes. The ability to weed out the lookers and shoppers from the bonafide potential buyers is a broker's responsibility. Brokers take a lot of flack from buyers who know they are not qualified but are persistent in the belief that it is their God-given right to look at properties that they are told are financially over their heads. Brokers who show unqualified buyers are cab drivers as opposed to matchmakers. The conscientious broker who performs the weeding-out task efficiently saves the seller a lot of pain and strain and rightfully earns the sale commission.

There are salespeople who never learned to distinguish the several kinds of buyers with whom they do business. Let's look at a few who should be easily recognized.

The buyers that I have labeled the students inspect the property with a tape recorder in hand and a large legal-size pad under arm, and ask every question under the sun. I cannot recall, in over a 40-year period, one student type who has ever purchased a property from me.

Next in line are the purchasers I call the plumbers. Between the husband and the wife they turn on every water faucet in the house and flush every toilet, at the same time if possible, and then apologize for the inconvenience. Since 99 percent of the time they cannot find anything wrong with the water pressure, they depart saying that the master bedroom is too small or that they need a five-car garage to accommodate their fleet. The ad they responded to clearly indicated there was a two-car brick garage.

Then there are the kind of people that will never buy because they don't intend to, or say they are waiting until they can save enough money to pay all cash. Many of them have been looking and waiting for the right housing opportunity since the end of World War II. I assume, and properly so, that house hunting for them has become a weekend pastime.

On the other hand, there are the red-hot buyers who are in a hurry to move. They have been transferred into town or have just sold their house and are being charged $100 per day for use and occupancy. Many of them have successful careers based upon their ability to make a quick decision. They usually buy or reject the proposition right on the spot with no horsing around in between.

One never forgets the cool buyers who show no sense of urgency. They are looking for a special deal, or more frequently, for a bargain-basement deal. They may even try to go behind the realtor's back and attempt to deal directly with the owner to get out of paying the brokerage commission. Too often they are grave stompers looking for widows who are desperate to sell, and someone they can con into making a deal at thousands of dollars below the fair market value.

Let's not forget the ceiling watchers. They are the people who, from the moment they enter a home, never take their eyes from a room's heaven. When they discover a hairline crack in the ceiling, they shout, "What caused that defect? Is the building shifting from its foundation?" The ceiling watchers remind me of the oldtime Sunday morning automobile tire kickers: there is little to nothing they can learn about the general condition of a car by kicking its tires, or by scrutinizing ceilings for anything other than leaks. In searching for leaks, a glance will tell you all you need to know. When your eyes are on the sky, you sometimes miss something under your feet.

Last, but not least, are Mr. and Mrs. Homebuyer, people who are sincerely looking for a house, perhaps their first home, at market price. They are willing to abide by traditional rules of the market place as long as they have confidence that the real estate broker will treat them fairly. Most house hunters fall in this category.

The broker who can recognize the various types of buyers relieves the seller of both pain and strain in the process of selling their homes, whereas some real estate agents create more problems than they solve. Be very careful when choosing a real estate agent; selecting the wrong one can prove very painful and costly. Real estate agents, like dentists, lawyers, auto mechanics and surgeons come in all sizes, shapes, and shades of intelligence and abilities. Many of them could not sell a hot dog at a baseball game or a beer at a jam-packed football stadium on a warm Fall afternoon, although they may represent a member firm of a nationally advertised brand name real estate franchise.

When you employ a real estate salesperson, you don't hire a brand name product that has been tested in a laboratory, you hire a person. Therefore, it is up to you to administer the test, and you don't do it by hiring the first real estate person that walks through the door. Interview the leading sales representatives in your area from at least three different real estate firms. You might begin with recommendations from recent sellers or check the real estate ad sections in your daily and weekly newspapers. Call those firms that seem to be most active in your area and ask a principal of the company to send you his top agent.

During the interview, find out whether the agent sells full-time or part-time, and ask for names and addresses of the buyers and sellers involved in deals the agent has closed within the past 60 days. If the agent has sold fewer than four properties in two months, I suggest you continue your search unless you sense that the salesperson has the ability, but may have hit a streak of bad luck, or no luck at all. I know we all have to start somewhere, but remember, if you take pot luck, past performance is an excellent barometer of future success.

The high-water test of a good agent is the ability to sell your house within 2 percent of the listing price. Be skeptical of salespeople who quote you pie-in-the-sky prices and then ask you for an 180-day exclusive agent agreement. The professional knows the market and will not quote an inflated price and hope that time will wear you down to the point where you are ready to confront the facts of life. It is my experience that any property that doesn't sell within 90 days was listed wrong, or that the marketing program was hampered by bad weather.

A broker who accepts an overpriced house listing is either unethical or ignorant. A salesperson who engineers a seller into that position in order to acquire the listing is guilty of unprincipled behavior. It may not be a bad idea to call your state's board of ethics or the Better Business Bureau to check whether any complaints have been filed against a firm that you are considering for an exclusive agent's agreement.

Agency agreements between the broker and the seller come in many forms. One is the exclusive right to sell under the contract agreement. The listing agent is entitled to a commission no matter who sells the property, including the owner. Even if another agent produces a buyer, the seller owes only one commission, which is shared between the listing and selling brokers. On the other hand, there is the exclusive agency agreement in which the seller doesn't pay a commission if a buyer is found without assistance from the broker. Then there is an open listing agreement, usually oral. The seller agrees to pay a commission to any agent who produces the first acceptable buyer. In this arrangement, no commission is paid if the seller finds a buyer.

High-profile and successful realty companies will accept only exclusive right-to-sell agreements. Sellers who have obtained an employer's guarantee to buy their house at a discount if the asking price is not met should insist that the E.R.S.A. contract includes a clause that prohibits the agent from claiming a commission in the event your company purchases your home.

No matter what form the agreement takes, the time limit should not exceed 90 days, even though many agents will attempt to get as long as six months. If the firm has put forth its best effort, you can always extend your listing agreement for an additional 90 days if necessary. Don't forget to check the small print on the agency agreement to make certain that you're not agreeing to an automatic extension. The agent's compensation is based on a percentage of the sales price, which for typical sales may vary between 6 percent and 10 percent.

Who determines the price a house will sell for? It is neither the seller nor broker. The actual sales price is the number of dollars a buyer will pay and a seller will accept at a specific time in a given market. Since markets are fluid, the buyer and seller need a scorekeeper. That person is the broker, whose stock in trade is to maintain a score board on the real estate prices at all times. In the absence of a realtor as the middleman, sellers have been known to sell their properties substantially under current market value because their only price reference is what they paid 30 years ago. On the other hand, I can cite numerous cases where pseudosophisticated buyers have paid thousands of dollars over the market price while trying to cut the real estate broker out of the deal. The success of the professional realtor is contingent upon an ability to set the asking price within 1 to 3 percentage points of the actual selling price.

There are sellers who think that their houses were made in heaven, who get hot under the collar when a realtor suggests a sales price below what their friends and relatives say they should get. I frequently remind them that I can identify with their right to dream, but selling dreams is not what I get paid for, and suggest that we restrict our conversation to realities of the real estate marketplace.

Sellers seem to forget that the real estate brokerage commission is based on a percentage of the sales price. The broker does not benefit by listing a $100,000 house for $50,000. In the reality of the real estate world, the seller and broker are partners who rise or fall together. Therefore, select your broker as carefully as you choose any professional whose services directly affect your life and the way you want to live it.

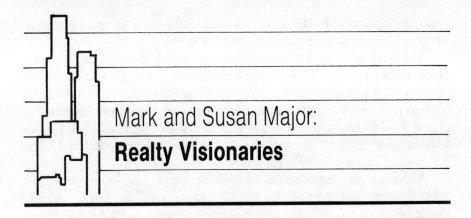

# Mark and Susan Major:
## Realty Visionaries

*"Real estate was my escape route from the underclass."*

Mark and Susan Major are native Chicagoans. They met and married while employed by the National Equipment Manufacturing Company that had its headquarters in their home town. Susan worked in the front office as an accounting clerk and he worked in the plant as a lathe operator.

Mark's mother, Mary Ann, was a day housekeeper for Sarah Boute, who owned a two-flat building. Mrs. Boute, who suffered from a severe case of glaucoma, was anxious to move back to her birthplace in New Orleans, before her eyesight deteriorated much further.

Mrs. Boute asked Mrs. Major to arrange for her son and daughter-in-law to meet with her and discuss the possibility of buying her two-flat frame building, located in the Morgan Park section of Chicago. At the initial meeting, Mary Ann's employer, who was partially blind, said to Mark, "Your mother has been a godsend to me, and I want to do something for you because of her kindness. Therefore, I am going to let you buy my building for $8,000, which is what I paid for it 20 years ago."

Mrs. Boute made the generous offer to the Majors in October 1975. The couple wanted to buy the property, but flunked the most important prerequisite: they were not financially able. The Majors collectively—Mary Ann, Mark and Susan—did not have $1,500 in their bank accounts. Mark suggested to his wife that each of them borrow $2,500

---

*These case histories are documented; only the names were changed to protect the confidentiality of the real estate broker-client relationship.

from the company credit union and take advantage of the once-in-a-lifetime opportunity that Mrs. Boute was offering.

The Majors owned a ranch house in Markham, Illinois. On their credit applications they submitted to the credit union's loan committee, they stated the purpose of the loans was to make interior improvements, such as new carpeting throughout and wood paneling in the recreation room. The fabrications on the loan applications were hatched by the Majors because they knew that the credit union bylaws prohibited loans for making down payments on real estate.

Although the loans were approved promptly and they now had $5,000 to apply on the two-flat, the Majors were still short of the money needed to close the deal. Mark visited several banks and savings and loan associations in pursuit of a $3,000 loan. He was turned away at each institution faster than a potential lover with bad breath.

One morning, after his umpteenth loan rejection, Mark walked slowly out of Tri-State Bank in Harvey, Illinois, with a hung-dog expression on his face. An elderly banker caught him by the sleeve just before he reached the exit. The white-haired gentleman spoke slowly and deliberately:

> They won't loan you any money to purchase real estate. However, since you own a home out in Markham, why don't you ask for a home improvement loan and make sure the improvements are made on the inside of the house. Remember, you must arrange never to be home when they come by to make an inspection of the completed work.

The Majors were soon approved for an additional $4,000 improvement loan. They closed the $8,000 deal on the two-flat frame building and had $1,000 left over to deposit in their bank account.

From 1975 to 1978, Mark and Susan rented the building for $600.00 per month and, over the same period, they spent $8,700 on such repairs and improvements as replacing the old furnace, installing storm windows and doors, improving the plumbing system, and painting the interior and exterior, thus giving the building the appearance of being loved by somebody.

In 1978, the Majors sold the 80-year-old two-flat frame building purchased three years earlier for $8,000 for the grand sum of $39,500. The couple's interest in real estate escalated and they both enrolled in Real Estate Principles 101 that I was teaching at the Olive-Harvey Community College. They became two of my best students.

In the fall of 1978, Mark and Susan decided that they were ready for the big time, avidly reading the real estate ads in the *Chicago Sun-Times* and the *Chicago Tribune*. When they spotted an ad for a 12-flat building in the Park Manor area advertised by Travis Realty Company for sale at $70,000, the Majors used $20,000 of the $39,500 generated from the sale of the two-flat as the down payment on the apartment building. With their excellent credit history, they had no problems with securing a first mortgage for $50,000 from the First Federal Savings and Loan Association of Chicago, now Citicorp Savings.

The Majors turned the real estate management chores over to Travis Realty. Mark devoted his spare time after completing eight hours on his regular job to perform general maintenance work around the newly acquired building. Between 1979 and 1986, they spent $19,200 on improvements on the 12-flat building. They also gave their best efforts to satisfy the building department whenever some irate rent-delinquent tenant made a complaint to the city that there was some imagined code violation in their apartment.

To minimize the harassment of the building inspector, the Majors met the basic city codes and beyond: new kitchen sinks and vanities in all 12 apartments, carpeting in the public hallways, storm windows and doors, landscaping in the front and rear of the building, wrought iron fences around the perimeters of the structure, a new electric system, timers on the boiler, new plumbing where necessary, low-sodium fluorescent lights in the hallways and exteriors, and a new roof.

With the renovation of the building, Mark and Susan were able to attract high-quality tenants and generate approximately $4,300 per month in income. The building was grossing $51,300 annually, just a shade over two-thirds of what they had paid for the property initially. The bottom line that resulted from the improvements made over a period of eight years became very visible when they sold the building they had bought for $70,000 for $180,000, or $15,000 per apartment unit. This converts into 3½ times the gross rents.

The Majors netted somewhere in the neighborhood of $85,000, not counting the return on the investment that they received from the rents, or the tax write-offs from depreciation. Susan and Mark were indeed moving into the big time although after 20 years with the National Equipment Manufacturing Co., their joint incomes never exceeded $39,000 per year.

Major found his job both boring and a dead end, two conditions that drove him closer to career possibilities in the field of real estate. He reasoned:

As a lathe operator, I was turning steel, forming parts and that type of stuff. It was very repetitious. It was like walking up a dead-end street at midnight. Moreover, it was debilitating to watch old men performing the same type of work that I was doing. Many of them had been performing the same old repetitious daily task for 30 to 35 years. I watched them walk out the door and die waiting on their pension. Sometimes they would die within three weeks after they retired from the job.

It was while attending one of my fellow-worker's funeral that I promised myself and seven other responsible people that I would not let my life end in that manner. I knew there had to be a higher plane.

Subconsciously, when I started acquiring property, I was looking for a means of escape. Real estate was my escape route from the underclass.

When I first met Mark Major, I recognized that he was young and highly-motivated, a driven man with a wide-eyed look of someone in search of something. He didn't really know where he was going but was anxious to go somewhere, anywhere, but where he was. My real estate office became Mr. Major's second home. During one of his regular visits, he recalled:

I walked into Mr. Travis' outer office one crisp fall afternoon in 1980. He was talking on the phone, clearly becoming irritated at the person on the other end of the line. I heard him snap, 'The building is completely occupied and if the roof wasn't any good, how the heck do you think people would be living in the building?'

Mr. Travis continued, 'I'll tell you what, never mind, never mind,' and hung up the phone. Then he turned and looked out the door and said, 'Mr. Major, would you come here a minute? I have a building for you. You're just the person I wanted to see.'

After Mr. Travis told me that some widow was asking $41,500 for an 18-flat building at 62nd and Langley, I jumped in my car and drove by the building and said to myself, the land the building is on is worth that price. I felt this was a very good real estate investment.

The following day, Mr. Travis arranged for my wife and me to inspect the interior of the building. To tell the truth, I was somewhat disappointed and frightened at what I saw during my excursion through the four levels of the structure. The basement was under water at least one foot deep. The sewage or something had backed up. There was graffiti on almost every inch of the hallway walls. The rear porches were in need of repairs. It was a holy mess, but I was determined to buy the building. The price was $41,500. We closed the deal in December of 1980. It was bitter cold and Chicago's hawk (wind) was singing "Tobacco Road." I decided because of the extreme cold weather that I would rehab the inside of the building during the winter months. I put in new kitchen sinks and cabinets, dry walled where the plaster had been totally shot, carpeted or sanded the floors in each of the 18 apartments. I put in new doorbells, an intercom system and mailboxes.

In the spring of 1981, I tore down the old back porches and built new ones, and sandblasted and tuckpointed the entire building. I spent approximately $30,000, which means that I put a little over $70,000, including the price, into the property. The building had a good return, approximately $7,500 per month, which was a very fair rent for the west Woodlawn area. On April 4, 1986, I sold that property for $127,000 or $7,055 per apartment. The wife and I realized a profit of $52,000.

In the meantime, the manufacturing company that the Majors were working for moved, throwing out of work all the people in the Chicago plant who did not want to move to the new plant operation in Georgia. Major decided that it was time to create his own employment and work full-time on his buildings. Susan decided to return to school and get a bachelor's degree in business administration. The Majors could afford to make a deep right turn in the road because their real estate ventures had made them financially independent.

Mark Major became a jack-of-all-trades in the building construction business, tackling independent contracting. He purchased a single-family HUD-owned home at 102nd and Morgan—a sound house with four bedrooms, 2½ baths, and full basement. Mark decided to renovate the building from the basement to the roof, spending approximately $10,000 plus his own labor on repairs. The initial price of the HUD property was $30,000, and he subsequently sold it through Travis Realty Co. for $57,000. Although Major realized that $12,000 for a few months' work, he felt that he had been taken by HUD.

Mark did not seek a professional opinion before getting into the HUD deal. Had he done so, he would have known that the government does not throw real estate bargains around for him or anybody else to get fat on. Moreover, he also would have learned that if a conservative appraisal value of $50,000 is placed on a HUD foreclosure house, the bidding will start somewhere between $47,000 and $48,000. There is very little cushion between the appraisal value and the bid price.

On the other hand, if Mark Major had purchased the four-bedroom house at the right price, he would have realized at least a $20,000 profit on the $10,000 that he put into rehabbing the structure. A good rule of thumb to remember is that for every dollar that Mark put into rehab he should have planned to get 2 to 5 dollars back at the time of sale. Mark Major would have had to search among hundreds of VA- and FHA-foreclosed properties to find one with any real profit potential.

As a result of Mark's initial HUD experience, he made this observation:

> I discovered that HUD was also in the real estate business. And their whole scenario has changed as far as the sale of property is concerned. What I mean is that HUD is selling properties that are in need of repair for an exorbitant price. They are making little or no allowance for the deteriorated state of the properties in their pricing. They are making every effort to maximize the amount of money they can get for their properties and, in turn, they are lowering the incentive for individual entrepreneurs or families seeking to buy a home to go in and attempt to fix up the orphan properties and come out with their pants or skirts. In other words, it seems to me that they are selling 'as is' properties at market value. If a contractor or entrepreneur is trying to make a buck for his labor by buying HUD properties, he's in the wrong ball park. A contractor can get hurt in the HUD game and an amateur can be financially murdered. Beware!

Despite the negative experience Major had in his construction efforts with the HUD property, he was determined to become a general contractor. In Janury 1987, he and his wife purchased a 55-flat building that a bank had on its foreclosure shelf for $75,000, or $1,364 per apartment. The building was fully occupied with people Major described as totally undesirable tenants. Some of them had not paid rent in two years.

Major was in too big of a hurry to go through the regular court procedure for evicting each tenant, so he and his lawyer went to court and a judge gave them a vacate order for the entire building. With the help of some uniformed friends, Mark put every tenant and his belongings on the street in March 1987. Major and his friends, with their kangaroo court process, accomplished in one day what under ordinary court procedure would take two to three months.

I would not advise anyone to use Major's eviction method because it is definitely against the law and it is also dangerous. You should never be in such a hurry to succeed that greed outreaches your need. I maintain that pigs get fat and hogs get slaughtered. Pray that you never become a hog.

I sincerely hope that Mark's eviction process was his last illegal short-cut because he has a very bright future in the housing rehabilitation business if he does not make another U-turn.

Major is rehabilitating his newly acquired 55-unit apartment building at a cost that will probably run in the neighborhood of $300,000. Although he is not physically doing the work himself, he's directing and orchestrating the methods that he wants the job to be done, and buying and supplying all the materials for the tradesmen. By acting as his own general contractor, Major could very well cut anywhere from 25 percent to 30 percent off of the cost of rehabilitation.

The Majors' building rehabilitation program is a family affair. Susan and their 21-year-old son are on the job every day, just like Mark. She notes:

> If you're going to be in the real estate business, especially if you're just getting started, you cannot be afraid to get your manicure messed up. You cannot wear clean clothes and get the job done. You have to be in there working with your people and letting them know that you don't mind participating in order to see that it's completed. The tradesmen will work effectively with you if they see you're about taking care of serious business. You must put on your jeans and roll up your sleeves and get down and work.
>
> I am usually on the job site everyday. I'm looking at things maybe that Mark missed, minor details. I'm offering suggestions as to interior decorating and the exterior landscaping. I take care of the book work, keep all the contractors and contracts and everything filed appropriately so if there are any questions, I can handle them. I intercept all calls from the bank or from the contractors. I do all of the accounting work in preparation for it to go to our certified public accountant for finalization and pay outs. Whatever it takes to get the job done, I'll do it. I'm down picking up paper off the lawn one minute and up on the roof the next. Nobody sits around the job with me looking pretty.
>
> When Mark has to leave the job, he leaves the keys with our son. We are bringing him up gradually in the business so he will know that he's a part of what we're doing. When we feel that he is ready to take on more responsibility, we will give it to him.

Moreover, it's our opinion that for him to appreciate what we're going through, he has to be on the job and participate. He's learning an awful lot just by being on the job site. Some day the experience will prove very beneficial to him.

When I made an inspection of the Majors' 55-unit building in 1987, I estimated that they were perhaps 90 percent through with the total rehabilitation program and within 20 to 30 days of launching a full-scale rent-up program. The work that they've done is certainly a major improvement for the area, something they should be proud of. However, the final chapter of the story will not be known until after the rent up is completed and the building has had an opportunity to settle with highly desirable tenants. If this development is as successful as we hope it will be, the Majors will truly have made some giant strides.

As I parted company with the Majors, Susan cautioned:

If anybody is serious about real estate, they must be able to get rid of their immediate gratification mentality. You will rarely buy a piece of real estate that will make you rich overnight. It's just not going to happen. It takes time to grow. The whole procedure takes time. Moreover, you are a lot more certain of coming out a winner in the real estate market than you are of coming out a winner in a state lottery.

## Samuel & Lucille Cross:
## The Real Estate Strivers*

### *"Don't fall in love with the bricks or the tenants."*

Samuel Cross was born July 15, 1927, in Chicago. Lucille Cash was born in a rural area outside of Vicksburg, Mississippi on January 10, 1930, just three months after the big 1929 stock market crash. Both were members of middle-class families. As early as Sam can remember, his father had owned several apartment buildings. Lucille's father was a man of property and a landlord, too. Fourteen tenant sharecroppers lived and worked on Mr. Cash's 800 acres of Mississippi farm land.

Sam Cross spent three years in the U.S. Army. Soon after his honorable discharge in 1946, he took a job as a $1.26-an-hour clerk at the main post office in Chicago. Sam and Lucille married in 1954, moved in with his parents at their home in the Park Manor section of Chicago, and began to accumulate savings.

In 1957, Lucille gave birth to their first child. Their baby girl was not six months old when Lucille decided that it was time for the growing family to find laughing room in a house of their own. After they purchased a five-room Chicago-style brick bungalow in the 7600 block of South Michigan, they were blessed with another daughter and a son.

Nine years after they bought their first home for $13,500, the Crosses sold it for $19,500. They took half of their $6,000 profit and purchased a newly constructed six-room house at 79th and LaSalle. Less

---

*These case histories are documented; only the names were changed to protect the confidentiality of the real estate consultant-client relationship.

than a year after buying their second home, they purchased a four-flat building on the same street as an investment.

Lucille Cross reflected:

We thought that real estate would be a good source of extra income. I was not working and I had to think of ways to supplement my husband's income and also raise the children in a desirable community. We always entertained the concept that we were going to let the profits from each building be a stepping stone towards our next investments. In other words, my husband's salary was used to maintain three children and ourselves. The profit from the four-flat building was put into our bank account with the intent of buying bigger and better buildings at each step along the way. Out of the four-flat building, we were able to net approximately $3,600 a year.

In a year and a half, we had accumulated enough money to buy a second four-flat building. We did not have to put but $3,000 down. The seller agreed to hold a $3,000 second mortgage on the side. At that time, some savings and loan associations would not permit second mortgages. Therefore, the seller did not record his mortgage until about five months after the deal closed.

There was another plus on our side because my husband was very handy. Sam had learned building maintenance when he was a young boy helping his father after school. So we were able to save an awful lot of money by doing so many things ourselves. Plus, you must keep in mind the fact that we had three children, all going to the University of Chicago Lab School. It became obvious that we had to live frugally because our only sources of income were my husband's salary from the post office and the two buildings.

It was costing us $2,000 per year per child to keep the kids at the University of Chicago Lab School. They did not enroll at the Lab School from grade one. My daughters started going to the Lab after they reached high school age and my son started in the third grade. The good education paid off because my oldest daughter is a practicing physician and my son and second daughter are both practicing lawyers. My husband and I don't feel that the sacrifice we paid to educate our children was too high. As a matter of fact, we know it was one of our best investments.

We can certainly give credit to our real estate investments for making those educational opportunities possible. I think we should point out the fact that we didn't take vacations for 18 years. My husband drove the same car for 12 years, and did not think about getting another until old faithful broke down. Even then, we bought another second-hand car. Our striving to get ahead was by no means the days of wine and roses.

With the thought of expanding our real estate investment plans, I started going to Chicago State University during the period of time that my kids were in school. I would go to school at 10 in the morning and always be home by 3 when they got out of class. Over a period of years that now seem like forever, I earned my bachelor's, master's and doctorate degrees while going to school on a part-time basis.

Now with the extra salary coming in from my teaching career, we really began to look at real estate and all of its ramifications and possibilities. We sold both four-flats and invested the monies in a 36-unit building, which to this day has proven extremely profitable.

Sam and I did not realize at the time that when we purchased the four-flats we were not really into investment property. You don't begin to see a significant return on your real estate dollars until you get into 12 or more units. The economy of size makes a big difference on your net return. After only three years, we got an opportunity to parlay the profits out of the 36-flat and buy a 60-unit building. Then, on the side, we began to pick up small properties in the Gap area, between 31st and 37th Street and east from King Drive to Indiana Avenue. We purchased one Gap property at 36th and King Drive through Travis Realty Company for $13,750, held it for approximately 14 months and sold it for $60,000, and netted $40,000.

Samuel Cross interrupted his wife Lucille at this point and said:

One of the biggest mistakes we ever made was not buying the Ida B. Wells Landmark building, which Travis Realty was marketing. I guess the thing that influenced me against buying it was the fact that my original intention was to gut it and totally rehabilitate it before moving in. My wife did not want to live in the area until the proposed 1992 World's Fair opened. Although the World's Fair has been aborted, we still missed a grand opportunity to have bought a building that easily would have sold for four times the asking price after just a little fixing up.

Mrs. Cross patted Sam on the shoulder warmly and interjected:

Although we lost on the landmark property, we ultimately hit a real estate bonanza when a very prominent Hollywood, stage and TV star decided to sell all of the properties he owned in the Chicago area. Through Mr. Travis we were able to package the whole deal and get the seller to hold the mortgage in the bargain. This turned out to be a very good deal for us. We sold one of the properties out of the package for which we paid $38,500 for $150,000. Of course, we had made improvements on the property such as tuckpointing, putting in a new furnace and a new roof. At the closing we walked away with an $80,000 net profit, which was no small accomplishment when you consider it all started with a $3,000 down payment on a five-room bungalow.

Samuel and I cannot take total credit for our accomplishments because we were kind of stumbling around and searching for direction in the real estate market when we met Mr. Dempsey Travis, who sold us our first building in 1957. I am using the word 'sold' loosely because Mr. Travis never really gave us a sales pitch in that his style is more or less that of an advisor or consultant who introduces you to the options and then leaves you on your own. For example, we purchased the second four-flat without seeking Mr. Travis' advice. When we subsequently brought our newly acquired property to his attention, he simply asked, 'What investment objective were you planning to reach by owning two four-flat buildings? If your interest was to maximize the return on your dollars, you made the wrong turn in the road.'

It took Sam and I a little time to catch up with Mr. Travis' thinking on the fact that it costs less to heat one eight-flat building than it does to heat two four-flat apartments with the same gross income. Also, the real estate taxes are less on one eight-unit than on two four-unit structures. As simple as it may sound, it's hard for most people to realize that it is not the number of free standing buildings you own that counts, but the number of units in each building that gives the biggest bang for your buck.

Many people, like the Crosses, fall in love with buildings and it sometimes takes a lot of rethinking and undoing to break up the "I am in love with bricks" affair. Once the Cross family crossed that bridge, it did not take me long to convince them that it was to their benefit to sell the two four-flat buildings and invest the monies into a 36-unit brick three-story walk up.

Samuel Cross gave the following rationale for purchasing the second 4-flat building:

I bought the four-flat because it was attainable. It did not require a lot of work. I wanted to stay away from three-story buildings because you have to provide garbage and scavenger service if it is six units or more. With the two-story brick, the tenants carry their own garbage down and that eliminated another chore that I would have to perform. Buying the second four-flat unit, in my opinion, was not a mistake at the time. Today, under my present financial circumstances, it would be a mistake.

Another big mistake made by the Crosses, and many other owners who manage their own properties, is that they figuratively fall in love with their tenants. One of the early signs of a tenant-owner love affair is the owner's refusal to raise the rents to meet the annual cost of living index. In making rent surveys on buildings that are being put on the market, I have seen some extreme cases where some tenants have not received a rent increase in 15 years. This occurred even though the tenants are on a month-to-month tenancy, which means that the owner could have raised the rents by simply giving the tenants a 30-day notice.

The usual response I get when I ask why the rents have not been raised to the market level is: "They are such beautiful tenants and they have been with me ever since I bought the building." These love affairs must be mutual. What tenant would not be madly in love with a landlord who is charging 1970 rent in 1987?

A classic case of penny-wise and pound-foolish developed years ago when a prominent real estate lawyer asked me to manage his 20-flat building for 4 percent of the annual gross rents. I told my friend I could not afford to do it for less than 6 percent. Twenty-seven years later, in 1987, he asked me to sell his building. Would you believe that this brilliant attorney who refused to pay a 6 percent management fee was still collecting 1960 rents?

One of the several diamonds in the real estate crowns of Lucille and Samuel Cross is good judgment. They learned early to hire professional management services for their properties, and through the years, they have encouraged every member of their family to take this vital step.

The economic moral of this case: "Don't fall in love with the bricks or the tenants."

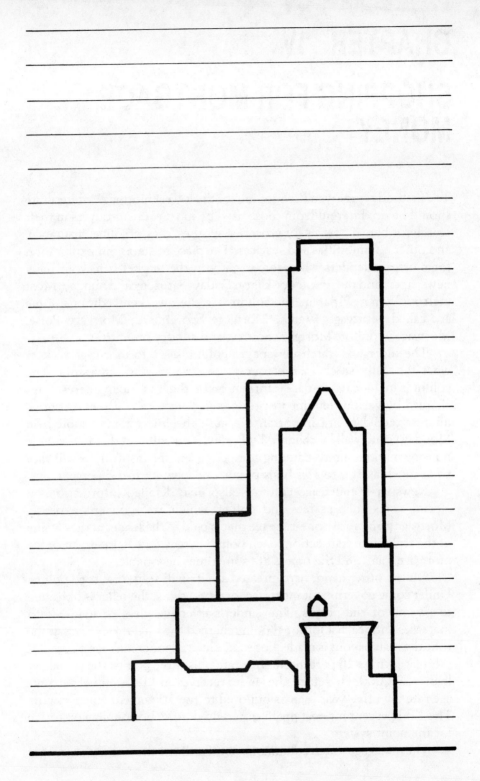

# CHAPTER IV

# SHOPPING FOR MORTGAGE MONEY

The methods employed in shopping for the lowest mortgage interest rate should be no different from those used by most prudent buyers in their search for bargain prices for groceries, clothes, cars, gasoline, insurance, and other commodities and services. The place to start your exploration for mortgage lenders who are currently in the market is in your daily newspaper, and the time to look is on Friday, Saturday and Sunday. Most metropolitan newspapers run columns in their weekend editions; some are called Mortgage Watch, Mortgage Scoreboard, Mortgage Pulse, Mortgage Monitor, Mortgage Source, and sundry other titles.

The mortgage watch newspaper columns are to mortgage seekers what the daily stock market quotations are to stock investors. The columns include up-to-date information on the home loan interest rates charged by various lending institutions in your area. Current mortgage interest rate data are important because the interest rate quoted on Monday could well be changed by Friday. You will find that in the same housing market, interest among competing lending institutions will vary by as much as 100 to 150 basis points or 1 percent to 1½ percent.

Newspaper mortgage columns also give detailed information on closing costs such as fees and points, which are a buyer's expense. Mortgage points are a one-time fee that is paid to the lender at the closing of the real estate transaction. Each point charged equals 1 percent of the mortgage loan, and the points are sometimes negotiable.

On the other hand, hard-pressed sellers will split or absorb points. Under some government mortgage loan programs, the seller is obligated to pay all of the points. The lender's effective yield or loan return increases with each additional point charged the buyers or sellers at the time the loan payout is made. For example, if a lender makes a $100,000 mortgage with a 10 percent interest rate plus three points, the actual net loan is $97,000 Therefore, the lender receives an 11.33 annual percentage rate on a five-year loan as opposed to the 10 percent contract rate. The 1.33 percent interest profit differential is the bottom line objective for the point system.

The mortgage watch columns also will indicate the lender's charge for processing the loan application, known as a processing fee. The fee could range from $350 to several thousands of dollars depending on the size of the loan. The mortgage processing fee is non-refundable. In addition to points and fees, the columns offer information on prevailing interest rates and the various types of mortgages available.

For decades, the only type of home financing instrument available was the fixed-rate loan, which is a mortgage agreement with a fixed annual percentage interest for the life of the loan. The monthly loan payments were level (same amount each month), and the loan was fully amortized (paid off) at the end of a specific period. For example, a $600 per month payment (including principal and interest) at 10 percent per annum would pay the mortgage in full in 30 years.

In 1980, when double-digit inflation hit the money market and prime interest rates rose from 8 percent to 21.5 percent, fixed-rate mortgage loans in bank portfolios became an income drain and passbook savers were being siphoned away by attractive interest rates of other financial instruments such as stocks, bonds, and treasury notes. Money movement from lending institutions to other financial instruments is known in the industry as disintermediation. During periods of disintermediation, depositors withdrew funds at record levels from the mortgage lending institutions. Hence, the savings and loan industry was forced to create some new products to compete for the dollars in the market place. In the process, the thrift banks shifted the impact of the inflation risk to the borrower.

Here are some new mortgage products that are utilized as hedges for lending institutions during inflationary periods:

1. Adjustable Rate Mortgage (ARM). The mortgage, as the name implies, permits the lender to increase the interest rate semiannually or annually as dictated by general money market condition.

ARMs have a ceiling, or a maximum level of how much a rate can be raised. If you purchased a home with an 8 percent ARM, the contract has a ceiling, or cap, of possibly 13 percent to 14 percent. One of the pitfalls in the ARM is that you cannot plan a budget because, unlike the old stand-by fixed-rate conventional loan, you cannot predict how inflation is going to affect the mortgage market from year-to-year.

Several types of ARM loan products are available. The most popular is the contract with a 6 percent life-time ceiling, which means that during the life of the mortgage contract, the maximum interest charged cannot be more than 6 percentage points higher than the initial rate. Under this plan, the lender can adjust the interest rate only once a year and under no circumstances can the adjustment exceed 2 percentage points annually.

ARM loans are purchased by the Federal National Mortgage Association, a national company with the mortgage portfolio estimated at $94.8 billion as of the third quarter of 1987 and currently holding $12.53 billion in ARM loans. The loans must have an interest cap of 1 percentage point per adjustment, which can be made every six months, and the rate may not be increased more than 5 percentage points over the life of the loan.

Such a move by the largest mortgage buyer in America could very well standardize the ARM program. On the other hand, the lending institutions have done a masterful public relations job for the ARM program and 65 percent of the current market has bought it. In my opinion, the apparently successful ARMs are dangerous because they turn the borrower into a risk-taking entrepreneur, diverting risk from the banking establishment, whose primary job is predicting the money market.

2. Balloon Mortgage. Under this plan, the buyer makes equal fixed payments for a short period of time, usually five to 10 years, then must pay off the entire remaining balance. Most lenders usually roll the loan over or renegotiate the terms of the loan for another five- or 10-year-period.

The balloon mortgage predates the 1930 Depression. During the 1930s, many borrowers could not meet their mortgage obligation when the note became due and the end result was a rash of foreclosures. The foreclosure crisis gave cause for the creation of the Federal Home Loan Bank system in 1932 and the Federal Housing Administration in 1934.

However, this program can also be dangerous because there is nothing in the mortgage contract that could prevent the lender from foreclosing on your property if you did not pay the loan off on the mortgage in full on the final due date. The balloon loan is a useful financing vehicle if you plan to sell your home within the term of the mortgage or expect the property value to appreciate rapidly.

3. Federal Housing Administration (FHA) and Veterans Administration (VA) mortgages. Under these programs, mortgages are conventional and usually have a payout period of 30 years, with a fixed rate.

A 1987 policy implemented by the Department of Housing and Urban Development has liberalized limitations for buying down interest rates on Federal Housing Administration-insured home loans. The purpose of the change in policy was to allow an increase in interest rate buy downs and thus make it easier for marginal borrowers to qualify for an FHA mortgage under the current government's new tough credit standards.

Buy downs were used extensively during the 1980-82 period when the mortgage rates soared to as high as 15.5 percent per annum. During these years, builders paid mortgage lenders substantial buy down fees in order to move their finished housing products in a historically tight money market. Buy downs were a very practical way for builders to people thousands of acres of brand new empty houses.

In buy downs, a builder deposits funds in a lender's escrow account to make up the difference between the borrower's monthly payments and the amount that would have been paid in the absence of the interest buy down. Typically, the buy down cost to the builder amounts to 3 percent of the loan amount, reducing the borrower's interest rate by 2 percentage points the first year and 1 percentage point the second year.

Commencing with the first month of the third year, the buy down ends and the borrower starts paying the going FHA rate, currently 10.5 percent on a 30-year-fixed mortgage. Since there is no such thing as a free lunch, the builder packs the cost of the 3 percent buy down into the price of the house. The 2-1 buy down would cost the builder about $2,618 on the maximum $87,250 FHA loan in the Chicago area.

Under the liberal buy down program, the Federal Housing Administration permits the borrower to qualify for the first year's monthly mortgage payment based on a buy down interest rate of 8.5 percent. Prior to the liberalization, the FHA permitted 2-1 buy downs but the borrower had to qualify for the loan based on an income that would support the full percentage rate payment and not the buy down rate. In other words, the borrower would have to qualify for a 10.5 percentage rate mortgage, which eliminates a large number of marginal buyers.

4. Graduated Payment Adjustable Mortgages. GPMs usually are employed by young buyers who are on the fast track and anticipate that their income will be upward bound. With a graduated payment mortgage, the monthly payment starts at a low level and gradually increases 2 percent a year until reaching a level slightly above the prevailing conventional mortgage rate.

5. Bi-weekly Mortgage. This is simply a fixed-rate loan requiring half a monthly payment every two weeks. Under this plan, you accelerate your equity build up and reduce your interest costs over the life of the loan. Many people borrow where they bank and make arrangements for the lender to deduct the bi-weekly payments out of their savings or checking account.

6. Shared Equity Mortgage (SEM). Under this agreement, the investor provides part or all of the down payment, portions of the monthly payment or both. In return, the investor receives an equity interest in the property and some of the tax benefits. Many lenders make it a prerequisite that the investor or co-borrower be an immediate family member.

Equity sharing is an excellent way to finance a mortgage. It enables parents to help children who have not accumulated any funds to make a down payment and simultaneously protect themselves. However, it need not be limited to parents. A cousin, a nephew or niece, or a stranger can participate in the equity arrangement. Equity sharing can be reversed and used by children who have done well and want to help their parents who couldn't accumulate any money during their working years because they spent most of their savings sending their children through college.

Let's assume that a prospective purchaser, a homeowner, wants to buy a house for $100,000. The lender requires a 10 percent down payment of $10,000. The homeowner gets the $10,000 from the investor, and agrees to pay 10 percent interest, or $1,000 a year, to the investor. At the end of the five years, the home is sold for $120,000. The investor gets the initial $10,000 back in addition to the $5,000 interest payment. The homeowner, who had no equity, gets a home he or she could not have afforded otherwise and makes a $15,000 profit when the house is sold.

In part II of the scenario on equity buying, the co-purchaser becomes co-owner when the mortgage papers are actually signed. The investor then becomes part owner, usually 50-50, and part landlord. The person who occupies the property is part owner and part tenant. The investor receives some rent, one-half of the fair market rental rate, plus tax deductions for one-half the interest payment on the loan. The basic concept of the equity arrangement is excellent, but legal counsel is advisable in drafting the supporting equity agreement.

7. Growing Equity Mortgage. The GEM is a fixed-rate mortgage with a fixed schedule of payments that gradually rise over time. The increase in payments is applied to reducing the principal. Extra principal payments allow you to decrease the pay-off period of the mortgage by five to 15 years. A GEM is a growth-equity mortgage in that you might make payments of $400 a month for the first year, $650 the second year and $800 the third year. This type of loan is of great benefit to young professionals who are certain that their incomes will increase dramatically within a relatively short period of time. On the other hand, this type of loan would not be good for public school teachers, college professors, commercial bankers and other people in non-growth salary industries. For the fast tracker, this type of loan instrument is tailor made.

8. Flexible Loan Insurance Program (FLIP). The FLIP loan is a fully amortizing, graduated payment mortgage that treats the down payment in a unique way. Instead of using the down payment as equity in a building, a major portion (say, 80 percent) is deposited in a savings account pledged as additional collateral for the lender, and as the source of

supplementary payments for the borrower during the first few years of the loan.

The lender can advance up to 100 percent of the purchase price, and each month withdraw a set amount from the savings account, which added to the borrower's reduced payment, comprises a normal loan payment. There is an interesting feature of the FLIP account: the mortgagor generates interest from the pledged monies that can be applied against the mortgage interest rate, and actually reduces the interest rate cost the mortgagor has to pay.

9. Home Equity Mortgages. HEMs are basically second mortgages that are collateralized by the equity in the borrower's home. This type of loan is particularly attractive to the elderly because of the initial bait and trap low interest rates that are tax deductible under the Tax Reform Act of 1986. The kicker for most elderly persons is that because their income is low, the Tax Reform Act of 1986 is practically meaningless to them.

A home equity line of credit is a convenient and flexible second mortgage for a person who does not need all the money at one time. Borrowers pay interest only on the amount borrowed, not on the total credit line available. The amount of credit available is based on the mortgagor's equity in the house minus the balance on the first mortgage, if one exists.

The minimum home equity loan is $5,000. The line of credit usually is limited to 75 percent of the market value of the home. According to consumer advocates, very few lenders quote fixed rates on home equity loans. Most rates are adjustable, based on the prime lending rate, which was 8.75 percent as of mid-Novembr 1987. The initial interest rate on most home equity loans is set between 1 percent and 3 percent above the prime, that is, the rate that banks charge their most credit-worthy customers.

Very few lenders set caps on how high the interest on a home equity line of credit may rise. The prime rate soared above 21.5 percent in 1980, and equity loan interest bounced up dramatically. Home equity loans in the early 1980s made mob juice loans look like bargains; interest rates eat equity like termites eat wood.

Some new equity products tailored to fit the elderly are:

a. Reverse Mortgage Program. The loan carries an above-market interest rate and requires full repayment of accumulated borrowing plus interest at a fixed date, say five or 10 years from the start of the loan. If the borrower is alive at the end of the amortization period, the lump sum repayment could put the elderly homeowner in the position of having to sell his or her house.

b. Shared Equity Long-term Reverse Mortgage. This program, known as IRMA (Individual Retirement Mortgage Account) is available only in a handful of states. The program offers guaranteed monthly payments for life. Although it is the most innovative commercial undertaking in the seniors' equity field, IRMA does take a portion of equity appreciation plus a double-digit basic interest rate when the time comes for repayment or for selling.

c. The Older Homeowners Line of Credit. This plan is a creation of a Washington, D.C.-based non-profit group known as the United Seniors Health Cooperative. This program, launched in early 1988, has some interesting features that might revolutionize credit for senior citizens.

1) Age and income standards are between 65 and 70 years of age or older and for people who have an income that is no higher than $20,000 to $30,000 a year.

2) The maximum credit line is tied to age. The older the applicant, the higher the percentage of home equity the account will allow to be drawn down. For example, an 85-year-old widow with $150,000 worth of equity in her home might get a $100,000 line of credit. A 65-year-old man might be allowed only half that amount.

3) There is some flexibility on draw downs in that seniors needn't touch their approved credit line until they want to. However, there will be limits on the maximum draw down of some percentage of the total line, possibly one-third in any given year.

4l) There is no requirement to repay a single dollar until the borrower dies, moves voluntarily from the house or has to move to a nursing home or similar facility. Repayment of all principal amounts borrowed, plus an interest rate hopefully in the single digits, would come from the proceeds of the home sale.

The key to the widespread availability of the senior credit program, according to the sponsors, is the willingness of state home financing agencies to set aside start-up financing for it. Even a modest initial amount of $1 million per state can initiate a national program such as the one in the state of Maryland. Many state agencies have tax-exempt, bond-generated dollars that can keep the underlying interest rate on the elderly credit line well below 10 percent.

The preceding background information should prove helpful in your search for mortgage money that fits your particular circumstance.

Keep in mind that various types of loans may be obtained at the mortgage institutions whose names appear in various newspaper financial scoreboards. After reading the newspapers, your next step is the yellow pages of the telephone book. They list hundreds of lending institutions under such categories as savings and loan associations, savings banks, commercial banks, insurance companies, mortgage brokers, and mortgage bankers.

With the telephone directory in hand, you can canvass lending institutions by phone. Ask basic questions about the interest on fixed-rate loans, and adjustable rate mortgages, and about other mortgage products, such as the senior citizen credit line. After calling from 25 to 40 loan officials over a period of several weeks, you will sound like a professional with a feel of the real estate mortgage market and its language.

I must emphasize that your search for a mortgage loan should begin where you have savings. Don't bank where you cannot borrow. On the other hand, you should not accept a loan, even from your bank, without making a comparison of interest rates, points and escrow requirements offered by other institutions in your city. Remember that many lenders will offer good rates but flunk the service and public relations tests. There is a lending institution in Chicago that I think of as the bank with a smile, but I know others that appear to wear perpetual frowns. While friendly banks welcome you with open arms, you have to crowbar your way through the loan officer's door in other institutions. The personality differences of lending institutions cannot be discovered in one visit. You can save time and energy by vicariously using the mind and eyes of your real estate broker.

You can also learn a great deal by talking with friends and relatives about the kind of services they get from their respective banking institutions. They may caution that the best price may not always be the best bang for your buck. For instance, some automobile dealers who offer the best showroom prices give terrible service when you need repairs. Although a mortgage is not likely to break down like a car, extenuating circumstances might sometime force you to make special arrangements with your lending institution. Friendly, service-minded banks make adjustments for emergency needs without giving you a difficult time in the process.

If your efforts to deal with a bank fail, you must employ creative ways to finance the purchase of real estate. First, there is the use of a contract for a deed, which eliminates the necessity of a large down payment. Second, you could assume existing loans with a minimum or no-cash down payment. Third, you might obtain a loan from your stock broker or bank using your own stocks and bonds as collateral for a non-purpose loan. Fourth, you could employ the wrap-around mortgage, which is a second mortgage wrapped around a first mortgage. This would enable you to reduce your down payment to a minimum without actually assuming the existing loans. Fifth, there's a blended mortgage that permits you to assume an existing first and second mortgage, and perhaps blend the rate differential between the two. Finally, there is the bridge loan, a temporary mortgage usually made for 30 to 90 days. It would provide quick cash for a deal that you ordinarily could not make through the regular process. A bridge loan usually can be arranged within a 72-hour period, whereas the regularly processed loan may take six to eight weeks, and that might be too long to hold down a very hot deal.

In this chapter, there is a large arsenal of financing tools that you can use when you go hunting for your friendly mortgage institution. Good hunting!

# Strickland Davis:
## The Real Estate Parlayer*

*"The real estate determines the wisdom of the investment."*

Strickland Davis was born on a farm in the Mississippi Delta. The share-cropping shack in which he spent his nights after working all day in the cotton fields was so deep in the bowels of Mr. Alex Ridoff's cotton plantation that Strickland's parents would not permit him to go to school until he was 8 years old. He was such a small child his folks felt that it would be too dangerous for him to walk the nine-mile round trip by himself to a one-room redwood schoolhouse plunked near the county line.

Looking back, Strickland feels that his folks were overprotective and did not realize the situation they were creating for him to wrestle with during his adolescent period. When Strickland came to Chicago in 1951 at the age of 13 and enrolled in elementary school, he discovered that he was four years older than anyone else in his fourth grade class. Little Strickland did not graduate from grammar school until he was 17 years of age and the other members of his class were 12 and 13 years old.

Late one afternoon while enroute to a part-time job cleaning washrooms and sweeping floors in a box factory, young Strickland stopped dead in his tracks and said: "What am I going to do with myself? I am already four or five years older than my schoolmates. If I go to college and ultimately graduate, I will be 27 or 28 years old. I have got to find some alternative to fulfill my life."

Strickland was fortunate in meeting a school counselor who empa-

---

*These case histories are documented; only the names were changed to protect the confidentiality of the real estate broker-client relationship.

thized and recognized that he had a problem because of his late start in acquiring a formal education. The counselor suggested that Strickland go to a vocational school where upon graduation at age 21 he would be prepared to enter the work force.

In September 1955, Strickland enrolled in the Chicago Vocational High School on East 87th Street. He was serious about becoming a top student and making up for lost time. At Chicago Vocational, he was exposed to some phases of all the trades. Strickland believes that his rural background may have given him a deeper insight into such basics as trees, animals, nature, more so than possessed by a person reared in the city. Davis felt that his early exposure to the cycles of nature in the rural south enabled him to sap out quickly a great deal of knowledge about the different trades. His love and major in vocational school was auto mechanics. He feels that if you understand the mechanism of a car, you are a world beater, because to understand a car you have to know a lot of things. For example, you have to have a certain amount of knowledge about both the electrical and heat transfer theories. If you don't take the heat off of a engine through the cooling system, the motor will burn up. The same basic concepts, he rationalizes, are applicable to the heating system of an apartment building.

At the age of 27, Strickland purchased his first piece of real estate because the landlord had asked him and his wife to give up their one-bedroom apartment. Davis' wife was seven months pregnant with their first child and their landlord did not want any children in his building. Strickland had the grand sum of $500 with which to buy a house, and wondered how to go about it:

> How in the heck am I going to buy a house when all the money I got to my name is five one hundred dollar bills? I ran around to different real estate companies in different neighborhoods trying to find somebody who would let me have a house for my wife and heir. My wife wanted the very best for $500. Finally I ran into a two-bedroom duplex at 88th and Kenwood. The building had been vacant for 10 years. Wild trees had grown in the backyard that were 15 to 20 feet tall. There were at least eight inches of dirt, grime, and filth on the floor and I had to shovel through the dirt to see the grain of wood.
>
> My training at Chicago Vocational High School enabled me to look through the grit and grime and see the basic construction. Moreover, I remembered reading an article by Dempsey J. Travis in *Ebony Magazine* entitled, "Don't Buy Other People's Paint." I applied that principle.

I told my wife I thought I could handle the deal. They were asking $10,000 and I wanted to offer $7,000. My wife said, 'No! No! No! Give them what they are asking because this is the end of the road and I am going to have our baby in two weeks.'

I called the real estate broker and told him if he could make the deal with $500, I was ready to buy. Through some miracle, the deal was closed in a relatively short period of time and we never looked back until we made the decision to buy another house in 1971.

In 1971, the Strickland Davis family was mentally ready to buy a second house but were financially strapped because they had not saved any money. To acquire a house at 90th and Yates, Strickland borrowed $8,000 from his dad and $8,000 from his wife's uncle. He later sold his first house to his brother-in-law for $29,000. He made a net profit of $19,000 from the sale of the first house, out of which he repaid his relatives.

Strickland decided that after going through that episode of borrowing money from his kinfolk, he would never let himself get in that position again. He considered being broke a bad scene, especially since in addition to his regular job as a mechanic, he was the owner of a service station business on the side. Strickland shared his experiences in the service station business as follows:

I attempted to run a tight shop by cutting expenses to the bone. However, I ended up being the biggest prostitute on the street in that after I fed the light company, a national gasoline and oil company, plus my employees, the profit that I realized was minuscule.

To get that monkey off my back, I decided to get rid of the chain-controlled service station and build an oversized garage on the rear of my second house and operate an auto repair shop with a minimum amount of overhead.

I was able to get my neighbors to cooperate with me by giving the ladies free service whenever anything went wrong with their cars. My alley garage business prospered and I was able to bank $10,000 in the first year of operation. Between 1971 and 1975 I salted away $30,000.

In June 1976, the Davis family was ready to seriously start looking for some real estate investment property. He realized that with $30,000-plus in the bank he could negotiate whatever kind of deal he wanted. He found a 10-year-old, eight-apartment building on East 73rd Street, where the seller was asking $40,000 but accepted an offer from Strickland for $32,000.

Strickland was able to assume an existing $24,000 6 percent mortgage with a remaining five-year amortization period. The building was a perfect fit for Strickland's buying philosophy because he did not want a long amortization period and he did not want anything so old that it would require a lot of money to fix up. The only improvements that were needed on the structure were cosmetic and the unit dollar price of $4,000 per apartment was right in the ball park for that neighborhood. Another plus was the oversupply of potential tenants who wanted to live in a decent neighborhood.

Strickland and his wife were so pleased with the quick financial turnaround they were realizing on their first piece of investment property that they decided to buy an eight-unit apartment in December 1976, six months after their first purchase.

The Davises ran into a lot of problems attempting to buy the second investment property although they were credit worthy. This was during the 1970s when banks and savings and loan associations refused to make loans to minorities on apartment buildings with more than four units. If a minority happened to own a 20-apartment building during that period, the capital was frozen because the only way he or she could sell the property was either on contract or to take back a purchase money mortgage.

It was with a purchase money mortgage held by the sellers that enabled the Davises to buy their second investment property. In this case, the seller reduced his price from $40,000 to $30,000 when they agreed to make a 50 percent down payment upon the closing of the deal. In addition, the seller agreed to accept an 8 percent interest rate as opposed to the prevailing 16 percent. With a bundle of cash in his pocket, Strickland fashioned a tailor-made deal to fit his buying philosophy.

Strickland describes his capital accumulation formula:

> The time span between acquiring new investment properties becomes shorter and shorter as you add buildings to your portfolio. Initially, it took me 4 to 5 years to accumulate enough money to buy an apartment complex. Now I can recoup my capital in one year and buy at least one additional building a year if I wish.
>
> My third purchase was a 20-flat. The seller wanted $225,000 for the property. I offered him $175,000 with $40,000 down,

providing he hold the balance in a 9 percent note and trust deed payable over a 10-year amortization period.

The seller was motivated to accept my offer because he was a man 62 years old, in ill health and ready to retire. Plus, the neighborhood was changing and he was anxious to get out. For the seller, my offer to pay him $2,000 a month with no headache was a retirement plan made in heaven.

Strickland Davis is a good negotiator who adopted the philosophy "He who cares less always wins."

I think that can be interpreted to mean that you must go into a negotiating session with the notion that if they don't accept your offer, you will walk and not look back. In that sense, you are a winner, because if you look back you are subject to become a loser.

He gave this rationale for investing in real estate:

I found that I could work a job and invest in real estate and make a good return on my investment and not change my working pattern. In other types of businesses, it was always a question of whether it was the job or the business. If I put the time into the business, the job suffered. If I put the time into the job, the business suffered. With real estate, I can do both and do both relatively well. Moreover, I got good family backing, my wife and my kids.

My real estate is a family business. Having two daughters, it was a little difficult to get the daughters to get in there and paint and help decorate and so forth. I started them out early enough so now that is no problem. The wife has played a significant role, both as a secretary and advisor. If I made a decision to buy some investment property, she was 100 percent supportive.

The real estate investor further observes:

If your primary reason for buying real estate investment properties is tax shelters rather than the inherent safety and long-term appreciation potential of the property, then you shouldn't buy any more real estate in this tax season. Under the 1986 Tax Reform Act, the only reasons for buying real estate are 1) appreciation in market value (either by immediate upgrading or long term market value increase) and 2) positive cash flow.

Today I would not buy anything unless 1) the property is a below market price bargain that can be upgraded to increase its value or 2) it offers positive cash flow. The real estate determines the wisdom of the investment.

Another axiom Strickland Davis follows is that he always purchases a building that is well-located. If possible, he purchases the largest building in the block because he feels by owning such a property, he can control the real estate environment. In addition, he solicits the assistance of his neighbors to help maintain a wholesome surrounding. As a matter of fact, of the 10 buildings that Strickland Davis has purchased, only one was not the largest in the block. In some instances, he bought the largest building in a three-block area.

Mr. Davis' determined purchase of the biggest buildings on the block is driven by an early real estate venture. He was burned one time when he purchased a small building next to a 36-unit building that was owned by an absentee landlord who ultimately abandoned it. Of course, the abandoned building had a very negative effect on the value of Davis' property. Now, he figures that if he owns the biggest piece of property, that experience probably won't be repeated.

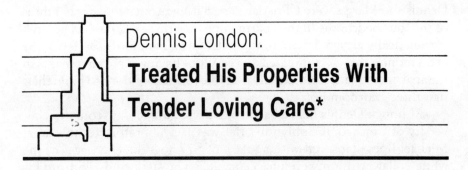

# Dennis London:
## Treated His Properties With
## Tender Loving Care*

### *"I was sick and tired of living in a windowless cubicle."*

Dennis London was born in Chicago, and was reared on the south side of the city in a one-room kitchenette. He and his father, a very religious man who worked in the stockyards as a laborer for Swift and Company, shared a community kitchen and bath with several other families. Throughout Dennis' years in elementary and high school, he refused to bring anyone to his home because he was ashamed to let his friends know the conditions in which he and his father lived.

The young man's luck did not change even after he was drafted into the U.S. Army during World War II, because there he shared bed space in a large, open barracks room with 96 other soldiers. To make bad matters worse, the army latrine was wide open and inferior to the one he had become accustomed to at home because it did not afford him any privacy at all.

Housing opportunities did not improve for Dennis even after he was married to Margie Hardwick in 1946. Like millions of other veterans, he could not find an apartment, and the couple ended up moving into a one-room kitchenette. The Londons became dog-sick and tired of being cramped into a small, windowless cubicle. Finally, Margie, a graduate of the University of Chicago, was befriended by a former classmate whose father owned a three-flat building and who offered them a large seven-room apartment with four bedrooms and 2½ baths. The Dennis Londons knew three other young couples who had been married about the

---

*These case histories are documented; only the names were changed to protect the confidentiality of the real estate consultant-client relationship.

same time as they and who were also apartment hunting. Since both Dennis and Margie were Christian and sharing people, they rented three of the four bedrooms in the apartment to the three couples, an act that automatically elevated them to the status of sublandlords. By 1955, the extra monies they accumulated as a result of having three subtenants in the apartment made it financially possible for the Londons to build their first three-bedroom home.

Although Dennis held a bachelor's degree in biology from the University of Chicago, his only job offer was as a laboratory technician at Michael Reese Hospital with a salary of $77 a week. The wages of the white-collar position were unacceptable, so he stepped down from his academic ladder and took a blue-collar job as a milkman for the Bowman Dairy Company. The dairy used horses and wagons on their residential delivery routes during the 1950s, and London delivered milk on the southeast side of Chicago from 1952 until 1973.

A growing family of three girls and two boys soon confronted the Londons with the problem of making enough money to send their children through school. Dennis decided to become a part-time real estate agent for Travis Realty Company. He was quite successful in selling real estate sales in the afternoon and evening, after finishing his early morning to midday deliveries on his daily milk route. At the point when the last of the children reached school age, Mrs. London began her career as a public elementary school music teacher.

Having had a first-hand acquaintance with poverty and inferior schools practically all of his life, Dennis was determined to make enough money to put all of his children through the University of Chicago Lab School. The Londons decided that real estate investments would earn that extra money needed to properly educate their offspring. Dennis had learned to fix doors and faucets and make other repairs around the house to save money, and loved doing it to the extent that building maintenance became a hobby.

In 1969, the Londons bought an 18-flat building from Travis Realty Company. The apartment complex was sold at $65,000 with $20,000 down, but when they entered the contract, the Londons only had $12,000, a fact they shared with the broker after the deal was closed. Luckily for them, it took four months for the deal to actually close. In the interim, Margie borrowed $4,000 from the Chicago Teachers Union and Dennis borrowed $4,000 from the People's Co-op, only to find out at the closing of the deal that they were still $2,000 short. Again, lady luck came to their rescue: $2,500 in rent security deposit credits due them from the seller made up the shortage, and they were able to close the deal without asking for an extension or a second mortgage loan.

The real estate transaction hadn't been closed 30 days when the boiler broke down and the Londons needed $5,000 to buy a new one. They sought direction from their broker at Travis Realty Company, who referred them to the Seaway National Bank of Chicago. Since the bank held the real estate title on the 18-flat in trust, collateralizing the loan for the new boiler became rather simple. Nevertheless, Dennis decided that he could not continue to pay the old janitor and also make payments on a new boiler at the same time. He fired the janitor and began doing triple duty. London drove a milk truck six days a week from 4:00 a.m. until early afternoon, then spent several hours performing various janitorial duties at their apartment building before beginning his daily rounds of canvassing in the Park Manor and Chatham areas for real estate to sell.

The Londons bought their first car in 1951 and kept it for 10 years. "Even today, we usually keep a car about seven years," Dennis said. "When a car starts costing us money, it's time to get rid of it. I would drive a car for 15 or 20 years if it didn't give me a problem." Dennis and his wife believed in saving money: "So I said well, if we're both going to work, we should save one of the salaries. That is what we did. We started saving in '59 and by '69 we had five kids and $12,000 in the bank. My initial salary with the dairy was $3,000 and the wife, who had a master's degree, made $5,000 as a public school teacher."

In the spring of 1973, Dennis was looking through the real estate ads in the *Chicago Sun-Times* when he saw a 12-flat apartment building that was reasonably priced. He entered into a contract to buy the building and immediately turned to First Federal Savings and Loan Association of Chicago to arrange a mortgage. He told the loan officer that he owned an 18-flat building, and that he knew how to do all kinds of maintenance, and enumerated his other qualifications. The loan officer sitting across the desk smiled at Dennis and said, "I've got a better deal than this for you. I have a 24-flat building that needs some minor repairs that I will sell you for $10,000 more than you are paying for the 12-flat."

London reluctantly rose from his chair and said, "I can't handle it."

"Sit down," the loan officer snapped. "I will *show* you how you can own it."

He advised London to assign the titles of his home and his 18-flat building, both located in Park Manor, to the savings and loan association as collateral. The assignment action made it possible for Dennis and Margie to buy both the 12-flat and the 24-flat buildings without any additional up-front cash. The deals closed without a hitch.

The Londons now owned three apartment buildings containing 54 units, plus a house. And with this much real estate behind him, Dennis decided that he would retire from the milk business and his part-time real estate job and devote his full-time efforts to the upkeep and maintenance of his properties. The salary and benefits that he would have to pay three janitors exceeded his take-home pay from the dairy. Moreover, Dennis knew that there was an advantage in being your own maintenance man. People tend to act more responsibly when they have a vested interest. For example, you are more careful with your own car than a garage attendant usually is.

The same principle is operative with an apartment building, Dennis thought. When you walk down the stairs in your own apartment building and notice that a bannister is loose, you immediately take steps to have it fixed, before somebody gets hurt. The typical janitor would simply pass off the needed repairs as something to be done later, perhaps when the matter is brought to his attention again by the owner of the building or a representative of the management company.

Dennis London literally takes his maintenance chores to the roof, inspecting the roofs of his buildings at least twice a year for wind and sun damage. He points out that the sun draws the tar paper away from the fire wall; a problem that he resolves with a brush and a bucket of tar cement, a simple precaution that saves him thousands of dollars over the lifetime of the roof.

Dennis also learned routine plumbing tasks by watching the tradesmen he hired. He made it his business to stand close enough to observe them as they worked, and from time to time he would interrupt them with a question. The thrifty landlord maintains that once you see how a job is done, you can repeat the performance with a little mental and physical effort.

London recalls that when he purchased his first apartment building, he didn't know how to replace or put ropes on windows, and had to pay a handyman $10 a window to put ropes in the 12 windows that had been broken before he purchased the complex. London observed how the repairman did it, and in the process discovered it was a task he could do for himself, and hasn't paid a repairman for that chore again. Another point Dennis makes is that you have to pay for your education, but if you're smart, you don't have to pay to learn the same lesson twice.

Dennis London has never collected rents from any of his buildings because he knows that tenants would get to know him as both the owner and the maintenance man. And for reasons best known to themselves, tenants are reluctant to pay people they know, though they pay the real estate companies without any questions. He also believes that if he collected the rents, the tenants would treat him the way they did when he was collecting money on the milk route. "They would frequently say come back tomorrow or I will see you Friday," London quipped. "They kept me running back and forth and making trips to hear a thousand different kinds of stories. Management companies don't listen to that nonsense. They just simply have you evicted."

By 1985, the Londons had paid off all of their mortgages. They wanted to raise the roof of their home and add a super-sized luxury bedroom, a wood-burning fireplace and a sauna to enjoy during their golden years. Old faithful Dennis returned to the savings and loan association where he thought he had established enough credit to get a $25,000 loan, only to be told he would have to use his home plus two of his apartment buildings as collateral for the loan. Dennis' high blood pressure shot through the ceiling and he stormed out of the bank enraged.

Dennis felt that he was being unfairly mistreated because of his ethnic origin. All of the Londons' mortgages were paid off ahead of time, they had maintained a perfect credit record throughout the years and had accumulated substantial savings at the lending institution that was making what the Londons considered excessive collateral demands for a couple with their net worth. He could not understand why the firm demanded that he put his property in hock as collateral, and discussed the situation with Margie, who had a cooler head. They decided to document their case in a letter to the chairman of the savings association's board, and within 72 hours, they received a reply. The chairman had checked the Londons' record and found it to be excellent, and he assured them that they would not have to put up any additional collateral. The bank would simply place a first mortgage lien against the house upon which the improvement was to be made.

Such incidents force Dennis London to assert that blacks, often in spite of excellent credit records, have to prove themselves three or four times over, while whites generally receive favored treatment. He said to his wife, "I wonder why."

She replied, "Because we are black."

Dennis London maintains that if he had started his real estate investment program 20 years earlier, his net worth would be three times more than it is today. Judging from Dennis' track record, he is right in his retrospections.

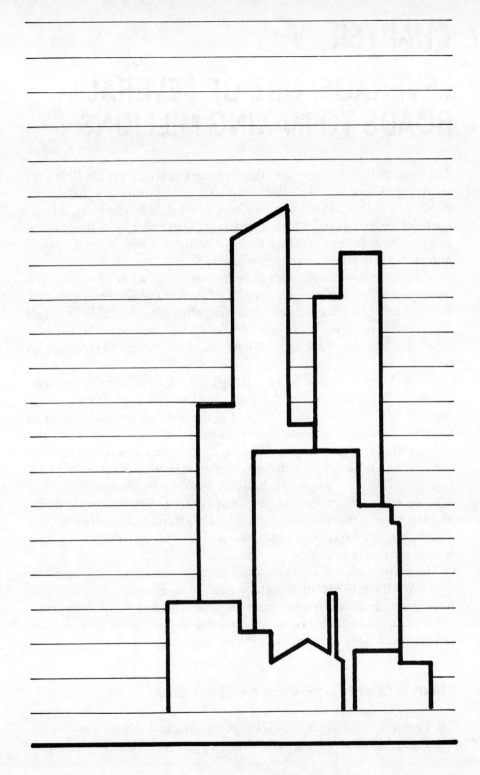

# CHAPTER V

# LEVERAGE: ONE OF SEVERAL ROADS TO MAKING MILLIONS

The leverage theory embodies buying as much real estate as possible with a minimum number of dollars. It also means putting the maximum number of dollars in your pocket after paying all fixed expenses, including taxes, principal and interest. Leverage is operating at its finest when you receive income or cash flow without having invested any of your own money. That is called leveraging to the hilt.

I know many people who have become millionaires by using the leverage strategy. I have never been an advocate of high leverage because I'm convinced that that particular money path leads up a cliff from which the leverager may plunge into a bottomless pit. I became a millionaire the old-fashioned way: I took the longer and more conservative route to reach the real estate gold.

This chapter can serve as a road map for navigating your chosen route to wealth. We'll discuss the advantages and disadvantages of the leveraging, and note some ups and downs of becoming rich without benefit of leverage. Leverage and conservative financial models move down the same road in the same direction, but at different tempos. Leverage may put a million dollars on the debit side of your balance sheet much faster than if you borrow money at a 30-70 or 40-60 ratio. Obviously the 0 to 100 percent leverager is not at risk for anything if he or she can tap dance without signing the mortgage note. The only thing that is at risk for the 100 percent leverager is his reputation and credit status. Preserving both is important in my opinion.

Unfortunately, when some individuals are reaching for the prize, they are willing to sacrifice both reputation and credit without asking how long a financial structure built on quicksand can stand. The answer in the majority of the many cases is not long, if they cannot back up their position with deep pockets of their own or somebody else's.

## EXAMPLES OF WHEN LEVERAGE IS AND IS NOT USED

Let's assume you have $50,000 in cash to invest. Let's further assume that the apartment building nets $4,000 a year, or an 8 percent return on the $50,000. Those who are sold on using leverage would consider you unsophisticated if you invested the entire amount in a 12-flat building. They would advise you to put little to nothing down.

The leverage-minded investor would have you build a half-million dollar building, using the $50,000 as seed money. If you obtain a 30-year amortized loan, it is conceivable that after the payment of all fixed expenses, including the interest and principal on the mortgage, the building would generate a cash flow of $7,500.

As the owner of the $500,000 building, you would be earning 15 percent on the initially invested capital, in addition to the increases in equity via the annual amortization on the $450,000 mortgage. On the basis of the $450,000 30-year mortgage, you would be paying off an average of $15,000 a year on the principal. When added to the 15 percent or $7,500-a-year cash flow average, this would yield a 45 percent return on your original $50,000 investment.

When you compare the 45 percent return on the highly leveraged $500,000 investment with the 8 percent yield on the zero-leveraged $50,000 12-flat apartment building, you can see how high-voltage leverage can get you to money heaven or debtor's hell faster than a 747 jet. John B. Connally, former Texas millionaire—a three-term Texas governor, U.S. treasury secretary under President Richard M. Nixon, and a failed presidential candidate—is living proof of the vulnerability of a highly-leveraged real estate empire building.

In the summer of 1987, Mr. Connally filed for bankruptcy in the U.S. bankruptcy court in Austin, Texas, seeking protection from creditors under Chapter 11 of the Federal Bankruptcy Code. His real estate investment firm, the Barnes/Connally Partnership, filed for liquidation under Chapter 7 of the code on July 31, 1987. Under Chapter 11, a debtor is protected from creditors while a plan of reorganization is worked out. Under 7, a trustee or committee is elected to collect and liquidate all property and examine claims. If a debtor hasn't been found guilty of any misconduct, the court grants a discharge releasing the debtor from most of the pre-petition debts.

The Barnes/Connally Partnership listed $1.8 million in assets and $39.4 million in debts. This is what I call leveraging wrapped around the red, white and blue. The 70-year-old Mr. Connally said:

Of all the creditors in these filings, 99.9 percent of those arise out of the partnership that I had in the development of real estate. If you look at my personal debts, I would not be in bankruptcy. As far as the partnership, we tried to refinance, to recapitalize. We went to Europe and the Far East looking for some avenues for refinancing. We found that everyone basically is afraid of Texas and Texas real estate.

Yes, we borrowed too much. And we undertook too much. But you can't look back. You can't go back. You do a lot of things in life that are a gamble. You take risks if you want to do anything or be anything.

You have to remember that I was one of seven children and that I came up out of Floresville, Texas, after walking barefooted behind a pair of mules pulling a horse-drawn plow. Along the way, you borrow money if you don't inherit any money or have no assets to go with.

People who came to Goliad and who came to the Alamo took a few risks, and for what? For what they thought was right. I will never quit taking risks. Occasionally you stumble. I have stumbled economically, but I will straighten up.

High leverage was John Connally's Achilles' heel, but the Texan declares he will make a comeback.

Debt is what high-leverage empire building is all about. Who is more likely to build a $500,000 building, one who has a half million dollars or one who has $50,000? Nine chances out of 10, it would be the one with the $50,000 who copied Connally's style of empire building. For that investor, there is more excitement and intrigue in creating a lot with a little than in risking a lot to gain a little. American capitalists have been conditioned to do big things with other people's money, like Connally.

Dollar pyramiding prevails in our society. For example, a person with one half million dollars in the bank plays it safe by depositing the money equally in five separate banks insured by the Federal Deposit Insurance Corporation at the prevailing passbook rate, or chooses other money market mechanisms considered almost as safe, or builds a $5- or $10-million building. One of the many blessings our economy grants to winners of the prize is that the favored few are encouraged to multiply assets through the leverage technique.

Leverage is really a license to manufacture money. For example, the Federal Reserve System permits its member insitutions to manufacture money through its open market by providing for reserve balances. Each dollar supplied by the Federal Reserve to a member bank enables that bank to multiply its lending capacity, and the real estate consumer benefits from this process.

On the other hand, dynamic leverage and money manufacturing schemes have built-in pitfalls. Under certain circumstances they can become very hazardous to your financial health. Thin equities of a small real estate owner or major institutions such as the $12.2 billion First City Bank Corporation of Houston, Texas, can be wiped out quickly by poor management, by an economic recession, by an illness or a break in their marital tranquility. A portfolio like the Texas bank's with $1.8 billion in bad energy and real estate loans can drown you in financial quicksand. You are treading on dangerous ground as an owner of highly leveraged properties because they are so delicately weighted between income and expense that a 15 percent drop in occupancy could put you in the red.

The investor who owns a building free and clear of mortgages can weather almost any economic storm. The owner of a 5-95 ratio leveraged building, however, can be uprooted from a real estate empire by a strong southern breeze. Leveraging in real estate means living on the edge of a cliff. It is like walking a tight rope between two mountain peaks, one called income, the other called expense. If the two don't stay in balance, you fall in slow motion to the debtor's hell at the bottom of the mountain.

Leveraging is not for the faint of heart because economic death has proven for some to be as fatal as physical death. I am definitely among the faint of heart. During my 40 years in the real estate business I have seen many of my highly leveraged friends go belly up and into foreclosure more times than I want to remember.

Many of us who have played it the old-fashioned way stay afloat without losing an investment, and stay around to play the game another day. As a matter of fact, among the thousands of people I have sold buildings to over the years, not one client has gone into foreclosure. This achievement can be attributed to the fact that I have never been an advocate of high leverage and the no-money-down theory. You cannot make many mistakes if you subscribe to the adage that there is no such thing as a free lunch. I am not saying don't borrow anything, because that is unrealistic. I *am* saying don't borrow more than you absolutely have to. If you have to borrow almost everything, in my opinion, you are not ready for whatever you are about to undertake.

The high-flying investors in the real estate market are not necessarily following my no-free-lunch strategy. The decrease in shelters and other tax benefits that resulted from the 1986 Tax Reform Act caused many real estate investors to seek a free dinner in addition to a free lunch. The free dinner comes in the form of an old lending game that predates the 1930 Depression years, recently resurrected as zero coupon financing. The zero coupon method is an alternative for minimizing equity investment and maximizing cash flow.

As an investor, your cash flow is maximized under zero coupon financing because you are not required to make any monthly amortization payment during the term of the loan. All interest and principal payments are held in the borrower coffers until loan maturity. The interest on the principal of the zero coupon begins to accumulate the day the moneylender makes the payout, and is generally compounded semiannually. On the day that the loan matures, the mortgagor (borrower) is expected to pay back the original borrowed amount plus the compounded interest. It is assumed by both the mortgagor and the mortgagee (lender) that the loan will be repaid by the borrower going out and getting a new mortgage on the appreciated property, or by selling the real estate to a third party.

The lender assumes protection by looking into a crystal ball, projecting that the property on which the loan is made will be worth the borrowed principal plus the compounded interest on the date that the loan becomes due. It was this type of forecasting by banks and private lenders in the roaring '20s and early '30s that caused the U.S. government to create the Federal Home Loan Bank System in 1932. This provided a central credit facility for the nation's devastated financial institutions.

Zero coupon lending by any name is very risky and you as a borrower are a classic leverager walking a financial tightrope and praying for appreciation. If your prayers are answered, you may make a bundle of cash. If there is no reply from on high, you are in serious financial trouble.

The epitome of the common man's leverage can be found in the no-money-down programs of the Veterans Administration and of the Federal Housing Administration. Millions of families have successfully used one or the other of these programs to buy their first homes, then leveraged the appreciated home value into dollars to buy bigger and better housing.

The key for being rescued from high leverage in a single family home market has been the inflationary spiral that housing has enjoyed over the past two decades. An increase in equity appreciation decreases the debt equity ratio. To get the full benefit of the housing appreciation cycle, the house must be in the right location. Location is critical when making a real estate decision because it can become your only springboard for "moving on up."

In contrast, I have seen hundreds of instances where families have purchased homes in the wrong location during the recent appreciation period and ended up selling them for prices much less than they paid. In addition, the unfortunate sellers usually must dip into personal savings to pay an agent to dispose of such mistakes. Buying the right house in the wrong location equals negative equity, which is an old formula for failing.

The basic way to accumulate equity in a single family home is via paying your monthly note, which is a method of forced savings and is "a long time coming" in a highly leveraged purchase. Consider, for example, a $60,000 mortgage with a 10 percent annual rate blanketing 100 percent of the purchase price. The buyer's cash equity, based on monthly payments of $526.24 in principal and interest, will be $333.53 at the end of the first year and $5,437.19 at the end of the 10th year. The total cash payment on a 100 percent leveraged $60,000 house will be over 300 percent or $189,555.00 at the end of 30 years.

Let's look at another house priced at $60,000 and requiring $30,000 down. The mortgage principal is $30,000 with a 10 percent per annum interest coupon payable in 30 years. The monthly payments are $263.77 including principal and interest. Equity at the end of the first year is $30,166.76 and at the end of the 10th year is $32,718.59. Total payments at the end of the 30 years on the 50 percent leveraged property are $94,777.73 compared with $189,555.00 on the 100 percent leveraged home. Both the mortgage interest and real estate taxes are 100 percent deductible on your income tax—and thus, a distinct advantage for the homebuyer. Remember, a renter pays mortgage interest and taxes for a lifetime indirectly without the benefit of such deduction.

Most real estate buyers don't realize that when they make a mortgage, they are actually renting money from the bank. Renting money to buy a house is expensive. The bank is the landlord that has agreed to give you a 30-year lease at a fixed or adjustable rent. If you fail to meet your obligation, the bank doesn't evict you, it simply forecloses. The end product for a tenant and home buyer is the same: miss enough payments and one evening when you arrive at your former home, you will find your furniture and other personal belongings stretched out in a disorderly fashion on the public sidewalk.

The flip side of that scene, where the banker throws the baby out the window with the bath water, is an optimistic picture painted with the following glowing assumption: The house will be sold within eight years, and the 1987 national medium annual rate for housing appreciation will continue at 4.5 percent.

A 1987 real estate survey revealed:

Median prices for existing homes ranged from below $55,000 to more than $180,000 in the nation's major metropolitan areas during the second quarter of 1987, according to the latest report from the National Association of Realtors.

The New York metropolitan area, including northern New Jersey and Long Island, topped the price list with a resale-home median of $183,000, moving up from its second place position during the first quarter of 1987. Boston, the first-quarter price leader, dropped to second place with a median price of $175,800.

The Orange County, Calif., area, including Anaheim and Santa Ana, ranked third with a median price of $167,300 for the second quarter. Hartford, Conn., was fourth with $157,000, and Los Angeles was fifth with $139,600.

Twenty-six of the 51 metropolitan areas surveyed by NAR had resale-home price appreciation rates exceeding the 4.5 percent national rate. Providence, R.I., with a median price of $109,800, topped all areas with a second quarter 1987 appreciation of 30.1 percent. Hartford, Conn., with a $157,000 median, ranked second with an annual appreciation of 23.0 percent. Albany, N.Y., including the Schenectady and Troy areas, had the third highest appreciation, 18.0 percent, with its median price of $86,500.

Washington, D.C., with a $120,400 median, ranked fourth with an apreciation of 17.1 percent. Detroit, with a $66,600 median, ranked fifth with 15.8 percent.

### Median Sales Price of Existing Single-Family Homes for Metropolitan Areas* (In Thousands of Dollars)

| | QUARTERS | | | | | Percent Change |
|---|---|---|---|---|---|---|
| | 1986 | | | | 1987 | 1986:2 |
| | II | III | IV | I(r) | II(p) | 1987:2 |
| Akron, Ohio | $58.2 | $56.9 | $56.7 | $54.7 | 56.9 | –2.2% |
| Albany/Schenectady/ Troy, N.Y. | 73.3 | 74.4 | 76.3 | 80.1 | 86.5 | 18.0 |
| Albuquerque, N.M. | 79.7 | 85.4 | 82.0 | 83.1 | 82.5 | 3.5 |
| Orange Cty (Anaheim/ Santa Ana MSA)** | 149.4 | 149.6 | 152.4 | 156.1 | 167.3 | 12.0 |
| Baltimore | 72.8 | 72.0 | 74.3 | 81.0 | 77.6 | 6.6 |
| Baton Rouge, La. | 73.3 | 69.8 | 68.5 | 68.3 | 68.1 | –7.1 |
| Birmingham, Ala. | 69.4 | 69.6 | 66.7 | 67.5 | 72.7 | 4.8 |

*All areas are metropolitan statistical areas (MSA) as defined by the U.S. Office of Management and Budget. They include the named central city and surrounding suburban areas.

**Provided by the California Association of Realtors

Source: National Association of Realtors Economics and Research Division

## Median Sales Price of Existing Single-Family Homes for Metropolitan Areas*
## (In Thousands of Dollars)

| | QUARTERS | | | | 1987 | Percent Change |
|---|---|---|---|---|---|---|
| | 1986 | | | | | 1986:2 |
| | II | III | IV | I(r) | II(p) | 1987:2 |
| Boston | 156.2 | 163.0 | 167.8 | 170.0 | 175.8 | 12.5 |
| Buffalo/ Niagara Falls, N.Y. | 54.0 | 52.8 | 53.5 | 55.6 | 57.0 | 5.6 |
| Chicago | 84.7 | 86.7 | 85.8 | 85.7 | 90.9 | 7.3 |
| Cincinnati | 64.2 | 64.5 | n/a | 63.8 | 65.9 | 2.6 |
| Columbus | 67.7 | 66.1 | 64.0 | 66.9 | 67.2 | -0.7 |
| Dallas/Ft. Worth | 93.6 | 92.4 | 89.8 | 91.2 | 90.0 | -3.8 |
| Denver | 87.3 | 87.5 | 85.8 | 89.9 | 87.5 | 0.2 |
| Des Moines, Iowa | 59.0 | 55.2 | 55.0 | 55.9 | 56.8 | 3.7 |
| Detroit | 57.5 | 59.9 | 60.1 | 64.3 | 66.6 | 15.8 |
| El Paso, Texas | 60.9 | 59.6 | 58.5 | 58.0 | 58.0 | -4.8 |
| Ft. Lauderdale/ Hollywood/ Pompano Bch, Fla. | 75.1 | 83.4 | 77.7 | 76.6 | 79.7 | 6.1 |
| Grand Rapids, Mich. | 51.6 | 50.6 | 49.7 | 51.7 | 53.4 | 3.5 |
| Hartford, Conn. | 127.6 | 132.0 | 134.6 | 136.6 | 157.0 | 23.0 |
| Houston | 72.0 | 70.4 | 67.6 | 64.7 | 67.4 | -6.4 |
| Indianapolis | 60.8 | 59.9 | 57.5 | 61.6 | 63.8 | 4.9 |
| Jacksonville, Fla. | 57.5 | 65.7 | 62.7 | 62.7 | 65.8 | 14.4 |
| Kansas City | 67.0 | 64.1 | 65.1 | 72.9 | 71.1 | 6.1 |
| Las Vegas, Nev. | 76.9 | 81.3 | 78.5 | 76.1 | 77.9 | 1.3 |
| Los Angeles** | 128.7 | 132.9 | 130.2 | 130.1 | 139.6 | 8.5 |
| Louisville, Ky. | 52.6 | 53.7 | 51.9 | 52.1 | 53.4 | 1.5 |
| Memphis, Tenn. | 71.3 | 71.5 | 69.9 | 70.6 | 76.9 | 7.9 |
| Miami/Hialeah | 85.7 | 85.5 | 79.1 | 74.7 | 84.4 | -1.5 |
| Milwaukee | 71.0 | 70.8 | 69.2 | 67.8 | 71.7 | 1.0 |

*All areas are metropolitan statistical areas (MSA) as defined by the U.S. Office of Management and Budget. They include the named central city and surrounding suburban areas.

**Provided by the California Association of Realtors

Source: National Association of Realtors Economics and Research Division

## Median Sales Price of Existing Single-Family Homes for Metropolitan Areas*
### (In Thousands of Dollars)

| | QUARTERS | | | | | Percent Change |
| | 1986 | | | | 1987 | 1986:2 |
| | II | III | IV | I(r) | II(p) | 1987:2 |
|---|---|---|---|---|---|---|
| Minneapolis/ St. Paul, Minn. | 79.0 | 78.1 | 77.4 | 80.4 | 80.2 | 1.5 |
| Nashville/ Davidson, Tenn. | 71.4 | 71.2 | 71.7 | 73.4 | 75.9 | 6.3 |
| New York/No. New Jersey/Long Island | 160.0 | 167.8 | 167.6 | 169.4 | 183.0 | 14.4 |
| Oklahoma City | 65.0 | 62.3 | 62.9 | 62.4 | 65.2 | 0.3 |
| Omaha, Neb. | 62.0 | 57.8 | 58.8 | 57.8 | 60.0 | -3.2 |
| Orlando, Fla. | 74.5 | 72.8 | 72.1 | 73.6 | 76.4 | 2.6 |
| Philadelphia | 73.6 | 75.6 | 77.1 | 79.8 | 84.4 | 14.7 |
| Phoenix, Ariz. | 78.8 | 79.1 | 77.9 | 78.4 | 81.4 | 3.3 |
| Portland, Ore. | 63.4 | 63.1 | 62.5 | 62.7 | 64.3 | 1.4 |
| Providence, R.I. | 84.4 | 91.9 | 96.4 | 101.3 | 109.8 | 30.1 |
| Rochester, N.Y. | 68.3 | 69.1 | 69.1 | 69.5 | 72.3 | 5.9 |
| St. Louis | 72.0 | 72.0 | 71.9 | 71.9 | 74.7 | 3.7 |
| Salt Lake City/Ogden | 67.8 | 69.9 | 69.0 | 68.1 | 69.4 | 2.4 |
| San Antonio, Texas | 69.1 | 69.3 | 70.2 | 67.6 | 73.2 | 5.9 |
| San Diego** | 119.9 | 121.1 | 118.8 | 121.1 | 127.1 | 6.0 |
| Syracuse, N.Y. | 64.9 | 66.2 | 66.4 | 65.2 | 68.1 | 4.9 |
| Tampa/St. Petersburg/ Clearwater, Fla. | 62.1 | 62.8 | 62.4 | 59.8 | 65.7 | 5.8 |
| Toledo, Ohio | 57.4 | 60.2 | 53.2 | 53.4 | 58.2 | 1.4 |
| Tulsa, Okla. | 66.8 | 65.6 | 63.4 | 64.1 | 67.4 | 0.9 |
| Washington, D.C. | 102.8 | 98.9 | 102.0 | 107.7 | 120.4 | 17.1 |
| W. Palm Beach/Boca Raton/Delray Bch, Fla. | 94.9 | 96.6 | 90.9 | 96.9 | 104.3 | 9.9 |
| United States | 82.0 | 80.7 | 80.2 | 84.2 | 85.7 | 4.5 |

*All areas are metropolitan statistical areas (MSA) as defined by the U.S. Office of Management and Budget. They include the named central city and surrounding suburban areas.

**Provided by the California Association of Realtors

Source: National Association of Realtors Economics and Research Division

But, before we all grab hands and walk off into the sunset singing, "Glory, glory, hallelujah," we should examine some statistics on the heavily leveraged homeowner. In making a case for or against leverage, the following data should be cranked into the equation:

### Mortgage Foreclosures by All Lenders+

| Year-End | Conventional Loans | FHA Loans* | VA Loans |
|---|---|---|---|
| 1965 | 0.08% | 0.50% | 0.40% |
| 1970 | 0.08% | 0.47% | 0.25% |
| 1971 | 0.07% | 0.68% | 0.30% |
| 1972 | 0.07% | 0.75% | 0.34% |
| 1973 | n.a. | n.a. | n.a. |
| 1974 | 0.15% | 0.57% | 0.40% |
| 1975 | 0.16% | 0.46% | 0.36% |
| 1976 | 0.18% | 0.48% | 0.41% |
| 1977 | 0.15% | 0.46% | 0.39% |
| 1978 | 0.13% | 0.42% | 0.32% |
| 1979 | 0.10% | 0.44% | 0.38% |
| 1980 | 0.17% | 0.53% | 0.46% |
| 1981 | 0.24% | 0.57% | 0.55% |
| 1982 | 0.39% | 0.88% | 0.76% |
| 1983 | 0.46% | 0.84% | 0.76% |
| 1984 | 0.47% | 0.98% | 0.82% |
| 1985 | 0.61% | 1.01% | 0.88% |
| 1986 | 0.69% | 1.22% | 1.14% |

n.a.=not available

+Percentage of loans in the foreclosure process

*For 1974-1978, FHA loans exclude sections 235 and 237 loans.

Source: Mortgage Bankers Association of America.

In spite of the administrative and underwriting problems that have plagued both the Veterans Administration and the Federal Housing Administration, those programs were conceived to make America a land of homeowners. Their goal has not been attained, but deep inroads were made because their philosophy was sound.

The FHA and VA plans were unlike the get-rich-quick and no-money-down schemes that are being peddled across the land by Gucci-shoed hucksters who are willing to share their secrets for $500 per listener. The real secret is that these golden-tongued speakers make an average of $7,500 per weekend telling you how to get over.

In a May, 1981 cover story, *Money Magazine* hailed Albert J. Lowry as a "real estate wizard" and estimated his net worth at $30 million. Ironically, the guru who made a fortune telling others how to get over by investing in real estate with no money down, filed a Chapter 7 bankruptcy petition May 13, 1987, in Los Angeles, California.

Remember, a huff and a puff will blow down a house that has been built on high leverage.

I realize that the huff-and-puff-line might be a good way to close this chapter, but I would be shortchanging you if I did not remind you that you have been using leverage for most of your life. Remember when you were a child playing on a seesaw. Recall what fun it was to keep your playmate's body elevated as long as you could while you kept your feet on the ground? You were using leverage then.

Leverage is employed when you enter a real estate transaction with superior knowledge. For example, a major development is planned for an area near the site that you are negotiating to buy. You are aware of the development, but the seller is not. Leverage is on your side.

I purchased a health club facility from a savings and loan association in 1966. The property had been boarded up with a for sale sign on it for three years. During that period nearly 100 prospective buyers inspected the property. What those real estate shoppers saw was a building with an olympic-sized swimming pool, a 12-lane bowling alley, an exercise room, and a health bar. The first time I inspected the building, I saw an excellent location for a commercial office.

Six months earlier, a health-conscious business executive made a high six-figure offer to the lending institution that held title to the foreclosed property, and it was rejected. Unaware of the earlier bid, I made an all-cash bid without any contingencies for 50 percent less. Following extensive negotiations and threats to withdraw my proposal and pick up my earnest money, the offer was accepted.

In retrospect, that deal was both a challenge and fun because I entered the transaction with leverage. I knew the community better than the bank officers did, and I was able to forecast its trends. In other words, leverage does not always have to be debt. It can be superior knowledge and/or a substantial net worth.

With some thought and effort, you too can accomplish successful transactions. Just stop and think, you use leverage every day in a personal way with your co-worker, your mate and the children.

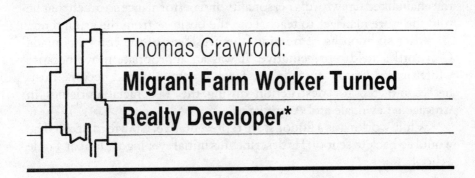

# Thomas Crawford:
# **Migrant Farm Worker Turned**
# **Realty Developer***

*"At age 35 I decided to become a millionaire by 40."*

Thomas Crawford's birthplace was Clarksdale, Mississippi. He arrived at high noon December 25, 1943, as the last in a line of 15 children born into the Crawford clan. Young Crawford dropped out of school and left home at the age of 14, and became a full-time farm migrant worker. He picked cotton and strawberries across the state of Mississippi, harvested tomatoes, watermelons and oranges in Florida and plucked beans and sugar cane from the earth in Louisiana.

While riding with other workers in the rear of a truck, Tom had many opportunities to watch the driver make repairs on the truck's engine. Because the engine was constantly breaking down, young Crawford started assisting the driver/mechanic with the repairs.

At the age of 20, Tom Crawford moved to Chicago and got a job washing cars at a service station. He was graduated without the benefit of ceremony from car washer to the position of service station auto mechanic one Monday morning when the regular grease monkey failed to show up for work. Crawford had worked with his hands all of his short life picking cotton or fixing cars and he was getting restless. His gut instincts told him he had a higher calling in life so he quit the job at the service station and went to work for a chain liquor store as a counter salesman. The sales position was his first white-collar job and he had every reason to become somewhat pleased with himself. The president of

---

*These case studies are documented; only the names were changed to protect the confidentiality of the real estate broker-client relationship.

the chain liked Crawford's personality and performance so much that he told the store manager to teach Tom the business from the ground up.

After six months of training, the president of the company made Crawford a field representative. It was an appropriate move because white-owned liquor stores in the black community had become businesses targeted for destruction during the '60s racial uprisings in Chicago's Lawndale and Austin areas.

While working as a liquor store representative, Crawford decided he would go back to school. He describes his initial evening at Dunbar Trade School:

I wanted to attend Dunbar night school and learn a trade. I was going to enroll in welding but the welding class was filled. I was on my way out of the building when I passed a room, stopped and looked through the window of a door at the maze of machinery in an electronics class. It was fascinating to me because I had never seen so much equipment in my life. Mr. Rulach, the instructor, saw me peering through the window and he came out into the corridor and asked, 'Since you're looking in the class, why don't you come on in and enroll? It's better than walking away from school.' I went into the room, looked around, and I decided to enroll.

I really got hooked on electronics when the instructor told me that the average person in the field doesn't really understand it until after they've been in it about two years. He said the majority of the students drop out.

Being the kind of person I am, I love a challenge for challenge's sake. As a matter of fact, my wife says that once I achieve something, I then want to move on to something else. I just keep moving.

Instructor Rulach was right in his dropout forecast because out of over 33 people who had enrolled at Dunbar Trade School for the electronics program, two years later only two of us graduated. With the electronics certificate behind me, I went to work for Zenith, and from there to Automatic Electric, finally winding up at U.S. Steel as an electronic engineer.

By this point, I decided to get married. I was sitting pretty at U.S. Steel, my wife was teaching school and Internal Revenue was killing us, yet we were living like millionaires. We traveled Europe on ski trips, and went scuba diving in the Caribbean every year.

I celebrated my 35th birthday in Innsbruck, Austria. It was on that day that I recognized that I hadn't achieved anything in life that was meaningful. When my wife and I went back to the hotel that night, I wrote a note to myself. It said, in effect, that my goal was to become a millionaire before I was 40 years old. However, in my note I didn't say how. I was just simply saying that I had to do something that would leave a mark, something that people would remember me by.

I was walking down Stony Island Avenue near 79th Street on the South Side of Chicago one afternoon when a community newspaper blew across my shoe. It flipped over in the wind and I saw something in large bold letters that read MARK OLIVER HENSON SAID, 'WAKE UP THE FINANCIAL GENIUS INSIDE OF YOURSELF.' So I reached down and picked up the paper. It went on to say how Henson became wealthy within a relatively short period of time. And that he had a formula that could teach others to do the same thing. All they had to do to get on the success track was send him $10 for his book on real estate. I took the paper home and showed it to my wife and she said, 'Well, that's how he got to be a millionaire. There are thousands of fools who will send him $10, and of course, that adds up to a whole lot of money.' I didn't say anything else to my wife about the subject. I just simply sent away the $10 and got the book. I call it my bible. I won't loan it to anybody. I read it over and over again.

The language of Henson's book has become my language. It's written in plain, simple, common, everyday words, which makes it easy to understand. What really stunned me was that it told me how I could negotiate with bank officers about buildings and possessions in their language so they would respect me as a knowledgeable person who knew what I was about. Sure enough, when I went into a bank and started talking almost verbatim from the book, it was almost like I was reading a script from a play. I would make a statement and then the banker would respond with a statement that sounded as if it was also out of the pages of Henson's book. I thought, my God, I guess this thing really works.

After my first meeting with a banker, I set out to buy my first building. The wife and I had, and I still got the bank book, $250 to our name. We had paychecks coming in but that was all. Henson's book said you have to sell yourself, and I went out to sell myself. I met a man named Eddie Spraggins from a South Side realty company and discussed with him a building that was located in the 7900 block on South Essex.

I actually convinced Mr. Spraggins that I was into all kinds of investments. I was lying, but he believed me. I was following Henson's book and selling myself. I gave Mr. Spraggins a $2,000 check for earnest money with instructions not to cash it unless he gave me three or four days' notice. In addition, I handed him $100 in cash that I drew out of our $250 savings account for him to order a credit check. The credit check showed that both my wife and I had good jobs and that our credit was excellent.

My next step was to try and come up with the $9,000 Mr. Spraggins wanted as down payment on the building. I tried almost everything imaginable and came up with zero. Through a stroke of luck, I learned that one could borrow $15,000 under the Department of Housing and Urban Development (Title I) Loan Program* to rehabilitate a building. Although I did not hold title to the building, I arranged through the South Shore Bank and Trust Company to close both the first mortgage and Title I rehab loan at the same time. I used $9,000 of the Title I loan money as my down payment. I did not take any money to the closing on September 18, 1978 because I did not have any. That in a nutshell is how I acquired my first building.

Realtor Spraggins was so taken with Thomas Crawford's Barnumlike personality that he never cashed the $2,000 earnest money check. The check was not worth the paper that it was written on. Crawford won Spraggins' confidence through their discussions of things that were of common interest. The two were avid skiers and skied at the same resorts in Switzerland, and in the Austrian Alps. Both were expert scuba divers and talked for hours about their underwater experiences in the the clear blue Caribbean Sea. Crawford and Spraggins even shared a passion for flying. Realtor Spraggins was a millionaire and owned a plane; Crawford flew with a flying club. Though Thomas Crawford's delusion of wealth was a facade, he had an extraordinary ability to persuade without being obnoxious.

The next real estate man that I asked to hold a personal check was Dempsey J. Travis of Travis Realty Company. Mr. Travis told me that a personal check in a real estate transaction had less value

---

*Home Improvement Loan Insurance (Title I)—HUD insures loans to finance major and minor improvements, alterations and repairs of individual homes and non-residential structures (whether owned or leased). Currently, the loans may be up to $17,500, and may extend to 15 years and 32 days. Loans on apartment buildings may be as high as $8,750 per unit, but the total for the building may not exceed $43,750, and the terms may not exceed 15 years. Lenders process these loans. Loans of not more than $2,500 are generally unsecured personal loans. Legislation establishing this program was enacted in 1934. The cumulative activity of the program through September 1983: 33,592,159 loans insured with a value of $33.2 billion.

than a roll of toilet paper. I started to challenge Travis that day and let him know that I was going to be a millionaire in five years. I decided not to push my luck, and Travis subsequently came to my aid. I was having problems with the loan processing department at First Federal Savings and Loan office down at 7 South Dearborn. They were giving me all kinds of runaround and standing on my very last nerve. I came back to Travis Realty and told Mr. D. J. Travis my plight. He simply picked up the phone and called somebody he obviously knew very well and told that person that Thomas Crawford was all right. When I went back down to First Federal the next day, all the doors were open and I was literally welcomed with open arms.

Crawford purchased his second six-flat building in December 1978, with a first mortgage loan from the First Federal Savings and Loan Association of Chicago. The purchase of the second piece of real estate was exactly three months after he had purchased his first one. He used the $6,000 that he had left over from the initial Title I Loan on the South Essex building as the down payment on his second six-flat building which was located in the 6700 block on South Cornell. He applied for and received a second Title I Loan to make improvements on this newest acquisition.

One hundred and eighty days after the Mississippi native purchased his first bulding in Chicago September 1978, he bought his third property, a six-flat building at 70th and Clyde. All of Crawford's properties are in the South Shore area, on the Southeast Side of Chicago and within a couple of blocks of one another. Owning buildings in one area is very advantageous for those who plan to do the maintenance work themselves.

Crawford made the following observations:

I bought three six-flat buildings back-to-back because that's the way Henson's book said I should do it. I made a kind of dumb mistake in that after I got the buildings working, I began feeling somewhat comfortable, enjoying a sense of security, and I didn't have to worry about finances anymore. I was still working on the job at U.S. Steel plus doing 90 percent of the work at the buildings when I suddenly found myself in Jackson Park Hospital. It was not until I got out of the hospital and saw the results of my tests that I realized that I was working 10 to 12 hours at the steel mill and then working 8 to 9 hours on the buildings.

Late one Thursday afternoon, I collapsed on the floor of the third-floor apartment of a building in the 6700 block on Cornell. I couldn't move. I couldn't talk. But I could think. It taught me a lesson. And, my doctor warned me, 'You're going to make your wife a rich widow.' I kind of backed off my 20-hour-a-day schedule with some reluctance because I fully enjoyed working around the buildings and improving them. Doing something that I like, I really can't define that as work. I have a tendency to overdo and stretch myself out to the limits both mentally and physically.

Thomas Crawford talks fast, walks fast, thinks fast, and is constantly on the move, riding from place to place, riding his motorcycle. During our two-hour interview, he must have received a dozen beeper calls and we were interrupted an equal number of times by his pocket cellular telephone. I asked Mr. Crawford why he was so wired. He replied:

After I purchased my first building I had to learn to do construction work. I did not have any money left from the Title I loan because I had used it as down payment on the second building. Hence, I had to cover myself by physically doing the work myself since I had spent the money. I had not put a nail in the first piece of wood to rehab the buildings. Remember, there is nothing in the Title I agreement that says who has to do the rehabbing. It simply says that the home improvement must be made in a workmanlike fashion. As a committee of one, I filled both the rehabilitation and the construction requirements.

Back to your question about my being wired. As a result of teaching myself the construction business by reading how-to books, today I have six construction crews working for me all over the city. To stay in touch with my foremen and they with me, I became wired and carry both the beeper and cellular phone with me all the time.

To befriend someone is not the usual manner in which one acquires real estate, but, that is the method by which Thomas Crawford acquired his fourth six-flat building. Here's the scenario according to Crawford:

Mrs. Winnie Smith owned a six-flat building on 67th Place near Stony Island. I occasionally did work for her because she was an old lady and her husband had passed. Some unscrupulous real estate people were trying to take advantage of her. They had her sign a lot of papers which in effect would have taken her building without giving her very much consideration at all. One day while I was repairing some plumbing for Mrs. Smith, she brought the contract to my attention. I told her she didn't have to go through with that deal because on the face of it, it was blatantly unfair. I also told her I would help her to sell her building and get a fair market price. Mrs. Smith asked me if I wanted the building. I told her I had just bought another building and I just couldn't afford it.

One morning, attorney Wayman Cross called me. He said that he represented Mrs. Smith and that she had wanted him to contact me and that I should come down to his office. I asked, 'For what?'

'Well, aren't you buying her building?' he asked.

I said, 'No. I can't buy it because I just bought a building and I don't have any money.'

He said, 'Well, come down anyway.'

So, I figured what did I have to lose. I went down. Mrs. Smith, through her lawyer, practically gave me that building. They made me an offer I could not refuse. All she wanted was $30,000 for the building and $5,000 down. She was willing to give me credit for the security deposits, approximately $1,200. Her attorney said, 'We will have the deal set up to close after the rents are due which means that you'll get another credit for approximately $1,200.' He asked, 'Can you come up with approximately $1,800 and pay $330 a month for 10 years on a six-flat building?'

I said, 'Of course.'

Attorney Cross said, 'All she wants you to do is guarantee that she can retain her apartment as a place to stay for the rest of her life.'

I said, 'I don't see that as being a problem. I'll take care of everything. And she can live there free.'

He said, 'No, she don't want to live there free. She wants to pay you fair rent, which is $275 a month, and you can take that off the first mortgage payment. You'll only have to pay her $55 a month.'

Mrs. Smith, who was around 75 years old, told me that she probably had 10 more years to live and she wanted me to have the building. She passed away seven years after we closed the deal. I still have a couple of years to go to finish paying for the building. Mrs. Smith had a brother by the name of Bernard Coleman who lived in the apartment with her. After she passed, Mr. Coleman got an apartment in a senior citizens' building. However, I still pay him the full mortgage amount of $330 on the first of every month, the same as I would have paid her. I go down to see him from time to time or whenever he calls and tells me that he's got a problem or has some paperwork to be done. I just kind of look out for Mr. Coleman the same as I would have looked out for his sister.

I have a basic philosophy about being nice to old people. I

believe that if you are nice to them, it will come back to you in some fashion, not necessarily by receiving a piece of real estate. But you will be rewarded. Remember in Chapter 20 of Exodus, in the 12th verse it says, 'Honour thy father and thy mother that thy days may be long upon the land which the Lord thy God giveth thee.'

Crawford's empire building is going to need God's help along with a lot of prayer, street smarts, luck and hard work because his acquisitions of buildings five, six and seven have led him down a dark alley that is loaded with pit bulls. Buying mortgages on buildings that are already in receivership is not smart. To make bad matters worse, he began rehab construction on the properties without the benefit of being in title. He compounded his troubles by entering a demonstration program that dictated he vacate the buildings in order to qualify for a $245,000 rehab loan on each property. The rehab program was subsequently scrapped and buildings five, six and seven are currently being stripped by vandals.

Another axiom about real estate—one that Crawford never learned or perhaps forgot—is that you can build a structure on quicksand and it may stand the test of time if you don't build it too high.

Thomas Crawford was attempting to build a real estate empire without taking time out to dig deep enough in the sand to strike bedrock on which he could have laid a solid foundation for his expanding projects.

# Clinton Robertson:
# The Money Manufacturer*

*"I always buy at a good price, looking forward to selling what I bought at a better price."*

Clinton Robertson was born December 19, 1947 on a farm near Gallion, Alabama. He was the eighth of 12 children. His earliest exposure to entrepreneurship came from observing his maternal grandfather. Grand-dad, Emmett Sims, was the father of 15 children. What fascinated young Clinton was that Grandpa Sims, a sharecropper, had maneuvered himself into the position of owning a 1,200-acre plantation.

Clinton was even more astounded when he realized that though his grandfather could neither read nor write, the old man had no problems with counting money rapidly in any and all denominations. As a matter of fact, Grandpa Sims was in such good financial shape that he gave all of his 15 children a house on his plantation and some start-up money.

Clinton Robertson vividly remembers the following:

> My father accepted the house that Grandpa gave my mother but then decided that he did not want to farm anymore. So he moved his family to a town called Demopolis, Alabama, where he was able to get a job in a cement plant. Although Dad did not have any savings, he started talking about buying a house shortly after we moved to Demopolis. Looking back, I suspect that Dad moved away from Gallion to get my mother out from under the wings of

---

*These case studies are documented; only the names were changed to protect the confidentiality of the real estate broker-client relationship.

her father. And his desire to buy a house was an effort to prove to his family that he was as much a man as my maternal grandfather.

Dad finally purchased a house but he did not win the race against Grandpa. When my mother's father died, he willed 35 acres of land to each of his 15 children and 12 acres to each of his 39 grandchildren.

Soon after my grandfather died in 1967 I moved to Chicago and got a job as an assistant manager working in a laundromat on the night shift. In that fall I enrolled as a full-time day student at Chicago State University to pursue a degree in education. Shortly after I received my degree in 1971 and started teaching, I was offered an opportunity to buy the laundromat where I had been working for four years. The price was right and the terms were reasonable.

I had not owned the business six months before all of the wet elements in the sky found refuge inside my business establishment. The real estate management agent moved so slowly in resolving the roofing problem that I took it upon myself to call the owner of the building. I reached him at his California home and said, 'It looks like we have a roofing problem here. As a matter of fact, we've had it ever since I've been here and something has to be done.'

The owner said, 'Well, Mr. Robertson. I don't have the time nor the energy, nor am I concerned enough to come to Chicago and check out a roof. If you are calling me to talk about a purchase, let's talk about a purchase.' I said, 'No, that was not the reason for the call. But I would like to purchase the building.'

We handled the whole transaction over the phone. He called his attorney. I instructed my attorney to offer him $40,000 with the understanding we would reduce the price by the cost of the roof repair. I also wanted the closing date to be set six months from the date the contract was signed. That would give me ample time to accumulate additional capital from the earnings of the business.

After purchasing his first piece of commercial property, Robertson decided that he would never put a laundromat or any other business in a building that he didn't own. His rationale was that he knew a lot of people who developed successful enterprises only to have the owner of the building plug into the business with such a high rent that the entrepreneur became an employee of the landlord. Moreover, Robertson wanted to own the land under the business as a base for leveraging in other investments. If he should decide he didn't want to operate the business anymore, he would have an opportunity to lease the property to another entrepreneur, doing unto others what he would not like to have done unto himself.

Before buying his second piece of commercial property, Clint said:

> I always buy at a good price, looking forward to selling what I bought at a better price. I am not trying to rip off anybody. I simply see it as a sound method of doing business. I look at property as an investment, something that will not necessarily make you rich quick but could be the gold in your future.

Clinton employed leverage in the purchase of the second parcel. His leverage was a by-product of the appreciation of the real estate in which his business was located coupled with his successful laundromat business.

Mr. Robertson was now bankable. Eugene Dunn, the real estate man, approached him about buying a third property just a few blocks from Clint's first laundromat.

"How much are you asking for the property?" Clint responded.

Dunn snapped, "The price is $110,000."

Clinton recoiled, "I will give you $90,000."

Dunn retorted, "I will take it."

Clinton was now able to negotiate in an auction-like fashion because he knew that he could go to the bank and get $90,000 based on his personal signature and balance sheet.

Clinton Robertson was on a roll when he purchased his fourth piece of real estate, a vacant building in need of substantial improvement. At the time he decided to buy the building, he did not actually have a need for it. However, because the real estate was in a good location and on a corner with a high traffic count, he envisioned that eventually he would put a new store on that site. He immediately tore the old building down and then waited three years before moving forward with the construction of a new one.

The timing was right. There had been an increase in family formations and a decrease in the number of empty-nesters in the area, and the families with small children were ready for a major chain-store sized laundromat. This turned out to be Clint's most successful location.

The construction loan on this property was made because Clint had established himself with the local bank by carrying large balances. He had become the kind of client a banker loves to see come through the door. No wonder the banker always welcomed Mr. Robertson with a smile.

Clint's fifth piece of property was a 75-unit apartment building, which marked the first time that he had deviated from a 100 percent commercial property.

He bought the large building at a very good price after I had prevailed on him over two months to purchase it. Usually when I have to argue and persuade a person over an extended period of time, I end up buying my own recommendation. Mr. Robertson can consider himself lucky because that was a good deal in spite of the deferred maintenance that had created a need for extensive rehabilitation.

As it turns out, Clinton's apartment building is grossing as much per year as he initially paid for the property. Plus, he recovered the $250,000 in rehab money that he put into the building within 18 months after Travis Realty Company completed the rent up. The returns from the money invested in the apartment building are so good that Clinton calls the complex his money-manufacturing machine.

The next time opportunity knocked at Clinton Robertson's door, he refused to open it. I will never forget the day that the Federal Deposit Insurance Corporation called my office and asked me to handle several large buildings they had recently foreclosed. After inspecting the properties, I called Clinton and told him that I would like for him to look at a specific property because I thought it lent itself to a buying pattern that I had seen developing when he purchsed his first four properties. The subject property had good location, great future potential and was an ideal investment for a young man in his mid-30s. I told him that, if I were his age, I would buy this piece of property because I saw it as a valuable asset that would serve well until the year 2000. I pleaded with him for two or three months, but he just wouldn't listen.

So I approached another young man just a couple of years older than Clinton who, in my opinion, ranked high among the top young businessmen in America. The structure was in an ideal location for his enterprise. He, like Clinton, could not see beyond the peeling paint and the water marks on the ceiling.

I have always maintained that you have to look beyond flaking paint to see the future. In other words, I maintain that you should never buy a painted doll. Unsophisticated buyers who constantly fall into the trap of buying a coat of paint only learn that a multitude of flaws had been camouflaged.

The FDIC became jittery while I was trying to sell their property to Clinton Robertson. Their mandate to me was get it sold. A major institution was located within one-half mile north of the subject property, but I was reluctant to approach it in reference to buying the property. I felt that this was an opportunity for some young person who had a strong anchor in the community and who does not get many opportunities to buy prime property at a bargain-basement price.

I could not find such a person. I approached the FDIC official and told him that, since I could not find a buyer, I would personally make a cash offer for the property. The officer said he could not accept an offer from me because of my relationship with them as an agent. However, he agreed to consider it at a later date, providing I could wait eight weeks while they advertised in several major metropolitan newspapers in search of a bonafide buyer.

I felt that was the end of the road because I was certain someone else would see the ad and recognize the opportunity and buy the building. As luck would have it, the FDIC official came back to me after the ninth week and said, "Well, Mr. Travis, we have exhausted our advertising efforts and we are now willing to entertain your offer." I made the same six-figure offer that I had made earlier and they accepted it.

Two weeks after I acquired the building, Clinton Robertson came to my office and pleaded with me to let him buy the building or become my partner. I refused his pleas on both counts. Needless to say, that property turned out to be one of the best-located pieces of real estate south of Madison Street. It is almost unbelievable that I acquired it only because I could not find anyone who recognized the potential value.

Another factor that should have made the proposition attractive to Mr. Robertson was that a major institution was a tenant in that building, and it was paying enough rent for Clint to have met a mortgage note if he had gone that route. I suspect that both Clint and the other young entrepreneur felt that something was wrong if the big institution didn't buy the building. Something was wrong all right. Neither Clint nor my other young friend looked closely enough at the real estate to discern that what they thought was greasy water was actually oil.

A year after I purchased the building, the second young businessman entered a lease to rent 20,000 feet in the building and became the major tenant. The lease gives him an option to buy the building after 10 years.

The deal that I could not sell became even more attractive to me when I discovered that there was another block of property adjacent to the building that could be purchased. I hired the law firm of Earl L. Neal to unscramble the title interests of the various owners, who were stretched out across the southern part of the country from Florida to Texas. Putting the entire land package together made the initial building a heck of a lot more attractive, and of course, a lot more valuable.

The question came up of why anyone would buy blocks of property for which they had no immediate need. The underlying factor, as I said, is to be able to see through the paint. It is important to watch for three things in real estate: location, location, and location. When you are satisfied with a location, start looking at the actual balance sheet and income/expense statement. If none exists, prepare a pro forma statement based upon your own projection. If the location and the numbers make sense, you are in the right ballpark.

The only other investments you must make in real estate are hard work, time, and patience. With these as your assets, benefits will flow.

Clinton Robertson is taking a page out of my real estate book. He recently purchased a 24-flat building on a good corner location and is rehabilitating it. When I asked him why he had decided on that particular building, he said, "I selected it because of location and because of the success I have had with the 75-unit, the one I call my money-manufacturing building."

Clinton admits that his refusal to buy that commercial piece of property that I brought to his attention some years back was a big mistake.

He says that if a four-star opportunity ever knocks at his door again, he is going to open it fast and wide. Opportunity knocks at everybody's door at least twice in a lifetime. Unfortunately, most people do not recognize the knock. If you are alert enough to hear the knock, stop everything and grab the opportunity. You may never get another chance.

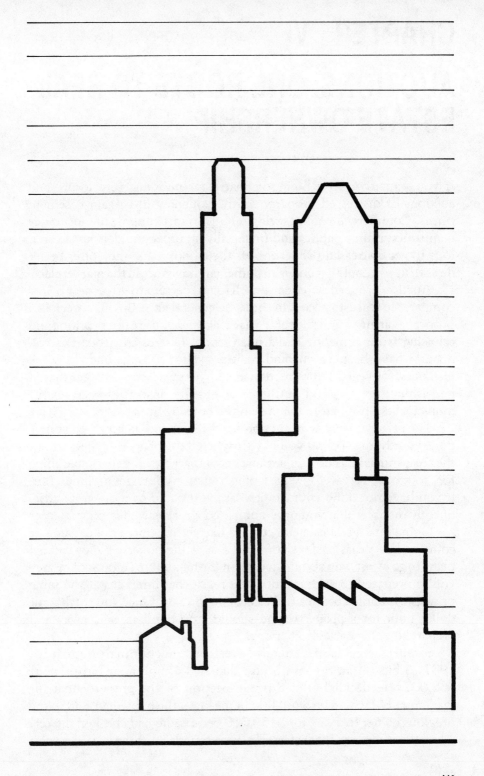

# CHAPTER VI

# AUCTIONS: ONE ROUTE TO REAL ESTATE OWNERSHIP

If you want to own a home or apartment building, foreclosure and auctions of distressed property can be your key to bargain basement prices. Commercial banks, savings and loan institutions, life insurance companies, municipalities and financially-strapped builders are so anxious to get distressed properties off their books that they offer better deals than you could get under any other circumstance in the marketplace.

Auction properties frequently sell for 10 percent to 90 percent below comparable real estate sales in the same general area. Buying foreclosed properties at auctions is not grave dancing, and you are not profiting and rejoicing from someone else's misfortune. Distressed properties frequently have been vacant and maltreated for months and, in some instances, for years. Your function as a buyer of sick real estate is that of nourishing, reviving and putting once-healthy properties back on the municipal tax roll before they reach the housing burial yard.

The price you pay at an auction sale will depend on how well you've done your homework. If you have inspected the property, checked out the area, and have a good sense of what comparable properties are selling for, you could very well emerge from an auction contest as a winner. But, if you have not done your homework, you could overpay and subsequently discover that you have purchased a real estate lemon.

Going into a real estate auction is like getting into a poker game or going to Las Vegas. Before you sit down at the poker table or catch a plane to go West, you should decide on the maximum amount of money you're prepared to spend. Once you reach that limit, stop. The same principle is applicable in a real estate auction sale. Once you reach your dollar limit for a property, you should stop bidding, walk away and prepare to come back another day.

Samuel Pierce, age 32, attended a real estate auction in the summer of 1987 to bid on an 8-room house that had a minimum bid price of $68,000. He decided after a pre-inspection of the property that his maximum bid would be $80,000. Pierce knew the house had sold to the previous owner in 1979 for $150,000 because he had checked the real estate tax records and transfers. He knew exactly what the last sales price was based on the dollar amount of revenue stamps affixed to the deed. Therefore, he was walking on solid ground when he arrived at the auction because he had thoroughly done his homework.

As the auction proceeded, the maximum price Samuel had set was surpassed by other bidders, so he dropped his hand and stopped his bidding. Then he had second thoughts: he was willing to go up to 60 percent of the original 1979 sales price of $150,000. When the bid reached $90,000, the other bidders dropped out and Pierce won the bid. Pierce got an excellent deal although the property had deteriorated. On the other hand, the area values had increased approximately 5 percent annually, that is 40 percent over a period of eight years due to appreciation. In the final analysis, after including the cost of rehabilitation, he had acquired the property in 1987 for a 1979 price.

Real estate auctions are now a national phenomenon. During the summer of 1987, 14,000 people registered with the Cook County Illinois treasurer's office to bid at an auction sale for tax-delinquent properties. In October 1987, 6,000 parcels in the Hyde Park area, which is located on the southeast side of Chicago went on auction; 10,000 parcels from the west side of Chicago were offered later. A total of 40,000 parcels were being auctioned countywide between October 5, 1987 and December 21, 1987. Everyone who registered was looking for an opportunity to get into real estate at bargain prices. The opening bids ranged from $50 to $50,000. The properties that were being auctioned by Cook County Treasurer Edward J. Rosewell's office were those on which taxes had not been paid for five years or more. There had not been a tax sale of delinquent properties in Cook County since 1983.

Tax sales occur because owners fail to pay real estate taxes for a prescribed period of time, usually five years. In such cases, the governmental body empowered to levy these taxes may file a tax lien against the properties and enforce them by conducting a tax sale. Like other forms of foreclosure proceedings, notice of a public auction is required so that some assurance exists that a price close to the fair market value is realized by the taxing body. The proceeds of the tax sale pay the delinquent taxes and any other recorded liens.

Buyers at a tax sale are warned by the Cook County treasurer that a successful bid is just the beginning of an expensive and lengthy legal process that generally requires hiring a lawyer and sending a barrage of notices to other parties interested in the property. They are also told that the former owner could buy back the property during a redemption period, which varies from state to state. Always check your state statute for information on the foreclosure act and the auction process.

Under the old Illinois Mortgage Foreclosure Act, the redemption period expires six months after the foreclosure sale. The sale ordinarily takes place about two to four months after the foreclosure case was filed, sometimes longer. Under the Illinois law that became effective July 1, 1987, the redemption period expires three months after the decree of foreclosure is entered, but not less than seven months after the foreclosure complaint and summons are served. It is important to note that under the new law, the expiration of the redemption period can come before the auction sale is held: real estate owners who sleep on their rights through the day of the auction sale may find that they have no rights left.

Individuals are not the only parties entering foreclosure auctions. Cities, towns, villages and counties are also competing. On September 3, 1987, Efraim Garcia, planning and development director for Houston, Texas, announced a city-sponsored plan to buy 1,500 HUD-foreclosed apartment units with $20 million in federal insured funds. The Houston plan has merit in that it makes affordable and attractive housing available while simultaneously putting graveyard properties back on the tax roll. In addition, it creates income tax breaks, equity and home ownership for many who individually could not have attained such goals.

Mr. Garcia noted, "The concept is ideal for Houston, where a soft real estate market and a long list of foreclosed properties facilitate the cheap purchase of vacant complexes that can be immediately renovated."

Home foreclosures in Texas and other oil-producing states have increased as much as 60 percent over the past year, and several housing industry leaders foresee a continuing tide of delinquent mortgage payments and foreclosures.

You cannot win in a mortgage foreclosure auction against a mortgage lender unless you understand the lender's objectives. Don't get into the auction arena before learning the rules of the game. If you are interested in a property that has a $50,000 mortgage in default, you can be certain as death and taxes that the first mortgage lender who is foreclosing is not going to let the property go at an auction for less than is owed, that is, the outstanding balance including interest and attorney's fees, that is, unless the property is a dog.

The most likely strategy would be to bid $5,000 to $8,000 above the outstanding delinquent mortgage in order to be within the ballpark as a winning bidder. Keep in mind that banks are in the mortgage business, not the property-owning business, so they will normally bid enough to protect their balance sheet. The exception to bidding above the indebtedness would be a VA or FHA mortgage where the lien represents 100 percent of the approved value of the property. In this instance, you bid below the mortgage balance in the hope of acquiring reverse leverage.

Another strategy to circumvent an auction war is to approach the mortgagor (borrower) who is about to lose the property and offer to pay off the debt, plus offer him a premium of perhaps $5,000 or $6,000. If you have done your homework, you may pick up a piece of real estate at a bargain basement price and perhaps make $25,000 to $30,000 in the process. This tactic will not make you an instant member of the nouveau rich, but it will certainly increase your net worth.

Many foreclosure auction buyers are not satisfied with simply increasing their net worth. They want to become instant real estate millionaires, and thus follow the teaching of those no-down-payment real estate gurus who say that they can show you how to triple your current income within one year, even if you have bad credit and are unemployed.

Greed will make some people believe anything that appears to have a leg up on beating the system without working. There are people who will pay to hear a lecture on how to turn green grass into green dollar bills. Some "gurus" claim that money-making miracles can be found in the home study courses that they sell for $390. They say that the only requirements for becoming a real estate mogul is to invest 30 minutes a day studying their high-priced materials and spend at least one afternoon every week looking at the tall, green grass surrounding distressed properties.

The get-rich experts do not tell you that the majority of foreclosed properties they preach about are in distressed areas and that they make more money giving you advice than they make from buying orphan properties. Charletons have become millionaires telling large audiences about the green-grass-no-money-down theory during the past two decades.

Let's assume that you got lucky, and became the successful bidder in a low- to no-down-payment foreclosure sale. The next thing you have to understand is how to detect a real estate land mine before stepping on it. Therefore, we should look at some of the most common booby traps in the field of foreclosures and review some measures you must take for protecting yourself.

Booby traps arise when you purchase a piece of property in a fore-closure sale that was executed under the uniform commercial code and the former owner files bankruptcy after the foreclosure. The decision of the Fifth Circuit Court of Appeals rendered in the case of Durrett vs. Washington National Insurance Company, 621 F 2nd 2001 (5th Cur. 1980), sent shockwaves through the mortgage and foreclosure markets. The court held that a non-judicial foreclosure sale, which is a sale without the benefit of a court order, is fraudulent if the transfer was made within a year before the debtor filed bankruptcy, and if the price for the property was less than its "fair equivalent value." The court argued that the basic principle of bankruptcy is equality of distribution of assets among creditors. The equality of distribution was undermined in foreclosure cases where only the first foreclosing lien holder can recover their losses, while the junior lien holders are cut off. In the Durrett case, the court established that a fair equivalent value is no less than 70 percent of the fair market value of the property.

The effect of this ruling on foreclosures in the mortgage market is that the courts can rescind the transfer of a property if the mortgagor (borrower) files for bankruptcy within a year after the foreclosure. The Durrett decision also had an impact on the availability of title insurance for homes that have gone through foreclosure within a year of application for a title policy. Many title insurance companies have decided that selling title insurance on property that has gone through foreclosure under a non-judicial sale is too great a financial risk. This could mean that if you are a successful bidder at a foreclosure auction, the asset you acquired in the auction could be tied up for years before you could obtain a title policy or get clear to title to refinance.

Another booby trap is federal tax liens. If a successful bidder fails to discover outstanding tax liens, and if the trustee fails to give the government 25 days' notice before foreclosure, the government can exercise its rights of redemption. This means that within 20 days after the foreclosure sale, a successful bidder can be forced to sell the property to the federal government for the bid price plus 6 percent annual interest and maintenance fee. The government takes such action when the tax debtor had a large amount of equity in the subject property.

The state of Illinois recognizes a land trust. Under this legal device, the legal owner of the real estate transfers the legal title to a trustee, which is usually a title company or a bank, and in return receives a beneficial interest in the trust that is legally considered personal property. Generally, the trustee's sole duty is to hold legal title to the property since the beneficial owner's interest becomes personal property. Hence, a pledge of one's beneficial interest in a trust is collateral in addition to the real estate as security for a mortgage loan. Typically, an assignment of beneficial interest gives the mortgage lender everything needed to protect a loan.

The beneficial interest in the land trust is pledged to a mortgage lender in much the same way one would pledge an automobile, television, VCR, household furniture or any movable object. If a party defaults under the terms of the mortgage, a lender would be able to use its remedy under Article IX, a Uniform Commercial Code (UCC). Article IX applies since the property involved is considered personal property, and it can be repossessed as quickly as they can back a tow truck up to an automobile and pull it away. In the assignment of beneficial cases, there is no need for the mortgage lender to engage in a lengthy and expensive foreclosure process.

Most lenders would rather have a collateral assignment of beneficial interest than a mortgage because there is no redemption period requirement under a UCC sale of beneficial interest. Title to the property transfers immediately to the successful bidder in a UCC sale while in a mortgage foreclosure action, the successful bidder must wait for the redemption period to obtain title.

There have been many cases in Illinois courts where lenders, as a condition of the loan, have required that the home owner place the property in a land trust and assign beneficial interest to the lender as security rather than execute a mortgage. In such situations, Illinois courts generally deemed the transaction to be in the nature of a mortgage, finding that the lenders were trying to circumvent the borrower's right to redeem. The courts, after determining that a transaction was in the nature of a mortgage, required the lender to go through the foreclosure process including the statutory redemption. It is important to know that in many cases judges have ignored the redemption right of the borrower and ruled in favor of the lender.

Other Protective Measures For A Bidder To Take In Foreclosure Sales

Step 1. Have your lawyer perform an extensive title search. A title search should uncover any outstanding tax liens that have not been erased by the foreclosure sale and other liens, such as junior mortgages and special assessments.

Step 2. The attorney usually examines the trust deed and notice of the deed of trust to insure that the trustee listed in the notice of trustee sale is indeed the one authorized to sell the property. It is also very important to make sure that the property's legal description in the deed of trust coincides with the one contained in the notice of trustees deed. Otherwise, you may buy the wrong building. That has happened.

The deed of trust should tell the auction winner if the notice of sale has been posted in the proper places. If the trustee ignores this provision, the sale could be jeopardized.

Step 3. Meet the trustee. Bidders should meet titleholders before the foreclosure proceedings if only to inform them they intend to make a bid. Such meetings alert trustees that there are serious customers, and enable bidders to recognize trustees among the crowd during the actual sale.

Step 4. Reinspect the property the day before the auction. Make a last attempt to inspect the interior and meet the former owner. Time may have eroded an initial hostility, and the owner may tell you the reason for the foreclosure. Also, talk to the neighbors and learn more about the history of the property, as well as of the neighborhood.

Step 5. Limit your personal exposure: Do not buy foreclosed bargains you cannot afford. I have known auction buyers who bought more than they could chew and ended up filing bankruptcy in an effort to save their shirts. I also have seen successful bidders of "as is" VA and FHA properties walk away from them and lose substantial monies because they could not obtain construction financing for rehabilitation needed to satisfy the municipal building codes within a reasonable time period.

As recently as December 1987, I received a call from a long-time client who had successfully bid for seven parcels containing 325 apartments units in the Cook County Tax Scavenger sale held in Chicago. He was looking for a partner to furnish him with money to close the deal within the 24-hour deadline, but was unable to find an angel. Bidding at a scavenger sale without a pre-arranged line of credit is not prudent, to say the least.

The plight of auction buyers seeking monies to rehabilitate sick properties was never fully documented until the *New York Times* profiled several cases in its September 13, 1987 edition.

The story revealed that 50 percent of the rehabilitators in the loan program sponsored by New York City in conjunction with the Dime Savings Bank have been households headed by single black women. "The women are doing very well—better than men," said Peter G. Florey, who administers the Dime Savings Bank program.

The second largest group of borrowers were Hispanic families. Three white households—two couples and a single woman—comprised the smallest group.

"I felt I was a woman in a man's world," said Brenda O'Brien, a single black woman with a 10-year-old son who was the Dime's first rehab loan customer. She bought her house in the Fort Greene section of Brooklyn in an auction in 1982, but could not afford to renovate it until the bank program was offered. With a city-subsidized 7½ percent $125,000 loan, the elementary school teacher renovated and moved into her brick house in 1986. "I always wanted my own house, but could not afford one in move-in condition. But I wanted a house for so long it gave me strength and courage to do this," said Ms. O'Brien.

Janice E. Henderson and her mother Adeline told of their experience in purchasing a property in Fort Greene, Brooklyn: In a February 1983 auction, the first bidders drove up the price of the four-story brownstone dwelling to $90,000, but they didn't have enough money to make the 10 percent deposit. When the house was put up for auction again, the bid climbed to $57,000, but the new buyer did not have enough money for the deposit. On the third go 'round, Janice and Adeline Henderson bid $51,000 and won.

"If I had seen the insides, we would never have bought it. It was a horror," Adeline Henderson said. "The front of the house had looked good," she said, so they passed up the opportunity to inspect the interior before the auction. That was a big mistake.

During the 10 years of city ownership of the Ft. Greene property, water had seeped through the roof and destroyed every interior wall, floor and ceiling and damaged the rear exterior wall. The Hendersons admitted they did not know enough about construction to worry. They hired an architect, who also acted as a general contractor, and work began after Dime Savings approved their loan 2½ years after their successful bid.

"We weren't there that often," said Janice Henderson, but they had confidence in their architect and the bank engineers, who inspected the project and approved payments to the contractor.

"I thought that was very helpful," Ms. Henderson added. "A lot of things probably went over our heads."

As in most rehabilitation projects, some things do go over everyone's head. The Hendersons spent $35,000 of their own money on unantici- pated extra expenses, including repairing the rear wall and replacing railings stolen during the construction.

Although the renovation cost $180,000, the contemporary interior with a restored exterior is much better than they had anticipated. The mother and daughter live in the upper three levels and rent out the garden-level apartment for $900 a month. This helps offset their $1,500 monthly mortgage payment.

It took three years for the Hendersons to move into their house, but transactions proceeded so smoothly that the two women subsequently became stockholders of the Dime Savings Bank of New York.

"One of the biggest property owners in Harlem is the city of New York, so you don't have much to chose from on an open market," said Marshan Mason Edwards, a business executive. In June 1985, she, her husband Wayne, who is a school teacher, and her mother-in-law Marie, a nurse, submitted sealed bids on three houses in a city auction of 148 houses, which gave precedence to Harlem residents. Their $51,000 bid, on their third-choice house, enabled them to buy a four-story brown- stone on West 131st Street. The building was in relatively good condi- tion, similar to one they had been offered privately for $100,000.

"All the mechanical systems have to be replaced, but the house isn't in terrible condition," Marshan said. "There is a lot of original woodwork intact. When we are finished, we will have a new house with seven working fireplaces; all except two have the original marble mantles."

By November 1987, the Edwards' had spent $15,500 on down payments and closing costs for their home, $8,000 on architect fees, $3,600 on mortgage payments to the city, and $1,000 on taxes and insurance.

The family had applied for a construction loan at the Chase Manhattan Bank in 1986. When the lender would not finance the entire cost of the renovation, they decided to apply for 100 percent financing offered through the city-Dime program. If they qualified for the full $60,000 subsidy on their $186,000 rehab loan, their $2,000 monthly payment could be reduced by about $400 a month. The Edwards' anticipate closing on the construction loan by January 1988, and moving in the following Christmas.

If New York and Chicago rehab experiences are typical, thousands of house-hungry people will make hundreds of bids. Many will bid on properties they have not inspected. Many will have no first-hand knowledge of the difficulty or cost of rehabilitating property that has been pillaged and unoccupied for years. More than a few bidders will be carried away by auction fever, and will not have enough money to make a deposit on their dream houses. Their dreams, like smoke, will fade away in the reauction process. Some will deplete their resources in their efforts to rehabilitate a ghost of a house.

Auctions have been held in New York City almost every month since 1980 by the Department of Housing Preservation and Development. Of the 2,300 properties auctioned, about half were one- to four-family dwellings, the remainder were five to 10 apartment buildings. In September 1987, the city of New York owned between 4,500 to 5,000 vacant buildings.

Data on a typical New York house auction support my premise. Out of 108 people who bid and won in a fall 1987 auction, 25 discovered to their dismay that they had bought dilapidated buildings in run-down neighborhoods and decided not to close the sale. They forfeited their deposit, which was 10 percent of purchase price. These properties were sold again at other auctions.

Two-thirds of the 108 properties will be renovated within the New York-required two-year period after the closing. Owners of the other houses must renovate or face foreclosure proceedings on the city's 7½ percent, 20-year-fixed-rate purchase money mortgage. Within 12 months, New York could possibly repossess and reauction or demolish two or three of the 108 properties for non-payment of the city-held mortgage and taxes.

Buying housing orphans at auctions is a road to building a healthy net worth for patient, stout-hearted real estate venturers.

# Frank Hunter:
# The Successful Real Estate Speculator*

*"Just the fear of being poor is enough to motivate me enough to fly to the moon."*

When Frank Hunter was nine years old, he recognized that whatever he got out of life he would have to earn himself. His parents were illiterate and poverty-stricken, and he sensed they could never offer him even a thimble full of assistance.

Frank's Aunt Matilda held up a brighter lamp for the young lad. She told him that if he went to school and made good grades, he would be rich some day. He made good grades and finished two years of college in the city of Port-of-Spain, Trinidad. Hunter was soon hired as an accountant at the school from which he had graduated, earning the grand sum of 30 British pounds, which was 84 American dollars a month. In 1954, that salary sounded like a ton of money to the youthful and ambitious Trinidadian.

At age 23, Frank Hunter was proud to be the first member of his family to get a white-collar job. It was something that he had always wanted. However, it did not take long for him to realize that white-collar salaries did not stretch much further than blue-collar salaries. The idea of buying a car or a house out of his earnings was totally out of the question. After several months on the job, Frank purchased his first piece of mechanical transportation, a bicycle bought on the monthly installment

---

*These case studies are documented; only the names were changed to protect the confidentiality of the real estate broker-client relationship.

plan. Hunter was not satisfied with his bike because his ambitions propelled him faster than the two-wheeler could carry him.

In 1956, Frank moved to Illinois and enrolled in a small liberal arts college where he graduated in 1959 with honors and a bachelor's degree in the liberal arts. Hunter's undergrad achievements enabled him to get a scholarship to a state university where he successfully completed the Master of Business Administration program. After receiving the M.B.A. degree in May 1961, he said to himself: "I am ready to cash in on my training."

In the summer of '61, Frank came to Chicago, looked around and found a fellow about his age who was just starting in the wholesale meat business. After an interview, the young entrepreneur said to Hunter: "If you wish you can come aboard, but I can't guarantee you anything because I don't know what I am going to do or if I am going to succeed or not." Frank accepted the job offer and both of them worked 12-plus hours a day on the docks.

The wholesale meat business moved very slowly for more than a year. Then a live-wire salesman was hired and the business took off like a 747 jet.

Hunter's first mistake was not to cut himself in for a piece of the action at the outset, even if it meant accepting one-third less salary. After five years on the job, Frank was made first vice president and controller of the firm, but his promotion did not entitle him to a single share of stock or a stock option.

On the other hand, the personal relationship between Hunter and his boss was good. A year passed before he approached his boss again about getting a piece of the stock action. It was during the winter of his sixth year with the company that Frank made this observation:

> The second time I asked for a piece of the action I met with partial success because he (Hunter's boss) agreed to sell me a certain amount of stock at what he called a fair market price, providing I paid for it within a relatively short period of time. In the interim, he had given some stock to several distant relatives who had just recently started working for the company. Moreover, they did not have to pay one red cent for it. I took that behavior on the part of the company president to mean that he looked at me different from the others and that I would never be a part of the group. It was at this juncture that I started thinking that if this is the way it is, I better start making another niche for myself. I decided that niche would be in real estate.
>
> My decision to start buying real estate was not based on a whim.

It was grounded on the fact that as an accountant, I had had the opportunity to file federal income taxes for others who owned property and see them succeed. In the Spring of 1968, I made the big leap and purchased a three-flat building. I thought I knew a lot about the business—only to find out I did not know anything. Being a quick study, I learned a lot in short order by asking other property owners how they handle this and that. During the summer of 1970, I purchased my second building; it was a four-flat brick. Everything went along very well until the gas crisis of 1974. The gas bills were so high they figuratively went right through the roof while the heat literally escaped between the cracks of the hungry mortar bricks and the ill-fitting windows of the 60-year-old buildings.

On a pleasant and mild Sunday morning in the spring of 1975, a very bright light came on in the head of Frank Hunter when he decided that with the escalating expenses, owning a three- or four-flat building as an investment was not very smart. Frank sold both the buildings and made a net profit of $14,000. However, the gentleman who purchased Frank's four-flat for $40,000 was more knowledgeable than Frank. He painted, buttered and shined the four-flat for about one year, sold it for $65,000 and made a profit of $25,000. Frank said, "Ah, ah-ha, that's the key."

In October 1976, Hunter purchased a 20-flat and an eight-flat building. The two buildings were too much for Frank to handle by himself while holding down his regular job as a vice president and controller at the wholesale meat company. So, he scouted around and found a guy who was knowledgeable about real estate maintenance and willing to work. The two men successfully maintained and managed the properties. Hunter, the real estate speculator, continued to buy properties for his portfolio.

Frank purchased all of his buildings the old-fashioned way: he used conventional financing because he did not like the added expense of carrying the heavy debt service on a maximum mortgage. Neither did he have the patience for the F.H.A. approach. He felt it was too cumbersome and consumed more time than he wanted to spend. Moreover, he could afford to have this attitude because he had been thrifty and saved over 50 percent of his $30,000 annual salary, and had established good banking connections.

In 1980, Frank decided that he would try his hand at purchasing buildings that had traveled the foreclosure route. He purchased a 15-flat that had been foreclosed from a bank for $70,000. After spending a modest amount of money on refurbishing the building, he was able to fully rent the once partially vacated building and netted $20,000 profit after the first year of full occupancy.

Frank received an offer to sell the building just 18 months after he had purchased it. The offer would net him a $90,000 profit. The decision he had to make was whether to take the $90,000 profit or continue owning the building and net $20,000 per year.

Frank decided to accept the $90,000, significantly increasing his capital formation. Had he kept the 15-flat building for four more years, he would probably have saved $80,000. By taking the $90,000 profit up front and reinvesting it in other foreclosed properties, he was able to quadruple his money to $360,000 in the same four-year period. In spite of the fact that Hunter has realized huge profits from buying and selling foreclosed properties, he still holds 30 or more apartment units in his private real estate portfolio to meet his personal day-to-day cash flow needs.

Frank Hunter became a multimillionaire by buying and selling foreclosed properties, piling up dollars in a relatively short period of time. The road he has taken is a well-beaten path, one that almost anyone who is genuinely interested in working hard and making money in the field of real estate can follow. After all, foreclosure information is available to the general public.

If you are interested in learning more about foreclosure, give me your hand and we will walk down the road a piece. I will point out the various signs that indicate a property is coming on the market via the foreclosure route.

The first public sign is a notice of default, which is recorded at the request of lender in the County Records Office in the county in which the property is located. The recorded information will appear in the legal notice section of your daily local newspaper and also in the Daily Law Bulletin. The default notices will denote the following: (1) the amount of the delinquency; (2) address of the property; (3) name of the mortgagor and mortgagee; (4) nature of the instrument, whether a mortgage, trust deed, or other document; (5) amount of the original mortgage; (6) legal description of the mortgaged premises and (7) date of the mortgage. The debtor now has an abeyance period, which varies from 30 days to one year depending on the particular state statute, in which to cure the indebtedness. In the time between the first public notice and actual foreclosure procedure, known as the publication period, heirs and claimants have an opportunity to respond. If they don't come forth, they can be defaulted.

The next sign on the road directs you to the foreclosure sale. In many instances, the lender is the only bidder. In many counties, the lender is permitted to bid up to the outstanding mortgage obligation without putting any cash on the barrel head. However, in states that have redemption laws, the lender will not get outright ownership of the property until the redemption period has expired. The redemption period can vary from state to state from 14 to 90 days.

Another road sign directs you to another type of foreclosure, a sheriff's sale where everybody bids. Some bidders are bidding with their eyes closed because hostile owners may deny them an opportunity to make an interior inspection of the property. Losing a building is a traumatic experience for any family and many former owners vandalize property when they vacate. If you cannot inspect the property interior before you purchase it, your bid price should be 30 percent to 40 percent below comparable properties or in the general area of the subject real estate to compensate for the unknown structural risk involved.

The heartbreak suffered in a tax foreclosure sale is vividly described in an article by Henry Locke that appeared in the *Chicago Daily Defender* of August 13, 1987:

## TAXBUYER WINS, HOMEOWNER LOSES

I.V. Taylor, 63, wept openly yesterday as he was evicted from his $66,000, single-family brick home of 14 years at 135 E. 119th St., for failure to pay about $350 for a tax assessment on an alley behind his home.

Taylor's neighbors labeled the ouster a 'cold-blooded and unconscionable eviction' by the taxbuyer who they said used the 'fine printing of a state law' to take the elderly man's home.

'I paid the money for the alley assessment,' Taylor said, 'but the county clerk's office sent it back, claiming I paid it after the deadline. But I was there on time, with Ald. Robert Shaw (9), and was assured by a clerk that everything would be recorded in a timely manner.

But I smell a rat in this case now because everyone is changing his story and I have lost my home,' he added, saying that he plans to hire a new lawyer 'to find out if there was a conspiracy to defraud me out of my home.'

David R. Gray, a Loop lawyer and managing partner of Midwest Real Estate Investment Co. which was awarded the house after paying the delinquent taxes, however, maintained that he attempted to 'work with the Taylors so they could keep their home.'

'It appears that the taxbuyer could have been a little more considerate, rather than striking out like a snake to take this house,' added Alf Wardlow, who called himself a fishing buddy and long-time friend of Taylor's.

'It is tantamount to murder, but just not first-degree' because the taxbuyer used the law to take the property, Wardlow added while assisting Taylor in carting away some of his possessions.

Still another neighbor expressed sadness and disappointment about the eviction, saying, 'I know the sheriff's department has a responsibility to carry out its duties, but I wonder if the people who do that dirty work can sleep at night.'

Taylor, who had fought unsuccessfully to block the eviction with the assistance of *Chicago Defender*, said, 'At one time I thought I would rather be dead than to lose my home because at my age, it will be too much of a handicap for me to start over again.'

Initially, Gray said, he was willing to allow the family to continue to live there by paying him rent until they could get the proceeds from an 'indemity fund,' but when Taylor refused to sign the agreement, 'there was nothing more to talk about.'

Because of the ordeal, Taylor and his wife separated. She had moved out of the house prior to Wednesday's eviction.

Gray explained that the proposed agreement called for Taylor to turn the money from the indemnity fund over to him, which would have allowed his firm to recoup its investment in the property.

However, during the past few days, Gray has refused to discuss the proposed agreement with Taylor or the *Defender*. As Taylor's furnishings were being removed from the house by the sheriff's department, Albert Nowicki, the receiver, observed the work.

Sheriff's Deputy K.L. Little said Nowicki was the receiver of the property, representing the taxbuyer. He previously told the *Defender* that he plans to rent the house until he can sell it at market value.

What is the safest way for you to enter the foreclosure business? How can you eliminate your chances of being a part of a heart-wrenching experience like Mr. Taylor's and avoid the risk of buying a vandalized building?

My best advice is to buy the property directly from the bank. After the bank has foreclosed on the property and it appears on the bank's books, it becomes an REO, or real estate owned property. Buying REOs off the shelf at the bank is the best way to get into the foreclosure business. The bank makes the deal almost risk-free because in the process of the bank's foreclosure, it clears up all outstanding liens, clears the title, and pays the back taxes and any other encumbrances that might be against the property. In other words, the property is free of all problems except deferred maintenance and possibly some vandalism.

Another advantage in investing in bank REO properties is that you can usually purchase them with a small down payment and occasionally with no money down. Other discount property opportunities may be found at real estate tax sales, real estate assessment tax sales, Internal Revenue Service sales, and probate sales. I have found that the best way to beat out all of the competition in discount sale competition is to be prepared to offer the title-holder an all-cash proposition and thereby be in a position to close the deal within 48 hours after the seller shows good title. The all-cash deal is attractive to the seller because you have eliminated all contingencies except the seller's ability to show good title.

There are exceptions to the general rule: Travis Realty has clients who have handled their own properties in such a professional manner that banks literally turn properties over to them because the real estate owners have been endowed with a brick thumb, a special capability for making real estate work. They know how to take the property off the sick roll and put it on the tax roll.

There have been occasions when banks make a no-down-payment deal and defer the principal and the interest payments for four to eight months to give the new purchaser an opportunity to refurbish the building. In other instances banks have actually increased the existing mortgage and advanced the monies for rehab.

Another plus for buying real estate owned property (REOs) from a bank is that the bank will usually handle most of the closing costs and various other fees that might be incidental to a purchase of real estate. Banks are motivated to get their REOs off their books as quickly as possible. An REO on the balance sheet is a red flag to both the state and federal regulators that the lending institution has not used the best judgment in putting the loans on the books.

As Frank Hunter demonstrated, profitable opportunities in real estate do not simply grow on trees, waiting to be picked off like ripe bananas. You have to make a concentrated effort to locate the opportunity, and then develop it. If you don't move when opportunity knocks, you will find yourself standing on the sideline watching the parade pass by without ever recognizing that your opportunity was in that unpainted building on the front line of the REO foreclosure parade. Hey! You missed it.

Hunter made the following observation about FHA foreclosure auctions on one- to four-unit properties:

> An FHA auction, well, it's kind of a frenzied way of dealing. I don't know if it's because of the unsophisticatedness of the people bidding, but they generally bid properties up beyond their reasonable worth. So I have not gone back to any of those in the past three or four years.
>
> But another point I want to mention is that it's dangerous to look at a building for its aesthetic value, you know, the beauty and the amenities that go along with owning a building. Buying real estate for what I call its gingerbread flavor is in ordinary language falling in love with a building. It is dangerous to do that. I look at a building only in terms of its basic intrinsic dollar value. I never have purchased a building that I loved so much that I could not sell it. That is a pitfall for the unsophisticated buyer. You should look at the building only in terms of its economic value and how much it can turnover. I find that failing to do that is one of the real estate traps that people continually fall into.

Mr. Hunter is not a showy person. He is presently driving a car that is five years old, and keeps most of his cars anywhere from eight to 12 years. He says as long as the body of the car is in good shape, doesn't rust too much and runs, he will keep it. However, his children do not share his affection for old cars and his respect for money. They may never understand the drive that keeps their father moving. Frank Hunter Sr. revealed his inner soul when he said:

> My early childhood was very meager. I did not enjoy it because of lack of funds from my parents. I have only one fear in life. And it's a fear of being poor again. The thought of that possibility drives me. That fear is the most overwhelming thing in my life. Just the fear of being poor is enough to motivate me enough to fly to the moon.

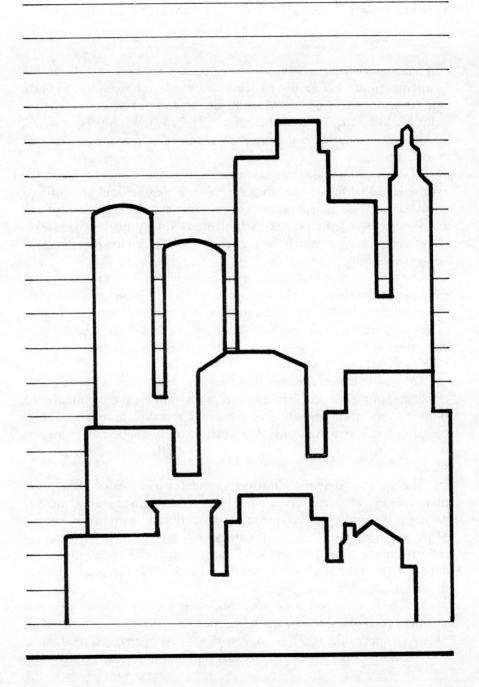

# CHAPTER VII

# MAIN STREET VS. WALL STREET

The stock market crash on Black Monday, October 19, 1987, decimated Wall Street and forced millions of investors to search elsewhere to find a safe haven for their money. Many turned to real estate because historically, as a long range investment, it has had greater immunity from sharp, sudden drops in value and from the volatility that frequently visits the stock market.

The owners of real estate may catch a slight economic cold with the rattling and shaking of the stock market but they seldom are inflicted with death-threatening pneumonia. The realty owner's greatest concerns are about how deeply pockets will be affected by a prolonged market disturbance and how much the turbulence will soften the rental market or weaken selling prices.

The turmoil that took place in the financial market in the fall of '87 gave a large number of real estate owners and developers the jitters. As the market continued its wild gyrations, the positive posture of some major corporate decision makers was abandoned and lease-making decisions were put on hold, negatively affecting the commercial and residential vacancy rates.

The residential properties that were the most affected were at the upper end of the market, with the exception of those at the pinnacle. At the very top, investors who lost a half million dollars in that market probably had several millions left to cushion the blow. Beware, however: when the big boys sneeze, a large segment of the population gets the sniffles.

The margin-buying Wall Street speculator in times of crisis prays that paper investments won't evaporate into thin air, a phenomenon that cannot threaten a realty owner or stockholder with deep equity. Moreover, housing is local and the stock market is nationally oriented, as reflected in the New York Stock Exchange Composite Transactions that appear daily in the *Wall Street Journal* and in the financial pages of every major metropolitan newspaper.

Unlike stocks, real estate is a basic commodity: when there is a shortage, prices tend to rise and when there is an oversupply, prices fall. Sheltered space, like food, is a necessity for every person, so real estate space ranks near the top of priority spending by the composite buyer. By comparison, products and services other than food and shelter are deferable and, under certain economic circumstances, downgraded in quantity and quality.

The tangible value of the real estate product in the market place is favored by investors because people turn to tangibles during times of uncertainty and inflation, and nothing surpasses the bricks and steel of real estate in tangibility and permanence. Admittedly, the real estate market, like the stock market, also has trends. Realty prices fluctuate but, unlike stock prices, don't change hourly or daily. Within the realty market, you will find quite a difference among the trends and prices of urban and rural properties, commercial and residential properties. These are much like the differences among the various listings on the daily stock market sans the brand labels.

To put the need for shelter as a commodity in bold relief, let's examine a story that appeared in the October 16, 1987 edition of the *Wall Street Journal* on the housing conditions in Japan.

Residential land prices in the Tokyo area soared an average of 93 percent in the year ending July 1, 1987, according to the National Land Agency. Prices tripled in Yokohama, Japan's second largest city, in the same period. A modest house outside of Tokyo now sells for as much as $2 million.

The problem has unsettling consequences far beyond the new generations of landless middle-class Japanese who despair of living their lives in cramped, rented living accommodations. Japanese money threatens to distort the real estate market across the world. Hawaiian condominiums and New York skyscrapers are dirt cheap to Japanese investors, enriched by the strong yen.

The debate over Japanese property inflation places much of the blame on aggressive land purchases by developers, including large concerns such as Sumitomo Realty. Also faulted are bankers, who offer easy credit for land speculation; urban farmers, who keep choice city turf off the market; politicians, who don't dare rescind tax breaks for those farmers; and government officials, who fail to apply available remedial legal measures.

The mania to concentrate business activity in the Tokyo area has also contributed to the property rush, as have the arrival of waves of foreign bankers who make frenzied demands on limited office space. Similarly accused is a tax system that discourages people from selling inherited land and encourages them to protect capital gains by pumping windfalls back into hyperinflated land market.

The real estate market and stock market have become inextricably linked. Investors borrow funds on the strength of real estate collateral to buy stocks, and the shares of companies with potentially valuable real estate are pushed sky high by stock speculators who ignore the companies' business prospects. As long as there is land involved, credit and equity are considered a safe bet.

A crash in the real estate market would have disastrous results in Japan and possibly send shockwaves to the financial markets world wide. However, such an occurrence is unthinkable to players of the real estate game. Because of the extreme shortage of land and dense population, Japan's belief is that what goes up must continue to rise.

Land prices have climbed since World War II with few exceptions, such as a brief dip after one of the oil shocks in the 1970s. Investors consider themselves exempt from the cycles of feast and famine that rule real estate markets elsewhere in the world.

Japan's stock market and real estate market are linked at the hip, and this could possibly prove fatal for the entire economy.

The New York City housing market, somewhat like Japan's, is very closely linked to the stock market. Individuals working for the giant investment houses in December 1987 and counting on year-end bonuses to finance the purchase of a $500,000 condominium or signing a six-figure lease for an apartment overlooking Central Park are in trouble. Stock market bounces have lit cautionary signs for both commercial and residential users.

For the investor who wants a foot in two worlds—the stock market and the real estate market—at the same time, the Real Estate Investment Trust (REIT) may be the answer. Since Black Monday, Real Estate Investment Trusts are getting a lot of attention from investors searching for a measure of protection from the volatility and economic uncertainty of the financial market place.

According to the Chicago Dock and Canal Trust, investors purchased more than 25,000 shares in a single day following the stock market collapse. The week of October 19, 1987 was one of the best weeks in the history of the trust. Santa Anita Realty Enterprises Inc., in California, also reported a heavy volume of inquiries from investors during the same period. Leavitt, Mitchell, Webb and Garrison, a Houston brokerage house, stated in a *Wall Street Journal* story that REIT stock sales were "up markedly since the market collapsed. We are generating orders on REITs for the first time in a long time," said Bruce

G. Garrison, senior vice president of the firm. "Every (REIT) stock on our list is a recommendation. That's never happened before."

Though REITs didn't totally escape the stock market plunge, they as a group weren't hit as hard as other stocks were. REIT stocks tumbled just 11 percent during the week ending October 23, according to the National Association of Real Estate Investment Trust Index of 96 REITs. By comparison, the Dow Jones industrial average, and Standard and Poor's Index of 500 common stocks declined 24.9 percent and 22.9 percent respectively, in the same week.

"The price volatility on the (REIT) stocks just isn't there," says Christopher Lucas, research director of REIT's national association.

"REITs are unique animals in the world of stocks because they are both stocks and real estate," says Mark Decker, executive vice president of the Real Estate Investment Trust Association. "And these days, many people feel more comfortable with real estate as they search for longer-term protection against economic uncertainty."

The relationship between the stock market and the real estate market has been center stage during and following the 1987-88 Wall Street debacle. Real estate companies across the country have experienced a 5 percent to 25 percent decrease in the number of customer inquiries. The stock market plunge definitely caused a small percentage of buyers to retreat from purchasing homes and businesses from signing long-term leases. Many prospective buyers adopted a wait-and-see attitude because their endowment plans were heavily invested in the stock market. There are legitimate grounds for some real fear about future economic conditions.

The fallout from the stock market shakedown resulted in an 18.7 percent decline in real estate values in the Northeast. James Christian, chief economist for the U.S. League of Savings Institutions, said part of the weakness may have been the impact of the market crash on housing in suburbs that cater to Wall Street brokers. In contrast, the Midwest sales soared during October, shooting up 47.7 percent to an annual rate of 112,000 units. This jump can be attributed in part to the improving fortunes of manufacturing companies whose export sales rose sharply in 1987.

David Seiders, chief economist for the National Association of Homebuilders, said surveys taken by his association before and after the stock collapse showed that builders are actually more optimistic now because of the easier money policies being pursued by the Federal Reserve System.

Immediately after the stock market collapse, the Central Bank moved aggressively to pump money into the economy to assure that the sudden loss of wealth from the record 508 point decline in stock prices would not threaten the U.S. financial system.

Builders believe that they will be able to get through the stock market mess in pretty good shape, providing the interest rates stay under control, as they presently expect.

In contrast to the good fortunes of the Midwest manufacturers, the Wall Street firm of Kidder, Peabody and Company said it would slash 13 percent of its work force, eliminating 1,000 jobs from its payroll of 7,500 employees. It would also close 10 percent of its branch offices and refocus much of its work, with the aim of saving $100 million a year.

Salomon Brothers slashed its work force 12 percent in October, and said it was pulling out of a huge Manhattan town real estate project in which it was to have been a partner and primary tenant. The firm announced December 4, 1987, that it would reduce office space needs and that lease cancellations would cost $51 million against fourth quarter earnings.

Charles Schwab and Co. Inc., the nation's biggest discount brokerage firm, reduced capital and operating costs because of lower earnings stemming from a fall in trading volume since the stock market crashed.

Other leading firms, including Shearson, Lehman, Brothers Inc.; Goldman, Sachs, and Co.; and Drexel, Burham, Lambert Inc., have also recently announced staff cutbacks.

On December 14, 1987, William Schreyer, chairman and chief executive officer of Merrill Lynch, Pierce Fenner & Smith Inc., said: "We are reducing total compensation costs by 10 percent. Undoubtedly, that will result in fewer people. We don't have an exact dollar tag on it."

The Black Monday nightmare punctured the 5-year-old bull market and halted the tremendous employment growth on Wall Street. The market turmoil has directly caused the loss of 3,700 securities industry jobs. In addition, an estimated 5,000 to 8,000 people will get fired because of the merger of Shearson, Lehman, Brothers and E.F. Hutton and Co.

The late Mayor Harold Washington of Chicago did not think it necessary to take the kind of drastic action that Mayor Ed Koch took in New York City. Following the stock market plunge, Mr. Koch imposed a hiring and salary freeze for city employees. Mayor Washington realized that the Chicago economy is not as dependent on LaSalle Street as New York is on Wall Street, although LaSalle Street has become an integral part of Chicago. Traders at the Chicago Mercantile Exchange occupy many of the 2,346 apartments in the newly-constructed Presidential Towers, located two blocks north of the Merc. They prefer cabbing or walking two miles to work to a 20-mile commute from the suburbs. Everett B. Harris, former president of the Chicago Mercantile Exchange, said, "The Exchange has sold half the real estate in the Highland Park suburb."

When the real estate market is compared to the daily movement of the stock market, it has to be considered a very stable long-term investment. Long term means just that and does not imply getting rich overnight. I am very much aware that both the stock market and the real estate market have suede-shoe artists who wave get-rich schemes before the public on a daily basis. Wise investors recognize the difference between investing and gambling, and are mindful that a steep, quick rise in the investment market can position them for an equally fast, deep fall. On the other hand, I have never seen prudent substantial equity investors in the real estate market ride a financial rollercoaster that parallels the one taken by so many investors in the '87-'88 stock market.

One of the arguments favoring the stock market over the real estate market is that real property is considered illiquid, meaning it is hard to convert to cash quickly. In my opinion, that's a very common misconception. Most solidly-built, well-located and realistically priced properties can be sold for market value in a cash sale within a 30- to 120-day period. There is a buyer for every piece of property. The trick is to find him or her. In addition, real estate can be converted into dollars quickly if the owner has some solid equity and selects to refinance the property with a new mortgage. The mortgage is tax-free because borrowed money against real estate is a debt that must be repaid. Moreover, if the property is in trust, you can arrange to get instant money as quick as you can sign over your beneficial interest in the trust and execute a bank note.

Essentially, one must think of real estate as a long-term venture and not as refuge for free money awaiting new opportunities. The rare instances of quick and profitable turnover should not be entertained or adopted as a given. Real property is a living, breathing thing, a business unto itself requiring hard work and continuous expert attention for the maximum attainable success.

There is no formal real market exchange as there is for stocks, where property can be sold quickly at quoted prices. Time, exposure, patience and realism are required to successfully sell or buy real estate. Remember, there is a buyer and seller in the land for every piece of property, provided the buyer is willing and able and the seller is agreeable to accepting a fair price irrespective of the original cost of his or her personal dreams.

# REAL ESTATE GLOSSARY

## A

**Abandonment**   The voluntary relinquishment of rights of ownership or another interest (such as an easement) by failure to use the property coupled with an intent to abandon (give up the interest).

**Abandonment of Homestead**   A recorded document executed by those claiming a homestead exemption, giving up said homestead. Not applicable in all states and procedure must be according to local statutes.

**Abatement**   A reduction or decrease. Usually applies to a decrease of assessed valuation of ad valorem taxes after the assessment and levy.

**Abridgement**   A synopsis; a shorter version retaining the original sense of the original form.

**Absentee Landlord**   An owner or lessor who lives away from the real estate from which rental income is derived.

**Abstract**   A summary; an abridgement. For the use of the photostatic copying, public records were kept by abstracts, or recorded documents.

**Abstract of Title**   A compilation of the recorded documents relating to a parcel of land from which an attorney may give an opinion as to the condition of title. Seldom used in Illinois, frequently used in the state of Michigan.

**Abut**   To touch or border on; as a piece of real estate abutting on a highway or sharing a common boundary with another property.

**Accelerated Depreciation**   Depreciation occurring or which has occurred at a faster rate than usual. The term is frequently used in the context of federal income tax.

**Acceleration Clause**   A condition in a loan contract or mortgage note that triggers the immediate repayment of the entire balance if the agreement is breached or conditions for repayment occur. For example, an assumption without the consent of the mortgagee.

**Accessibility**   The location of a site in terms of how easily it may be reached by customers, employees, carriers, and others necessary to the attended use of the property.

**Acknowledgement**   A written declaration by a person executing an instrument, given before an officer authorized to give an oath (usually a notary public) stating that the execution is of one's volition.

**Acoustical Material**   Materials having sound-absorbing qualities which are applied to walls and/or ceilings. They may be tile, Celotex, cork, special plaster, etc.

**Acoustical Tile**   Any tile having the inherent property to absorb sound.

**Acre-Foot**   A volume of water equivalent to one acre in area with a depth of one foot; 43,560 cubic feet of water.

**Act of God**   Damage caused by nature (floods, winds, etc.) rather than human destruction.

**Actual Cash Value**  The price that a property will bring in a fair and open market, sans duress, and after fair and reasonable efforts have been made to find the purchaser willing to pay the highest price.

**Addendum**  Something added. A list or other material added to a document, letter, contractual agreement, escrow agreement, etc.

**Adjustable Rate Loan**  Any loan on which the interest rate may be changed, either at set intervals or whenever movement occurs in a specified index.

**Ad Valorem**  According to value. A method of taxation using the value of the item taxed to determine the amount of tax. Taxes can be either ad valorem or specific. Example: A tax of $10.10 per 1000 of value per house is ad valorem. A tax of $10.10 per house (irrespective of value) is specific.

**Advance**  1. A loan of funds; in the savings institution business, usually a loan from a Federal Home Loan Bank to a member institution.
2. Money advanced by a mortgagee to pay the mortgagor's obligation of taxes, insurance or other items necessary to protect the secured property.

**Aesthetic Value**  The intangible, psychic enhancement of the value of a property due to such factors as a site offering an unusually pleasant view; a property located in a particular neighborhood, the overall layout and design of which is exceptionally attractive and all the properties therein are harmonious and in the same general price range.

**Affidavit**  A written statement or declaration, sworn to before an officer who has authority to administer an oath.

**Agent**  A person who acts or has the power to act for another person by the latter's written on oral authority. He stands in another's shoes as his representative.

**Agreement of Sale**  A written contractual agreement between a buyer and seller who have reached a meeting of minds as to the conditions necessary for the transfer of ownership of a piece of real or personal property.

**Air Rights**  The right to inclusive and undisturbed use and control of a designated air space within the perimeter of a stated land area and above a stated elevation. Such air rights may be acquired for the construction of a building above the land or above another building.

**Alley**  A relatively narrow way, publicly or privately owned, which serves as a secondary means of access and egress.

**Alternative Mortgage Instrument**  Any loan contract that differs from the traditional fixed rate, long-term fixed payment mortgage. The AMI may be written for a short term with a renewal clause; provide for changes in the monthly payment, term interest rate or other loan element; or contain some other creative provision.

**Amenities**  The qualities and state of being pleasant and agreeable. An intangible benefit of homeownership, such as satisfaction of possession and use derived from architectural excellence, scenic beauty, and desirable social environment.

**Amenity Value**  The increase in value above the utility or rental value attributable to the psychic value of home ownership.

**Amortization**  The process of recovering, over a given period of time, a monetary investment. The provision for the gradual liquidation of an obligation, usually by equal payments at regular intervals over a specific period of months or years.

**Amortized Mortgage**  A mortgage requiring periodic payments, frequently paid monthly, which includes a partial repayment without penalty of the debt and interest on the remaining indebtedness until the next payment period. It provides for the total debt retirement during a contractual term. It is characterized by equal dollar size payments in which the money for interest decreases constantly and principal repayment increases by the same amount that the interest decreases.

**Annuity**  1. An annual income as the result of an earlier investment.

2. The return from an investment of capital, in a series of periodic payments comprising interest and a partial return of capital.

3. An annual return, which may be in equal annual amounts, called a level annuity, or in increasing or decreasing annual amounts, is called an increasing or a decreasing annuity.

**Appraisal**  A valuation; an estimate and opinion of value. The act or process of estimating value. Usually, a written statement of the appraiser's opinion of value of an adequately described parcel of property as of a specified date. Synonym: valuation.

**Appraised Equity Capital**  The difference between the book value and market value of certain savings institution assets such as land and improvements; may be counted as net worth.

**Appreciation**  An increase in market value of a property.

**Assemblage**  The acquisition of contiguous properties into one ownership for a specific use.

**Assessed Value**  The dollar amount assigned to taxable property, both business and personal, by the assessor for the purpose of taxation.

**Assessment**  The valuation of property for taxation; also the value as assigned.

**Assessment Base**  The assessed value of all property within a designated area, such as an assessment or tax district.

**Asset**  Any property which is owned and has value. Assets are either financial, as cash or bonds; or physical, as real and personal.

**Asset Reserves**  Funds set aside against transaction account and other short-term deposit balances, as required by the Federal Reserve Board of all except very small depository institutions; held in the form of cash and non-earning deposits at a Federal Reserve Bank.

**Assignment**  A transfer to another of any property, real or personal, or any rights of estate in said property. Common assignments are of leases, mortgages, deeds of trust, but the general term encompasses all transfers of title.

**Assumption of Mortgage**  A buyer who takes ownership to real estate encumbered with a mortgage may assume the responsibility as the guarantor for the unpaid balance of the mortgage. The buyer is liable for the mortgage repayment, but the prior mortgagor is also liable if a written release has not been obtained by the mortgagee.

**Attractive Nuisance**    Anything on the property which may attract small children and is dangerous to them. Reasonable care must be used to prevent injury to children.

**Auction**    A public sale of land or goods to the highest bidder.

# B

**Balance Sheet**    A statement of the financial position of a person or corporate entity at a specified date, prepared from books kept by a double entry system of bookkeeping.

**Balloon**    In finance, the term refers to the unpaid principal amount of a mortgage or long-term loan which is paid off in a lump sum at the end of the agreed term. For example, a mortgage may have a 15-year amortization period but ballooned or became due within five years pursuant to the loan agreement.

**Balloon Loan**    A loan on which the entire balance becomes due after a specified time such as three or five years; the borrower pays interest regularly, and may or may not make small principal repayments during the loan's term.

**Bankrupt**    One who is adjudicated a bankrupt by a court having proper jurisdiction. The bankruptcy may be voluntary (petitioned by the bankrupt) or involuntary (petitioned by the creditors of the bankrupt).

**Bankruptcy**    Proceedings under federal bankruptcy statutes by which the property of a debtor is seized by the court and divided among the creditors. Voluntary bankruptcy is petitioned by the debtor; involuntary is petitioned by the creditors.

**Baseboard Heating**    A system of perimeter hot water heating with radiators, connectors, or air outlets located in the wall, replacing the baseboard; also called base panel heating.

**Bathroom**    A room containing, as a minimum, a toilet, lavatory, and a bathtub, with or without shower. Three plumbing fixtures equal one bathroom; two plumbing fixtures equal one-half bathroom, or powder room. In some areas, real estate brokers count a toilet, lavatory, and shower as three-fourth bathroom.

**Benchmark**    Surveying mark made on some object which is permanently affixed in the ground, showing the height of that point in relations to sea level. Used in topographic surveys and tidal observations.

**Beneficial Interests**    Benefits, profits, or advantages resulting from a trust agreement. The profits accrue to the real owner of the real estate as distinguished from the trustee who holds only legal title.

**Betterment**    An improvement to a structure which is not a repair, restoration, or enlargement. For example, the addition of a second bathroom, conversion of a basement into a recreation room, modernization of the kitchen or, similar improvements that increase the value of the property.

**Bilevel**    Two levels; for example, a split-level house.

**Bill of Sale**    An instrument by which one transfers personal property.

**Blacktop** Bituminous or asphalt material used in hard surface paving.

**Blanket Mortgage** A mortgage covering more than one property of the mortgagor, such as a mortgage covering several buildings. For example, an owner of a bungalow wants to purchase a 6-flat, and the mortgage on the 6-flat covers the bungalow as additional security for the lender.

**Blight** A reduction in the amenities or usefulness of the real property because of destructive economic forces, such as encroaching inharmonious property uses, infiltration of lower social and economic classes of inhabitants, and/or rapidly depreciating buildings.

**Blighted Area** An area characterized by deterioration or deteriorated buildings and/or environmental deficiencies, such as adverse land use mixture.

**Block Busting** A method of obtaining property at depressed prices in a changing neighborhood. It involves the introduction into the area of a family of another race or class and taking advantage of the fears and prejudices of the inhabitants to buy or list their property at low prices. Such property is resold to blacks or Hispanics at inflated prices.

**Blueprint** A working plan used on a construction job by tradesmen; an architectural drafting or drawing that is transferred to chemically treated paper by exposure to strong light, which causes the paper to turn blue and reproduces the drawing in white.

**Board of Equalization** A non-judicial board whose function is to review assessments to see that all districts are assessed at a uniform level of value; to raise or lower the assessments to achieve this purpose, so that a uniform basis of taxation is achieved. Also referred to in some areas as Board of Tax Review. In Chicago, it is known as the Board of Appeals.

**Bond-Type Security** An investment security, especially a mortgage-based one, that has the characteristics of a typical corporate bond, including long-term, fixed rates of return and repayment of principal at maturity.

**Book Value** The capital amount at which property is shown on the books of account. Usually, it is the original cost less reserves for depreciation plus additions to capital.

**Boom** Rapid growth in market values and expansion of business facilities and activity.

**Boulevard** A broad street or promenade, with rows of trees planted along its borders or in a median strip.

**Bridge Financing** A form of interim loan generally made between a short-term loan and a permanent (long-term) loan when the borrower wishes to have more time before making the long-term financing.

**Broom Cleaning** A term used to describe the condition of a building delivered to a buyer or tenant. As the term indicates, the floors are swept free of debris.

**Building Code** Locally adopted ordinance or regulation, enforceable by police powers under the concept of health, safety, and welfare, controlling the design, construction, alteration, repair, quality of materials, use and occupancy, and related factors of any building or structure within its jurisdiction.

**Business Cycle**   A recurring sequence of changes in business activity. Beginning with a period of prosperity, business activity declines until a low point, called a depression, is reached. A period of recovery follows when business conditions become more and more active until prosperity is again restored and a cycle is completed.

**Buyer's Market**   The condition that exists when, under competitive conditions, the schedules of supply and demand are such that market prices are at a relatively low level, giving the buyers an advantage.

# C

**Cabinet Work**   A term applied to any interior finish, usually in hardwoods, and which involves the skills of cabinetmakers rather than carpenters. For example, built-in fixtures, such as kitchen cupboards, counters, etc.

**Cape Cod House**   An architectural style developed from the one-story cottage. Generally, the main cornice line is at the second-story level, the roof slopes and there may be rooms on the second floor. Dormer windows are used. A detailed entrance features pilasters and cornices. These houses are most authentic when built of frame with clapboard or shingle walls, and painted white. In some sections, however, stone or brick is used for the first story.

**Capital**   Accumulated wealth. The entire stock of goods from which income is derived. Accumulated wealth is employed to produce other goods or additional wealth. Land, tools, machines, stocks, bonds, and any materials used to create, alter, extract, transport goods can be termed capital. Capital, in the form of raw materials, inventories, goods in production, securities, is referred to as circulating capital or current assets. Land, tools, factories, railways are fixed capital or fixed assets.

**Capital Gains**   The difference between purchase price and selling price in the sale of an asset; used primarily in income tax computations. It may be short- or long-term depending upon whether it occurs more or less than six months after the acquisition of the asset.

**Capitalization**   Determining a present value of income property by taking the annual net operating income (either known or estimated) and discounting by using a rate of return commonly acceptable to buyers of similar properties. For example, a net operating income of a property is $100,000 per year. Capitalizing at the rate of 10 percent, the property would be worth $1 million.

**Capricious Values**   In appraisal, a value based on whim or emotion and not reflective of the fair market value.

**Cash Flow**   Gross income less operating expenses and debt-servicing costs.

**Causeway**   A raised roadway on fill or a bridge-like structure over a low area, such as a swamp.

**Central City**   The primary city in a standard metropolitan area, and from which the name of the metropolitan area is usually taken.

**Certificate Account**   A savings deposit made for a fixed or specified minimum term, usually subject to a penalty (such as loss of interest) for early withdrawal.

**Certificate of Title** A document usually given to a home buyer with the deed, stating that the title to the property is clear. It is usually prepared by an attorney or qualified person who has examined the abstract of title for the property. It is only an opinion that title is good; not to be confused with title insurance.

**Chattel** Personal property such as household furniture, automobiles, horses, etc.

**Checking Account** A transaction account that permits unlimited withdrawals, transfers and payouts of funds but, by federal law, cannot earn interest.

**Closing Statement** The statement that lists the financial settlement between buyer and seller, and also the cost each must pay. A separate statement for the buyer and seller is sometimes prepared.

**Cloud on Title** An invalid encumbrance on real estate that, if valid, would affect the rights of the owner. For example, a mortgage that was intended to be a lien against house number two was recorded against house number one, thus clouding the title. The cloud may be removed by a quit claim deed or if necessary by court action in some instances by posting a bond.

**Club Account** A savings account program designed to help people save for specific goals such as Christmas or vacations, which provides for deposits each payday and a one-time lump-sum withdrawal, and earns interest at up to the passbook rate.

**Codicil** An addition to will, which modifies a will by adding to it, subtracting from it or clarifying it.

**Co-Executor** One who shares the duties of executors with one or more other executors.

**Coinsurance** The coinsurance or average clause in fire insurance policy is a device to penalize the underinsured. The most common clauses provide for insurance in the amount of 80%, or 90%, or 100% of the value of the building. The New York Standard Average Clause reads: "This Company shall not be liable for a greater proportion of any loss or damage to the property described herein than the sum hereby insured bears to eighty percentage (80%) of the actual cash value of said property at the time such loss shall happen, nor for more than the proportion which this policy bears to the total insurance thereon."

The "value of the building" means the cost to rebuild or reproduce the destructible portion of a building just as it was at the time of the fire, with the same kind and quality of materials, as of the date of the fire, less depreciation.

The cost, as here used, ordinarily includes architects' fees, superintendence during construction, and builders' profit. It does not include interest or taxes during the construction, legal expenses, or the cost of or interest on the mortgage. Those parts of the building foundations below the lowest floor usually are excluded.

The depreciation includes loss from wear and tear, exhaustion and deterioration, but, as a rule, does not include depreciation from economic causes, or actual or potential obsolescence. The bottom line under an 80 percent coinsurance policy means that in the event of a loss, the insurer will only pay for 80 percent of the fire claim and the insured will be liable for the balance.

**Collateral Assignment**   An assignment of property as collateral security, and not with the intent to transfer ownership from assignor to assignee.

**Collateralized Mortgage Obligation**   A mortgage-backed security that passes borrower payments into a trusteed pool, from which principal and interest are paid to security holders class by class, with one class completely paid off before any principal is repaid to the next greater maturity class.

**Commercial Loan**   A loan not secured by a pledge of real estate, made to a business for commercial purposes.

**Comparables**   An abbreviation for comparable properties, rentals, incomes, etc., used for comparative purposes in the appraisal process.

**Compensating Balance**   Funds deposited into a savings and loan association or other institution to induce the lender to make a specific loan or establish a line of credit. The deposit may be made by the party desiring the loan, or a third party.

**Compound Interest**   Interest paid both on accumulated interest as well as on the principal.

**Conditional Commitment**   A loan commitment given before a borrower (buyer) is obtained and subject to approval of the buyer by the lender. This is a common practice for FHA mortgages.

**Conservation**   As applied to real estate, the protection from blighting influences of good neighborhoods and structures, and their preservation in a safe and sound state.

**Consideration**   The price or subject matter which induces a contract; may be in money, commodity exchange, or a transfer of personal effort. In appraising, usually the actual price at which property is transferred.

**Consolidated Obligation (FHLB)**   A debt security issued by the Federal Home Loan Banks over the signature of the FHLB chairman; the financing needs of the various regional banks are consolidated into larger issues for the capital markets.

**Construction Loan**   A mortgage loan made to finance real estate construction; may include funds for land acquisition; may provide for permanent long-term financing upon completion of construction.

**Consumer Loan**   A loan made to individuals for any non-business purpose except the construction or purchase of real estate; also called a nonmortgage loan.

**Contiguous**   Adjacent; in actual contact; touching; near.

**Contingent Fees**   Fees to be paid only in the event of future occurrence. A broker's commission is paid only if the property is sold or leased (unless otherwise agreed upon). Attorneys (especially in negligence cases) may be paid based on winning the suit and collecting the damages.

**Contract**    An agreement of two or more persons upon a sufficient consideration to do or not to do a particular thing. When real property is involved, a written, signed agreement between two or more competent parties to do or not to do a legal act, for a legal consideration, within a specified time.

**Contract Sale**    A conditional sale. A sale in which the title to property or good remains with the seller until the purchaser has fulfilled the terms of the contract, usually payment in full.

**Conventional Loan**    1. A mortgage or deed of trust not obtained under a government insured program (such as FHA or VA).

2. A loan not insured or guaranteed by a government agency; may be privately insured.

**Conveyance**    A written instrument which passes an interest in real property from one person to another. Conveyance may be a deed, mortgage, lease, but not a will.

**Cooperative Apartment**    An apartment owned by corporations, either for or not for profit, or by trusts, in which each owner purchases stock to the extent of the value of his apartment, title being evidenced by a proprietary lease.

**County Records**    Public recorded documents by which notice is given of changes of title, liens, and other matters affecting real estate.

**C.P.M. (Certified Property Manager)**    A designation conferred by the institute of real estate management upon one who has completed certain required courses and has been active in property management.

**Credit or Equity Instrument**    Any direct market investment representing an ownership share in or a loan of funds to a corporation or government body, including stocks, bonds, bills, notes and debentures.

**Curable Depreciation**    Repairs which an owner of real estate should make to retain a high value, but which have not been made.

**Current Assets**    Readily convertible or liquid assets such as cash, public traded stocks and bonds, and also accounts receivable.

**Current Liabilities**    A liability that will be paid in the normal operation of a business; a short-term debt.

**Curtesy**    The estate to which, by common law, the husband is entitled in the lands of his deceased wife. The extent varies with statutory provision.

# D

**Death Rate**    The number of deaths per 1,000 persons in any given area during the period of a year. This is called the crude death rate. The refined death rate makes corrections for the number of people in each age group.

**Debtor's Position**    That portion of the market price of the real estate which is in excess of the balance due on the first mortgage. Better known as the borrower's equity position.

**Decentralization**   Dispersion from the center of a city. The movement of people, industry, and business from the central metropolitan area to the suburbs, rural-urban fringe, and/or to smaller cities. The movement of business from the central business district. The establishment of industrial parks away from large cities.

**Dedication**   The giving by an owner of private property for public use, and the acceptance by the property public authority. Most commonly, the dedication by a builder of streets in a subdivision.

**Deed**   An instrument in writing which, when executed and delivered, conveys an estate or interest in real property from the grantor to the grantee.

**Deed of Trust**   An instrument used in many states in place of a mortgage. Property is transferred to a trustee by the borrower (trustor) in favor of the lender (beneficiary) and reconveyed upon payment in full.

**Default**   An omission or failure to perform a legal duty.

**Default Judgment**   A judgment entered against a party who fails to appear to defend against the action.

**Defective Title**   1. Title to a negotiable instrument obtained by fraud.
2. Title to real estate which lacks some of the elements to transfer good title.

**Deferred Liability**   A liability arising from transferred real estate interests which does not become an obligation to the transferee until some subsequent period after the transfer.

**Deferred Maintenance**   Existing but unfulfilled requirements for repairs and rehabilitation to put the property in good condition.

**Deficiency Judgment**   The difference between a legally imposed indebtedness and the dollars received from a foreclosure sale of the debtor's assets. For example, if the sale does not yield enough cash to cover the mortgagor's outstanding balance to the mortgagee. The court awards the mortgage lender a judgment for the deficiency.

**Demise**   The transfer of an estate to another by a lease or will.

**Depository Institution**   A financial intermediary that accepts savings or demand deposits from the general public.

**Depreciation**   A loss in value as the results of deterioration and/or obsolescence.

**Depreciation Allowance**   As used in accounting it is either straight line or accelerated over a period of years. The term is often used in income tax cases.

**Depression**   The period of a business cycle when manufacturing is lowest, the rate of unemployment highest, prices hit rock bottom, and purchasing power is greatly curtailed.

**Depth Influence**   The effect of increasing depth upon the value of a lot or parcel having a given frontage. The increment or decrement of value arising from a depth greater or less than that of the standard lot. For example, in Chicago the standard depth is 125. A lot with a 175 depth may add value to the property or it may just add up to some additional grass to cut.

**Deterioration**   Impairment of condition brought about by wear and tear, disintegration, use in service, and the action of the elements.

**Direct Investment**   An investment made directly by an institution in a service corporation or for such purposes as the purchase of equity securities or real estate development.

**Direct Market Investment**   Any investment in a credit or equity instrument that is made directly with the seller or borrower and not through a financial intermediary.

**Disclaimer**   A denial or disavowal of any interest in or claim to the subject of action, such as renunciation of any title, claim, interest, estate, or trust.

**Discount Note**   A short-term debt security sold at less than face value but redeemed at maturity at full value; the difference between the purchase price and redemption amount is the equivalent of interest paid for the use of the funds.

**Domicile**   The locality in which a person or corporation is considered to have its legal residency.

**Donee**   One who receives a gift.

**Donor**   One who gives a gift.

**Dower**   That portion of, or interest in, the real estate of a decreased husband which the law gives to his widow for life. The extent varies with statutory provisions of each state or territory.

**Dry Wall Construction**   Any type of masonry work laid up without the use of mortar. A type of interior wall construction where the finish material used is other than plaster, such as wood paneling, plywood, plasterboard, or other types of wallboard.

**Ducts**   In building construction, metal pipes used for the transmission and distribution of warm or cooled air from a central unit to the rooms.

**Duplex**   A house containing two separate dwelling units, commonly one above the other.

**Dutch Colonial Architecture**   A style of home design featuring a gambrel roof and exterior wall of masonry or wood. Porches are at the side. It is adaptable to flat sites.

**Dutch Door**   A door divided horizontally in the middle so that the bottom half remains closed while the top is open or the reverse. This type of door was a common fixture in saloons in the last century and in the early part of this century.

# E

**Earnings-Based Account**   A savings deposit on which part of the interest payment is tied to the rate of return on earmarked assets; also called an equity account or equity certificate.

**Easement**   A nonpossessing interest held by one person in land of another person whereby the first person is accorded partial use of such land for a specific purpose. An easement restricts but does not abridge the rights of the fee owner to the use and enjoyment of his land. Easements fall into three broad classifications: surface easements, subsurface easements, and overhead easements. For example, a common driveway easement between two homes is a common surface easement in many areas and subdivisions with small lots.

**Economic Life**   The estimated period over which it is anticipated that a property may profitably be utilized. Also, the period over which a property will yield a maximum return on the investment. The economic life of real estate generally exceeds the projection made by the Internal Revenue and the lending institution. Many buildings that were endowed with an economic life of 50 years are still standing and productive after 80 years.

**Economic Rent**   The rental warranted to be paid in an open real estate market and based upon current rentals being paid for comparable space.

**Education Loan**   A non-mortgage loan made to a consumer to finance college or vocational school education or similar training.

**Effective Age**   The number of years as indicated by the wear and tear of the building. If a building has had better-than-average maintenance, its effective age may be less than the actual age; if it has had inadequate maintenance, it may be greater. An 80-year-old building may have an effective age of 20 years due to rehabilitation or modernization.

**Eminent Domain**   The right by which a sovereign government, or some person acting in its name and under its authority, may acquire private property for public or quasi-public use upon payment of reasonable compensation and without consent of the owner. The right or power of the government to take private property for public use on making just compensation therefor. The 1949 Federal Urban Renewal Act is the classic model for studying the utilization of eminent domain.

**Encroachment**   The act of trespassing upon the domain of another. Partial or gradual displacement of an existing use by another use; as locating factories in a residential district or vice versa.

**Encumbrance**   An interest or right in real property that diminishes the value of the fee, but does not prevent conveyance of the fee by the owner. Mortgages, taxes, judgments are encumbrances known as liens. Restrictions, easements, reservations are encumbrances, but are not classified as liens.

**Entrepreneur**   An employer or developer who assumes the risk and management of a business or enterprise; a promoter, in the sense of one who undertakes to develop.

**Environmental Deficiency**   Conditions, circumstances, and influences surrounding and affecting the development of an area which, in addition to structural deficiencies, promote blight and deterioration. Examples: overcrowding by converting large units into smaller ones or improper location of a structure on the land; excessive dwelling unit density; conversion of buildings to incompatible uses.

**Equity**   The net value of a property obtained by subtracting from its total value all liens or other charges against it. The term is frequently applied to the value of the owner's interest in property in excess of all claims and liens.

**Equity Build Up**  The principal repayment in loan amortization which decreases the outstanding indebtedness and increases the owner's equity. The equity increase is in the exact proportion that the interest payment decreases.

**Equity Loan**  Any loan secured by the equity in a property and made for purposes other than the purchase of that property regardless of the lien priority; may be structured as a second mortgage loan or as an open-ended line of credit with either variable or fixed rate terms.

**Equity of Redemption**  The right of a mortgagor by absolute deed to redeem the property by paying the debt, even after forfeiture but before sale, under foreclosure or transfer of title, or before this right is barred by statute of limitations.

**Equity Purchaser**  The purchaser of the equity of another in property and who may or may not personally assume all the indebtedness against the real estate.

**Escalator Clause**  A clause in an agreement providing for adjustment of price based on the cost of living index. For example, in a lease the provision to increase rent if operating expenses increase.

**Escheat**  A reversion of property to the state in the absence of an individual owner. Usually occurs when a property owner dies intestate, and without heirs.

**Escrow**  Money, securities, instruments, or other evidences of property deposited by two or more persons with a third person, to be delivered on a certain contingency or on the happening of a certain event. The subject matter of the transaction is the escrow; the terms upon which it is deposited with the third person constitute the escrow agreement; and the third person is the escrow agent.

**Estate**  1. A right or interest in property; it may be fee ownership interest or a lease interest for a period of years. An estate in land is the degree, nature, or extent of interest which a person has in it.

2. The property of a deceased person.

**Estoppel**  The prevention of one from asserting a legal right because of prior actions inconsistent with the assertion.

**Ethnic Group**  People of the same race having a common heritage of language and cultural customs.

**Exclusive Listing**  A contract to sell property as an agent, according to the terms of which the agent is given the exclusive right to sell the property. The term is also applied to the property so listed.

**Executor**  A person who is appointed by a testator to execute his will.

**Executor's Deed**  A deed court-approved under which the grantor is an executor

**Exterior Finish**  The outside finish of a structure. It includes such items as roof and wall covering, gutters, door and window frames. Generally, the term refers to the protective outer cover.

**Exterior Wall**  Any outer wall serving as a vertical enclosure of a building except a common wall.

# F

**Facade**   The "Sunday-dressed" or best-dressed side of a structure; the front or facade. The exposed surface of an object.

**Face Brick**   A better grade of brick which is used for the exterior wall of a building, usually only on the front or principal side.

**Fallow**   1. Land ordinarily used for crops which is allowed to lie idle during the growing season.

   2. The tilling of land without sowing it for a season.

**Federal Deposit Insurance Corporation (FDIC)**   The federal corporation which insures against loss of deposits in banks up to a maximum amount (currently $100,000).

**Federal Home Loan Bank System**   A system of 11 regional banks created under the authority of the Federal Home Loan Bank Act of 1932 to provide a source of credit for the banks' member home-financing and thrift institutions. Every federal savings and loan association is required to become a member of its regional federal home loan bank.

**Federal Housing Administration**   A unit of the U.S. Department of Housing and Urban Development which insures private lending institutions against loss or loans secured by residential mortgages and on loans advanced for repairs, alterations, and improvements which may be secured by collateral.

**Federal Savings and Loan Insurance Corporation**   A federal corporation insured against loss by depositors in a savings and loan association in much the same fashion the Federal Deposit Insurance Corporation insures against loss by depositors in banks.

**Fee Simple**   An estate under which the owner is entitled to unrestricted powers to dispose of the property and which can be left by will or inherited.

**Fee Tail**   An estate of inheritance that specifies the descendants or classes of heirs of the devisee who may succeed to the estate.

**FHA Loan**   A mortgage, mobile home or property improvement loan made by a private lender and insured by the Federal Housing Administration.

**Federal Home Loan Mortgage Corporation (FHLMC known as Freddie Mac)**   A federal agency purchasing first mortgages, both conventional and federally insured, from members of the Federal Reserve System, and the Federal Home Loan Bank System.

**Fiduciary**   One acting in a relationship of trust, regarding financial transactions.

**Final Decree**   A decree completely deciding all pending matters before a court, and obviating the need for further litigation.

**Financial Intermediary**   A corporation whose operating profit comes primarily from acting as a middleman between those with surplus funds to save or invest and those who want to borrow; accepts money from savers or investors and, in turn, lends the funds in the intermediary's own name to borrowers.

**Firebrick**   A brick made of fire clay that can resist high temperatures; used to line heating chambers and fireplaces.

**Fireproof Construction**   Designed to withstand a complete burnout of the contents of the structure, without impairment of its structural integrity.

**Fire-Resistive Construction**   Not combustible at ordinary fire temperatures; capable of withstanding ordinary fire conditions for at least one hour without serious damage to the structure.

**Fire Wall**   A brick or other incombustible wall built between buildings, or parts of a building as a fire stop; it should rise to three feet above roof, and be equipped with automatically closing fireproof doors.

**First Mortgage**   A mortgage which has priority as a lien over all other mortgages on a property.

**Fiscal Year**   Any 12 months selected as an accounting period, may or may not coincide with the calendar year.

**Fixed Liabilities**   Long-term debts; debts payable over a period exceeding one year as distinguished from current liabilities, which are usually due and payable within 30 to 60 days.

**Fixed-Rate Loan**   A loan made for a predetermined rate of interest that does not change over the life of the contract.

**Fixture**   A tangible thing, which previously was personal property, which has been attached to or installed in land or a structure thereon in such a way as to become a part of the real property. The legal interpretation of what constitutes a fixture varies among states.

**Flat lease**   See Straight lease entry

**Floor Load**   As commonly used, the live weight-supporting capabilities of a floor, measured in pounds per square foot; the weight, stated in pounds per square foot, which may safely be placed upon the floor of a building if uniformly distributed. This is also known as the live load. The weight of the building itself, including equipment, such as boilers, machinery, etc., is known as the dead load and is not included as a part of the floor load capacity.

**Federal National Mortgage Association (FNMA Fannie Mae)**   A private corporation dealing in the purchase of first mortgages at discounts.

**Forced Price**   The price paid in a forced sale or purchase; that is, a sale in which there was not enough time allowed to find a bonafide purchaser.

**Forced Sale**   1. The act of offering and transferring property, and for a valuable consideration, under conditions of compulsion.

2. Within specified time and place, frequently a sale at a public auction made by virtue of a court order.

**Foreclosure**   The legal process by which a mortgagee, in case of default by the mortgagor, forces sale of the property mortgaged in order to recover all or part of a loan.

**Forfeiture**   The taking of an individual's property by a government because the individual has committed a crime. In the United States, such action may be taken when a person is enriched by the sale and found guilty of selling narcotics. Otherwise, private property can not be taken except by eminent domain upon payment of just compensation or for nonpayment of taxes.

**Formica**   A trade name for a plastic material used primarily for the top of counter areas, but also used for wall covering, as a veneer for plywood panels, or as a wallboard where a fire-resistive material is desirable. Similar and competitive materials are produced under other trade names.

**Forward Commitment**   A definite promise to do something at a future time and within a specified period, such as make loans or purchase mortgages.

**Foundation**   That upon which anything is built; that part of a structure upon which the building is erected; usually that part of a building, that is below the surface of the ground and on which the superstructure rests.

**Foyer**   The lobby of a theater or hotel; entrance hall of a house.

**Free and Clear**   Real property against which there are no liens, especially voluntary liens (mortgages).

**FSLIC**   Federal Savings & Loan Insurance Corporation

**Fuse**   A protective device that controls the flow of electricity through a circuit, so constructed that it melts when the circuit is overloaded thus stopping the flow of electricity.

**Fuse Box**   The container that houses the fuses controlling the electric circuits of a structure.

# G

**General Reserves**   All reserve accounts on a balance sheet except those earmarked for specific potential losses.

**Good Will Value**   1. An advantage which a business has developed over a period of years which has converted into intangible values applicable to the specific going concern itself, such as name, certain types of patents, and trademarks, or similar rights or benefits. Primarily, these benefits are intangible nature and are not shared by competitors.

2. That portion when a period of prosperity, business activity declines until a low point, called a depression, is reached. A period of recovery follows when business conditions become more and more active until prosperity is again restored and a cycle is completed.

**Graduated Lease**   A lease calling for a varied rental, usually based on periodic appraisals or simply the passage of time.

**Graduated Payment Mortgage Loan**   A home mortgage loan on which the monthly payments start at a low level and gradually rise at a predetermined rate, based on the assumption that the homeowner's income will increase over time. In the early years of the loan, negative amortization may occur.

**Grantee**   A person to whom property is transferred by deed or to whom property rights are granted by a trust instrument or other document.

**Grantor**   A person who transfers property by deed, or grants property rights through a trust instrument or other document.

**Gross Effective Income**   The estimated gross income less allowances for vacancies and rent losses.

**Gross Income**   The scheduled income from the operation of the business or the management of the property, customarily stated on an annual basis.

**Ground Rent**   The net rent paid for the right of use and occupancy of a parcel of land; or that portion of the total rental paid that is considered to represent a return upon the land only.

**Growing Equity Mortgage Loan**   A home mortgage loan on which the payments increase according to an agreed-upon schedule, based on the assumption that the homeowner's income will increase over time; the initial payment level is sufficient to amortize the loan over a long term such as 30 or 40 years; the payment increase prepay loan principal, however, so that the loan actually is paid off in many fewer years.

**Gutter**   1. A channel at and running the length of the eaves of a building that carries off rain water, usually by means of downspouts.

2. The ridge formed by the edge of a street and a raised sidewalk or a depressed ridge in a road's shoulder which is a control for the flowage of storm water.

# H

**Hardwood**   Lumber cut from broad leaved trees, such as oak, mahogany, walnut, birch; and which is used in interior finishes and flooring. Term refers to type of tree, not to the actual hardness of the wood.

**Heir**   A person who inherits property, real and/or personal. Also the person designated by law to inherit the estate of one who died intestate.

**Highest and Best Use**   The use of land that will bring the greatest economic return over a given period of time.

**Hold Harmless Agreement**   A legally binding agreement in which the liability of one party is assumed by another party to the agreement.

**Hold Over Tenant**   A tenant who remains in possession of leased real estate after the expiration of his lease. In many states, the lease is automatically renewed if the lessor accepts another rent payment after the expiration of the lease.

**Home**   A residential structure containing one to four dwelling units; a condominium unit, regardless of the number of units in the building.

**Home Improvement Loan**   A loan to finance the repair, modernization or improvement of residential real estate; also called a property improvement loan. When secured by a mortgage, classed with other mortgage loans on the balance sheet.

**Home Loan; Home Mortgage Loan**   A residential mortgage loan secured by one- to four-family property or a condominium unit.

**Homestead**   The fixed residence or dwelling place of the head of a family, including the principal house, buildings, and land about it.

**Household**   All persons occupying a separate housing unit that has either direct access to the outside or a public area, or separate cooking facilities; when the members are related by law or blood, called a family.

**Household Funds**   In the Federal Reserve Board's Flow of Funds Accounts, the financial assets and liabilities of households, businesses, financial institutions and government units.

**Housing and Urban Development, Department of**   The federal department which is responsible for the major programs of housing and urban development, such as urban renewal, low rent public housing, mortgage insurance, metropolitan planning, etc. It is the 12th department in the president's cabinet, created in 1965 to replace the Housing and Home Finance Agency.

# I

**Improved Land** 1. Land which has been developed for some use by the erection of buildings and other improvements pertinent thereto.

2. Land that has been prepared for development as distinguished from raw land. This implies such things as grading and draining.

**Income Capital Certificate** An FHLBB certificate that is an agreement to pay back a corporation's loan, plus interest, when and it an association in financial difficulty gets into a better position. Payments are installments and are always less than the association's net income.

**Income Property** A property which, for its primary purpose, has the capacity to produce monetary income.

**Indemnity Agreement** An agreement by which one party agrees to repay another for any loss or damage the latter may suffer.

**Individual Retirement Account (IRA)** A trust-type savings deposit arrangement; exempt from federal income tax on account earnings and new funds deposited, up to specified limits, until the saver retires.

**Industrial Loan** A loan to a business for manufacturing or industrial, as opposed to commercial, purposes.

**Insurable Value** The term is used conventionally to designate the amount of insurance that may be carried on destructible portions of a property to indemnify the owner in the event of loss.

**Insurance Fund** The reserves accumulated by the Federal Deposit Insurance Corporation over the years to offset any claims made by depositors of defaulted insured institutions.

**Insured Institution** A savings association or savings bank whose deposits are insured by the Federal Savings and Loan Insurance Corporation or the FDIC.

**Interest Rate** A promised rate of return. The rate of yield earned from an investment. The annual interest rate is also referred to as the nominal rate. When this rate is divided by the number of annual payments, it is called an effective mortgage interest rate.

**Intestacy** The condition resulting from a person's dying without leaving a valid will.

**Involuntary Conveyance** A transfer of real estate without the consent of the owner such as in a divorce, or in condemnation, etc.

# J

**Joint Tenancy** An interest taken by two or more persons. The interest must be the same, accruing under the same conveyance, beginning at the same time, and held under the same undivided right to possession. Upon the death of a joint tenant, the interest passes to the surviving joint tenant without passing to the heirs of the deceased. Most married couples buy their property in joint tenancy as opposed to tenancy in common.

**Jumbo Certificate**   A market rate certificate savings account of more than $100,000.

**Just Compensation**   In incondemnation the amount paid to the property owner. The theory is that in order to be "just," the property owner should be no richer or poorer than before the taking.

# K

**Keogh Account**   A trust-type savings account for self-employed individuals and their employees; exempt from federal income tax on account earnings and new funds deposited, up to specified limits, until the saver retires.

**Kick Plate**   A metal strip placed at the lower edge of a door to protect the finish.

# L

**Land Trust**   An unincorporated association for holding real property by putting the title in one or more trustees for the benefit of the members whose interest are evidenced by land-trust certificates.

**Landscaping**   The features used to modify a landscape of an area or tract of land, such as trees, shrubs, flowers, lawns, paths, gardens.

**Lease**   An agreement by which an owner of real estate "lessor" gives a right of possession to another "lessee" for a specified period of time (term) and for a specified consideration (rent).

**Leasehold**   A property held under tenure of lease. A property consisting of the right of use and occupancy of real property by virtue of lease agreement. The right of a lessee to use and enjoy real estate for a stated term and upon certain conditions, such as the payment of rent.

**Lease with Option to Purchase**   A lease under which the lessee has a right to purchase a property. The price and terms of the purchase must be set forth for the option to be valid. The option may run for the length of the lease or only for a portion of the lease period.

**Legal Owner**   The owner of the title; a term used to distinguish the title owner from other interests, such as beneficial or possessory interests.

**Lessee**   One who possess the right to use or occupy a property under lease agreement.

**Lessor**   One who holds title to and conveys the right to use and occupy a property under lease agreement.

**Leverage**   The use of financing to allow a small amount of cash to purchase an interest in a large real estate investment.

**Lien**   A charge against property whereby the property is made the security for the payment of a debt.

**Life Tenant**   One who owns an estate in real property for a lifetime or for another person's life or for an indefinite period limited by a lifetime.

**Liquid Assets**   Assets which are immediately convertible into cash and therefore are immediately available for liquidating indebtedness. Synonym: quick assets.

**Liquidity**   Investments readily convertible to cash without significant loss; specified types of such investments held by member institutions to satisfy FHLBB requirements for short-term and overall liquidity.

**Loan Discounts and Fees**   Charges made by most mortgage and nonmortgage lenders for processing loan applications and writing new loans.

**Loans in Process**   The contra-asset account representing funds not yet paid out on existing loans.

**Lobby**   An entrance way to a theatre, public building, hotel, or office building.

# M

**Manufactured Home Loan**   A loan to finance the purchase of a manufactured (mobile) home; may include funds for associated costs such as transportation and setup.

**Marginal**   Situated on the border or edge. In economics the term refers to supplying goods at a rate merely covering the cost of production. In real estate, this applies to a property earning an income which is sufficient to merely cover the operating costs.

**Marquee**   A permanent hood that projects over an entrance to a building and is not supported by posts or columns.

**Mobile Home**   A house trailer: a complete livable dwelling unit equipped with wheels. The vehicle may be towed from place to place by a truck cab or automobile, depending on its size and the highway regulations of the states through which it will travel.

**Mobility**   In real estate, the term is used to describe the ease with which people can move from one location to another.

**Money Market Deposit Account**   A savings deposit not subject to rate ceilings, minimum balances or a minimum term; may have up to six preauthorized transfers a month.

**Money Market Fund; Money Market Mutual Fund**   A mutual fund that invests in short-term money market securities and sells shares in low minimum amounts to the public.

**Month-to-Month Tenancy**   A tenancy where no lease is involved, and rent is paid monthly. Some obligation as to notice of moving or eviction may still exist by statute. In Illinois, a 30-day notice is required.

**Mortgage**   A legal document pledging a described property for the performance of the repayment of a loan under certain terms and conditions.

**Mortgage-Backed Security**   Any of a variety of investment securities representing shares in a pool of mortgage loans; often guaranteed by the Government National Mortgage Association (Ginnie Mae) or privately insured.

**Mortgagee**   The party who advances the funds for a mortgage loan and in whose favor the property serving as security is mortgaged.

**Mortgage Loan**   An advance of funds to a borrower secured by the pledge of real estate. The pledge ends when the debt is discharged.

**Mortgage Warehousing**   A contra-asset account representing mortgages made by an institution and earmarked for inclusion in a pool that will underlie a mortgage-backed security; mortgages in the pipeline between origination and securitization.

**Mortgagor**   One who gives a mortgage as security for a loan.

**Multifamily Housing**   A residential structure containing five or more dwelling units.

**Mutual Capital Certificate**   A long-term debt security issued by a federal mutual institution, subordinated to all other claims on assets; not covered by federal insurance of accounts; may be counted as net worth for regulatory purposes.

**Mutual Institution**   A savings institution owned solely by its customers—current savers and borrowers—who elect the board of directors and, if the institution goes out of business, share pro rata in any assets remaining after all liabilities have been paid.

# N

**Net Income**   The difference between the effective gross income and the expenses, including taxes and insurance. Usually the term is qualified as net income before depreciation or net income before recapture.

**Net Lease**   A lease where, in addition to the rental stipulated, the lessee assumes payment of all property charges, such as taxes, insurance, and maintenance.

**Net New Retail Savings**   The total of funds placed in new and existing accounts except $100,000-minimum certificates, excluding interest credited, less withdrawals from these accounts, over a given period.

**Net New Savings**   The total of funds placed in new and existing accounts, excluding interest credited, less withdrawals from these accounts, over a given period.

**Net Worth**   The amount by which savings institution assets exceed liabilities, maintained at least at the minimum level required by regulation; a cushion to protect savers against any losses on loans and other investments; consists of federal insurance and general reserves, paid-in surplus, undivided profits, subordinated debentures, appraised equity capital, net worth certificates, income capital certificates and mutual capital certificates (for a mutual institution) or permanent stock (for a stock institution); now officially called regulatory capital.

**Net Worth Certificate**   A special security issued by a depository institution with a net worth deficiency; it is then exchanged for a promissory note from the FDIC or FSLIC; the institution redeems its NWC when it returns to profitability and can make all required allocations to net worth.

**Nominee**   Most commonly used in a deed or contract, such as to Mary Doe or nominee, when the actual grantee is not revealed. Has no legal meaning other than representative of another.

**NOW Account**   A savings account that allows check-like drafts (negotiable orders of withdrawal) to be drawn against the interest-bearing deposit. A regular NOW account has an interest rate ceiling, while a super NOW, with a $1,000 minimum balance, is ceilingless.

# O

**Obsolescence**   One of the causes of depreciation. It is the impairment of desirability and usefulness brought about by new inventions, current changes in design, and improved processes for production, or from external influencing factors, which make a property less desirable and valuable for a continued use. Obsolescence may be either economic or functional.

**Obsolete**   The state of being no longer useful or desirable; warranting actual and permanent disuse for reasons other than physical deterioration.

**Open-End Mortgage**   A mortgage permitting the mortgagor to borrow additional money under the same mortgage without paying an additional processing fee.

**Operating Expense**   Costs incurred in the normal operation of a savings institution or other business, as opposed to outlays and losses arising from extraordinary circumstances such as a lawsuit (nonoperating expense).

**Operating Income**   Income arising from the normal operation of a savings institution or other business, as opposed to funds received from extraordinary events such as the one-time sale of an office building (non-operating income).

**Operating Loss Carryback; Operating Loss Carryforward**   A provision of income tax law that allows businesses that experience an excess of operating expense over operating income in one tax year to use part of that loss to offset income in a past or future tax period.

**Option**   An agreement that for a consideration permits one to buy, sell, or lease something within a stipulated period of time in accordance with the terms of the agreement.

**Ordinary Savings**   The term used by some savings and banks to refer to passbook accounts.

**Over-the-Counter Savings**   Savings accounts and time deposits at depository institutions.

# P

**Parkway**   An arterial highway for noncommercial traffic, with full or partial control of access, and usually located within a park or a ribbon of parklike development.

**Parquet Floor**   A hardwood floor lain in various patterns, not a strip floor.

**Participations**   Mortgage loans made jointly by two or more lenders or owned jointly by two or more investors.

**Party Wall**   A wall erected upon and over a line which separates two properties and in which the respective owners have common rights of use.

**Passbook Account**  A no-minimum-balance savings account that permits the addition or withdrawal of any amount at any time without penalty.

**Pass-Through Security**  A security representing an interest in an underlying pool of mortgages, on which payments received on the underlying pool are passed through to the security investor.

**Personal Property**  Generally, movable items that are not permanently affixed to and a part of real estate. To determine what is personal property and what is real estate, usually there must be considered (1) the manner in which it is annexed; (2) the intention of the party who made the annexation (that is, to leave permanently or to remove at some time); (3) the purpose for which the premises are used. Generally, and with exceptions, items remain personal property if they can be removed without serious injury either to the real estate or to the item itself.

**Personal Savings**  In the Department of Commerce's National Income Accounts, the balance remaining after estimated outlays for goods and services are subtracted from the after-tax income of individuals and families.

**Power of Sale Clause**  Any mortgage or deed of trust given the mortgagee or trustee the power to sell the property in the event of default. There are laws which govern the sale which must be a public auction, but there is no court action necessary (judicial foreclosure).

**Primary Reserve**  With the secondary reserve, the funds set aside by the FSLIC over the years to offset any claims made by depositors of defaulted insured institutions.

**Private Mortgage Insurance**  Insurance offered by a private company that (a) protects a lender against loss on a defaulted mortgage loan up to policy limits, often 10% to 25% of the total loan amount; or (b) protects owners of mortgage-backed securities against losses on the underlying loans up to policy limits, often 5% of the total principal.

**Property Tax**  In general, a tax levied on any kind of property; that is, both real and personal.

**Public Housing Administration**  A unit of the U.S. Department of Housing and Urban Development which administers legislation providing for loans and subsidies to local housing authorities to encourage the creation of low-rental dwelling units.

**Public Unit Account**  A savings account containing the funds of a state, county, municipality, or other government unit or subdivision.

**Purchase Loan**  A mortgage loan made to finance the purchase of existing real estate, secured by a pledge of that real estate.

**Purchase-Money Mortgage**  A mortgage given by a purchaser of real property to the seller in part payment of the purchase price.

# Q

**Quarter**  In public land survey, a division of a section containing 640 acres, the quarter being 160 acres.

**Quasi**  A person or thing that is similar in some degree.

**Quit Claim Deed**   A form of conveyance whereby whatever interest the grantor possesses in the property described in the deed is conveyed to the grantee without warranty of title. For example, you can quit claim the Golden Gate Bridge although you do not have an interest.

# R

**Radiant Heating**   Method of steam, electric, or hot water heating consisting of pipes which are concealed in floors, ceilings, or walls.

**Radiant Heating System**   A system of warming of floors or other surfaces by means of hot air or hot water, usually the latter. Here pipes are embedded in the floor slab or in side walls with the air or water distributed by forced circulation. Lower temperatures are used.

**Radiator**   The term is accurately applied only to the type of exposed fixture which heats by means of a combination of radiation and convection effects. The common cast-iron radiator is an example. The several types of finned heating elements, such as baseboard heating, which are concealed within walls or in cabinets, are called convectors.

**Ranch Style House**   A one-story house, usually rambling and low to the ground, with low pitched gable roof or roofs, whose room plan is open with respect to the interior layout. It may have a basement.

**Rate of Return**   The percentage which the current year's annual net income from the operation of an enterprise develops upon the capital invested, or upon the appraised value or some other selected capital sum, or the net yield during investment life, giving effect to a finite period of economic life (of buildings), or to limiting time factors (such as the interval to maturity of a bond).

**Real Estate**   1. Land and anything permanently affixed to land such as a building, fences, and those things attached to the building, such as light fixtures, plumbing and heating fixtures, or any other items which would be personal if not attached. The term is generally synonymous with real property, although in some states a fine distinction may be made.

2. May refer to rights and real property as well as in property itself.

**Real Estate Mortgage Investment Conduit**   An issuer of multiclass securities similar to collateralized mortgage obligations but offering tax and accounting advantages, as authorized under the Tax Reform Act of 1986; savings institutions are authorized to issue and invest in Remic securities.

**Real Estate Owned**   Real property acquired by a mortgage lending institution as a result of its lending operations, after a borrower defaults.

**Real Property**   Refers to the interests, benefits, and rights inherent in the ownership of the physical real estate. It is the bundle of rights with which the ownership of real estate is endowed. In some states, this term as defined by statute is synonymous with real estate.

**Realtist**   An active member of a local real estate board which, in turn, is a member of the National Association of Real Estate Brokers.

**Realtor**   An active member of a local real estate board which, in turn, is a member of the National Association of Real Estate Boards.

**Recapture of Purchase Capital**   Recovery by an owner of money invested in real estate generally by a combination of mortgage amortization and the resale of the equity. The recapture of the mortgage component occurs according to the terms of the periodic installment contract (mortgage) without regard to fluctuations in market value.

**Receiver**   A person appointed by a court to exercise control over and administer a property or business when, in the interests of justice, it appears necessary to the court that some qualified and impartial person should assume such authority.

**Reconveyance**   An instrument used to transfer title from a trustee to the equitable owner of real estate, when title is held as collateral security for a debt. Most commonly used upon payment in full of a trust deed. Also called a deed of reconveyance or release.

**Recording**   The entering or recording of a copy of certain legal instruments or documents, as a deed, in a government office provided for this purpose; thus making a public record of the document for the protection of all concerned and giving constructive notice to the public at large.

**Redemption Period**   A time during which a mortgage, land contract, deed of trust, etc., can be redeemed. Usually set by statute and after judicial foreclosure.

**Red Lining**   The outlining of a map of certain "high risk" areas for real estate loan and insurance purposes. This means lenders will not extend credit or insurance in these areas for real estate regardless of the qualifications of the applicant or the subject property. Some states have passed laws against the practice. The use of the red pen or pencil for the outlining gave rise to the term. The victims of the red line practices were more frequently blacks and Hispanics.

**Registrar of Deeds**   A term used in some states to describe the person in charge of recorded instruments. More commonly called a recorder.

**Regular Deposit**   Any account at a savings bank except a checking, club or school account.

**Rehabilitation**   The restoration of a property to satisfactory condition without changing the plan, form, or style of a structure. In urban renewal, the restoration to good condition of deteriorated structures, neighborhoods, and public facilities. Neighborhood rehabilitation encompasses structural rehabilitation, and in addition may extend to street improvements and a provision of such amenities as parks and playgrounds.

**Reinstatement**   Payment of a note, mortgage, deed of trust, etc., to bring it from default to good standing.

**Rentable Area**   The area (square footage) for which rent can be charged. For example, an office would not rent the space used for stairways, elevators, public washrooms and hallways.

**Rental Value**   The monetary amount reasonably expectable for the right to the agreed use of real estate. It may be expressed as an amount per month or other period of time; or per room, per front foot, or other unit or property. Usually, it is established by competitive conditions.

**Request for Reconveyance** A request by a beneficiary under a deed of trust to the trustee, requesting the trustee to reconvey the property (release the lien) to the trustor, usually upon payment in full.

**Rescind** To void or cancel in such a way as to treat the contract or conveyance or any other object of the rescindsion as if it never existed.

**Reserve for Depreciation** An amount reserved before determining net worth to offset depreciation of fixed assets carried at values which were assigned before they had suffered the depreciation for which the reserve is provided. Also referred to as provision for depreciation and allowance for depreciation.

**Reserve for Replacements** A reserve set up before determining net worth to cover renewals and replacements of fixed assets. The object is to spread equitably over operations the renewals occurring irregularly.

**Restrictive Covenant** A private agreement restricting the use and occupancy of real estate which is a part of the conveyance and is binding on all subsequent purchasers. Such covenants may have to do with control of lot size, setback and/or placement of buildings, architecture, cost of improvements.

**Retail Savings** All savings deposits except jumbo certificates.

**Return on Assets** Net after-tax income for a given period of time, divided by average assets, net of contra-asset items.

**Revenue Stamps (documentary stamps)** Adhesive stamps issued by the federal or a state government, which must be purchased and affixed, in amounts provided by law, to documents or instruments representing original issues, sales, and transfers of stocks and bonds; and deeds of conveyances.

**Reversion** The right to possession of the residue of an estate and a grantor or successor of a grantor or testpator, commencing upon the termination of a particular estate, granted or devised.

**Revocable** Capable of being revoked or recalled.

**Right of Survivorship** The right of a survivor of the deceased person to the property of said deceased. A distinguishing characteristic of a joint tenancy relationship.

**Risk Factor** The portion of any given return or rate of return from capital invested in an enterprise that is assumed to cover the risks pertinent to the particular investment; as distinguished from and in excess of the return or rate obtainable from funds invested upon conditions of virtual certainty of the safety of principal.

**Row Houses** A series of individual houses with architectural unity and a common wall between each unit.

# S

**Sale-Leaseback** A sale and subsequent lease from the buyer back to the seller.

Although the lease actually follows the sale, both are agreed to as part of the same transition.

**Sale Price**   The price at which a property actually sold.

**Savings Account Loan**   A loan secured by a pledge of funds in a savings account at the same institution; often used by savers who want to avoid penalties for early withdrawal from a certificate account.

**Savings Association**   A state-chartered or federally-chartered financial intermediary that accepts deposits from the public and invests those funds primarily in residential mortgage loans; in various jurisdictions, also called a savings and loan association, co-operative bank, homestead society or building and loan association.

**Savings Bank**   A state-chartered or federally-chartered financial intermediary that accepts deposits from the public and invests those funds in a variety of secure investments, mainly mortgage loans; also often called a mutual savings bank.

**Savings Institution**   A savings association or savings bank.

**School Savings Plan**   A special account for young people, offered by some savings banks, that is exempt from most of the regulatory requirements that apply to other types of savings accounts.

**Second Mortgage**   A mortgage that ranks after a first mortgage in priority. Properties may have two, three or more mortgages, deeds of trust or land contracts as liens at the same time. Legal priority would determine whether they are called a first, second, third, fourth, fifth, etc. lien.

**Secondary Mortgage Market (FNMA)**   The market in home mortgages. Transactions in the secondary market are the purchases and sales of such mortgages after their origination by lenders. Commercial savings banks, insurance companies, and savings and loan associations, for example, are often buyers in the secondary market. Mortgage companies in particular and commercial banks to some extent are interested in the resale of mortgages. The ability of this secondary market to absorb mortgage loans into investment portfolios has a direct relationship to the amount of new mortgage loans made.

**Security Deposit**   Commonly a deposit of money by a tenant to a landlord to secure performance of a written or oral rental agreement.

**Sentimental Value**   An emotional relationship between a person (usually by the owner) and a property.

**Service Corporation**   A regulated business organization wholly owned by one or more savings institutions, which may engage in specified business activities that the parent(s) cannot or do not want to engage in, such as real estate development and management, insurance agency and brokerage services, or the sale of clerical and computer services.

**Set Back**   The term refers to zoning regulations which designate the distance a building must be set back from the front property line; or the height at which the upper floors of a building are recessed, from the face of a lower structure. There may be more than one set back in tall buildings.

**Sharecropper**   A tenant farmer who receives land and living quarters, in addition to seed, stock, and implements, from the owner in payment for shares the crops produced.

**Sharecropping Rent**   A compromise between renting and wage payments. Ordinarily, the tenant contributes only his labor and is managed and financed by the owner.

**Sheriff's Deed**   Deed given at a sheriff's sale and foreclosure of a mortgage. The giving of said deed begins a statutory redemption period. Also given at court-ordered sales, pursuant to the execution of a judgment.

**Site**   The area or the place on which anything is, has been, or is to be located.

**Slum Area**   A squalid, dilapidated, overcrowded area inhabited by a socially and economically deprived population. Slum areas usually are characterized by a coincidence of overcrowding in old, obsolete, deteriorated structures that lack natural light, ventilation, sanitary facilities, and few, if any, modern conveniences.

**Snow Fence**   A portable slat fence which is placed along the course of a highway or road at strategic points to keep off drifting snow.

**Soil Erosion**   The wearing or carrying away of the topsoil by running water or wind.

**Special Assessment**   A charge made by government against real estate to defray the cost of making a public improvement adjacent to the property which, while of general community benefit, is of special benefit to the property so assessed.

**Special-Purpose Property**   Property devoted to or available for utilization for a special purpose, but which has not independent marketability in the generally recognized acceptance of such a term. For example, clubhouses, church property, public museums, public schools, etc. Such property includes other buildings having value, such as hospitals, theatres, breweries, etc., which cannot be converted to other uses without large capital investment.

**Specific Performance**   An action to compel the performance of a contract when money damages for breach would not be satisfactory.

**Specific Reserve**   A balance sheet account containing funds set aside to absorb possible losses on a specific loan or business transaction.

**Speculatively Built Home**   A one- to four-family home on which construction has begun without a contract having been signed with any buyer.

**Speculator**   One who speculates; that is, one who buys any commodity, including real estate, in the expectancy of selling in a higher market.

**Split-Level House**   A house, the living areas of which are on two or more levels, with the levels being at heights less than a single story.

**Squatter**   One who lives on another's land without authority or claim of a right to possession. The land may either be private or public.

**Squatter's Rights**   Commonly confused with adverse possession. A squatter has no ownership rights and cannot, under the definition of a squatter, acquire any.

**Standard Metropolitan Area**   As established by the Bureau of the Census for the

1950 census, an area which includes a central city of a minimum population of 50,000 or two contiguous cities having a combined population of 50,000; and the county or counties in which they are located, but may include all or part of adjacent counties if they are economically integrated with the central city.

**Standard of Living**   The minimum of the necessities or luxuries of life to which a person or a group may be accustomed or to which they aspire.

**Statute of Limitations**   The law that limits the bringing of a court action (civil or criminal) to within a specified period of time.

**Straight Lease (Flat Lease)**   A lease calling for the same amount of rent to be paid periodically (usually monthly) for the entire term of the lease.

**Straight Line Depreciation**   A method of replacing the capital investment of income property by reducing a set amount annually from the income, over the economic life of the property.

**Straight-Term Mortgage**   A mortgage calling for principal to be paid in a lump sum (balloon) at maturity.

**Subdivision**   A tract of land divided into blocks or plots with suitable streets, roadways, open areas, and other appropriate facilities for development as residential, commercial, or industrial sites.

**Sublease**   An agreement conveying the right of use and occupancy of a property in which the lessor is the lessee in a prior lease.

**Sublessee**   One who enjoys the benefits, rights, and obligations of a sublease.

**Subordinated Debenture**   A long-term debt security issued by a savings institution, subordinate to savers' claims on assets; may be counted as regulatory new worth.

**Subrogation**   The substitution of one person for another, so that the former may exercise certain rights or claims of the latter. Used primarily when a relationship exists as insurance.

**Surplus Account**   A balance sheet account containing net profits from prior operating periods that were not distributed to savers in interest or paid to stockholders as dividends; a component of net worth at many savings institutions.

**Survey**   The measurement of the bounders of a parcel of land, its area, and sometimes its topography.

**Survivorship**   Gaining an interest in property by outliving (surviving) another who had the interest.

**Syndicate**   A combination of individuals formed to carry out some project requiring large sources of capital which individually none could undertake.

# T

**Taxation**   A system for raising revenues. Assessments upon property for federal, state and municipal purposes, and one of the four constitutional limitations on property.

**Tax Deed**   1. Deed from tax collector to governmental body after a period of non payment of taxes according to statute.

     2. Deed to a purchaser at a public sale of land taken for delinquent taxes. The purchaser receives only such title as a former owner had and strict procedures must be followed to prevent attachment of prior liens.

**Tax Exemption**   Total exemption or freedom from tax such as is granted educational, charitable, religious, and similar nonprofit organizations. Partial exemptions, such as the ad valorem tax exemption granted by some states on homesteads, as on the first $5,000 of value of a homestead in Florida.

**Tax Lien**   A lien which automatically attaches to property in the amount of property taxes unpaid on the property.

**Tax Preference Item**   The amount of tax saving generated by the use of certain loophole provisions in the tax code; a special minimum tax is imposed on users of these provisions to ensure that they cannot completely avoid federal tax liability.

**Tax Sale**   The sale of a taxpayer's property to collect delinquent taxes from the proceeds of the sale where the taxpayer has failed to redeem it within the statutory period.

**Tenancy**   Nature of tenure. The holding of property by any form of title. A lease or right to occupy for years; for a definite period, as one year and six months; at will, being ended at any time by landlord; at sufferance, when tenant remains after expiration of the lease; or for life, the right to occupy for one's life.

**Tenancy by Entirety**   A form of ownership by husband and wife whereby each owns the entire property. In the event of the death of one, the survivor owns the property without probate.

**Tenancy in Common**   The holding of property by two or more persons each of whom has an undivided interest which, upon the property owner's death, passes to the heirs and not to the survivor or survivors.

**Tenants at Sufferance**   One who comes into possession lawfully, by holdover, after the termination of interest.

**Tender**   The offer of money or performance in connection with a contract. If unjustifiably refused, places the party who refuses in default and gives rise to an action for breach of contract.

**Thrift Institution**   A depository financial intermediary that promotes thrift by offering savings deposit facilities to consumers; savings associations, savings banks and credit unions are included.

**Time Deposit**   Any savings deposit with a definite term or notice period; excludes transaction and passbook account funds.

**Title Insurance**   Insurance against loss resulting from defective title to a specifically described parcel of real estate. Defects may run to the ????? (chain of title) or to encumbrances.

**Title Search**   A review of all recorded documents affecting a specific piece of property to determine the present condition of title.

**Torrens System**   A system of land registration used in some jurisdictions in which the sovereign issues title certificates covering the ownership of land which tend to serve as title insurance.

**Transaction Account** A deposit from which payments may be made directly to a third party on the depositor's negotiable or nonnegotiable order; includes NOW accounts, checking accounts and third-party payment accounts.

**Trust** A fiduciary relationship under which one holds property (real or personal) for the benefit of another. The party creating the trust is called the settlor. The party holding the property is called the trustee. And the party who's benefit the property is held is called the beneficiary.

**Trust Agreement** A written agreement between settlor and trustee setting forth the terms of a trust.

**Trust Deed** A deed which establishes a trust. Generally an instrument that conveys legal title to property to a trustee and states the trustee's authority and the conditions binding upon the trustee in dealing with the property held in trust. Frequently trust deeds are used to secure lenders against loss; in this respect they are similar to mortgages.

**Trustee** A person who controls legal title to property under a trust agreement.

**Trust Instrument** Any writing—will, trust agreement, declaration of trust, deed of trust, or order of court—under which a trust is created.

**Tuck Pointing** The finishing of joints along the center lines with a narrow parallel ridge of fine putty or fine lime mortar.

**Turnover Ratio** The inflows from an investment portfolio over a given time period.

# U

**Unearned Increment** An increase in the value of property, not anticipated by the owner, due primarily to the operation of social or economic forces rather than to the personal efforts, intelligence, skill, or initiative of the owner; usually, but not necessarily, applied to land. This is a term developed by Henry George who believed that increases in the value of property ought not to accrue to the owners since they were due to social forces and hence "unearned." He did not, however, agree that losses were also due to social forces and that owners ought then to be compensated. Unearned increment, therefore, may be said to be a misnomer because the increment usually is a reward for the risk taken in such ventures.

**Unilateral Contract** A contract under which one party expressly makes a promise; the other party, although making no reciprocal promise, may be obligated by law or may have already given consideration.

**Upset Price** A legal term signifying the minimum price at which a property can be sold at auction, usually foreclosure.

**Urban Renewal Area** A slum area; a blighted, deteriorated, or deteriorating area, or an open land area, which is approved by Department of Housing and Urban Development as appropriate for an urban renewal project.

**Urban Renewal** A plan, developed by a locality and approved by its governing body, which guides and controls undertakings in a special urban renewal project area.

**Urban Renewal Project**   The name given to the specific activities undertaken by a local public agency in an urban renewal area to prevent and eliminate slum and blight. The project may involve slum clearance and redevelopment or rehabilitation or conservation, or a combination thereof.

# V

**VA Loan**   A mortgage or manufactured home loan made by a private lender and guaranteed by the Veterans Administration.

**Valuation Reserve**   An allowance set aside to cover the risk that the principal and interest on an investment such as a loan or security will not be repaid according to contract.

**Value**   1. The measure of value is the amount (for example, of money) which the potential purchaser probably will pay for possession of the thing desired.

2. The ratio of exchange of one commodity for another, for example, one bushel of wheat in terms of a given number of bushels of corn; thus, the value of one thing may be expressed in terms of another thing. Money is the common denominator by which value is measured.

3. The power of acquiring commodities in exchange, generally with a comparison of utilities—the utility of the commodity parted with (money) and that of the commodity acquired in the exchange (property).

Value depends upon the relation of an object to unsatisfied needs; that is, supply and demand. Value is the present worth of future benefits arising out of ownership to typical users and investors.

**Variable Interest Rate**   An interest rate which fluctuates as the prevailing rate moves up or down. In mortgages, there are usually maximums as to the frequency and amount of fluctuation. Also called "flexible interest rate."

**Variable Rate Certificate**   A certificate account on which the interest rate varies during the term of the deposit according to a predetermined schedule, formula or index.

**Variable Rate Mortgage**   A mortgage loan on which the interest rate may be adjusted periodically in accordance with changes in an agreed-upon index; also referred to as an adjustable rate mortgage.

**Vendee**   Purchaser or buyer, especially on a land contract.

**Vendor**   The person who transfers property by sale. Another word for "seller" commonly used in land contract sales.

**Ventilation**   The circulation of air in a room or building; a process of changing the air of a room by either natural or artificial means.

# W

**Waiver**   The relinquishment of a right. In construction, most commonly the waiver by a subcontractor of the mechanic's lien rights in order for the owner to obtain draws under a construction law.

**Wall Bearing**   A wall that supports any vertical load in addition to its own weight, such as a wall-bearing partition.

**Wall Tile**   A ceramic or plastic tile used as a finish material for interior walls or a wainscoting.

**Warm-Air System**   The most common type of heating system in which the air is heated in a furnace fired by coal, oil, or gas and is distributed to the space through a single register or through ducts leading to the rooms to be heated. Air circulation is maintained by a fan to amplify efficiency. In modern systems, particularly for dwellings, forced circulation with thermostats, humidity controls, and filters gives a degree of air comfort conditioning.

**Warranty Deed**   An instrument, in writing, by which title to real property is conveyed wherein the freehold is guaranteed by the grantor, his heirs, or successors.

**Watt-Hour**   The basis used to determine electric bills. Example: 100-watt light bulb means if the bulb burns for one hour, it will use 100 watts of electricity

**Working Capital**   Properly, the readily convertible capital required in a business to permit the regular carrying forward of operations free from financial embarrassment. In accounting, the excess of current assets over current liabilities as of any date.

**Wrap Around Mortgage**   A second or junior mortgage with a face value of both the amount it secures and the balance due under the first mortgage. The mortgagee under the wrap around collects a payment based on the face value and then pays the first mortgagee. It is most effective when the first has a lower interest rate than the second, since under the wraparound, the mortgagee gains the difference between the interest rates, or the mortgagor may obtain a lower rate than from refinancing.

# Y

**Yield**   The ratio of the dividends per share in dollars to purchase price per share in dollars. Income of a property is the ratio of the annual net income from the property to the cost or market value of the property. The return per acre in bushels, pounds, or ton of agricultural crops.

# Z

**Zoning**   The public regulation of the character and intensity of the use of real estate through the employment of the police power. This is accomplished by the establishment of districts in each of which uniform holding restrictions relating to use, height, area, bulk, and density of population are imposed upon the private property.

**Zoning Map**   A map depicting the various sections of the community and the division of the sections into zones of permissive land uses under the zoning ordinance.

**Zoning Ordinance**   The exercise of police powers by the sovereign to regulate and control the use of real estate for the health, morals, safety, and general welfare.

**Zoning Variance**   A change or variance in the use of property at a particular location which does not conform to the regulated use set forth in the zoning ordinance for the area surrounding that location. Variance is not an exception or change of the legally applicable zoning.

# SELECTED BIBLIOGRAPHY

## BOOKS

Allen, Robert G. "Creating Wealth," Simon & Schuster: New York, 1983.

Allen, Robert G. "Nothing Down; How To Buy Real Estate with Little or No Money Down," Simon & Schuster: New York, 1980.

Bloch, H.I., et al. "Inside Real Estate," Weidenfeld & Nicholson: New York, 1987.

Bockl, Joseph. "How To Use Leverage to Make Money in Local Real Estate," Prentice-Hall Inc.: Englewood Cliffs, N.J., 1965.

Bowly Jr., Devereux. "The Poor House, Subsidized Housing in Chicago, 1895-1976," Southern Illinois University Press: Carbondale, Ill. 1978.

Brandeis, Louis D. "Other People's Money: How the Bankers Use It," Harper & Rowe: New York, 1967.

Brouner, Dennis M. "Investing in Real Estate: How to Do it Right," Logman Financial Services Publishing Co., Inc.: Chicago, 1986.

Cadwallader, Clyde T. "How To Buy Real Estate for Profit," Prentice-Hall Inc.: Englewood Cliffs, N.J., 1958.

Conway, Lawrence D. "Mortgage Lending," American Savings and Loan Institute Press: Chicago, 1960.

Cook, Wade B. "How To Build A Real Estate Money Machine," Regency Books: Tempe, Ariz., 1986.

Cummings, Jack. "$1000 Down Can Make You Rich," Prentice-Hall Inc.: Englewood Cliffs, N.J. 1982.

Dooley, Thomas W. "Buy Now; How Alternative Financing Can Work for You," Real Estate Education Co.: Chicago, 1982.

" '87 Savings Institutions Source Book," United States League of Savings Institutions: Washington, 1987.

Fish, John Hall. "Black Power/White Control, The Control of the Woodlawn Organization in Chicago," Princeton University Press: Princeton, N.J., 1973.

Garrison, Marc. "Financial Free, Add $20,000 (Or More) Per Year to Your Income Through Part-time Real Estate Investing," Simon & Schuster: New York, 1986.

Grzesiek, David J. "Financial Independence Through Buying and Investing in Single Family Homes," Pelican Publishing Co.: Gretna, La., 1985.

Hanson, Arthur W. and Jerome B. Cohen. "Personal Finance, Principles and Case Problems," Richard D. Irwin Inc.: Homewood, Ill. 1954.

Hirsch, Arnold R. "Making the Second Ghetto; Race and Housing in Chicago, 1940-1960," Cambridge University Press: New York, 1983.

Kratovil, Robert. "Real Estate Law," Prentice-Hall: Englewood Cliffs, N.J., 1969.

Lowry, Albert. "Hidden Fortunes in Real Estate," Simon & Schuster: New York, 1983.

Macauley, Irene. "The Heritage of Illinois Institute of Technology," Illinois Institute of Technology: Chicago, 1978.

Maloney, Roy T. "Real Estate Quick and Easy," Drop Zone Press: San Francisco, 1980.

Mayer, Harold M. and Richard C. Wade. "Chicago: Growth of a Metropolis," University of Chicago Press: Chicago, 1969.

McLean, Andrew James. "Foreclosures, How To Profitably Invest in Distressed Properties," Contemporary Books Inc.: Chicago, 1980.

Milin, Mike and Irene. "How to Buy and Manage Rental Properties," Simon & Schuster: New York, 1986.

Miller, Peter G. and Douglas M. Harper. "The Common Sense Guide to Successful Real Estate Negotiations," Harper & Row: New York, 1987.

Nickerson, William. "How I Turned $1000 into a Million in Real Estate—In My Spare Time," Simon & Schuster: New York, 1959.

Nickerson, William. "Nickerson's New Real Estate Guide: How to Make a Fortune Today Starting From Scratch," Simon & Schuster: New York, 1963.

Nickerson, William. "Nickerson's No-Risk Way to Real Estate Fortunes," Simon & Schuster: New York, 1986.

Norton, Hollis. "The New Real Estate Game; Building Wealth Under the New Tax Laws," Contemporary Books Inc.: Chicago, 1987.

Pease, Robert H. and Homer V. Cherrington. "Mortgage Banking," McGraw-Hill Book Co. Inc.: New York, 1953.

Ramsey, Dan. "How To Make Your First Quarter Million in Real Estate in Five Years," Prentice-Hall Inc.: Englewood Cliffs, N.J., 1979.

Randel, Jim. "The Real Estate Game and How to Win it," Facts on File: New York, 1986.

Ratcliff, Richard U. "Real Estate Analysis," McGraw-Hill Book Co. Inc.: New York, 1961.

Snyder, Earl A. "Before You Invest; Questions and Answers on Real Estate," Reston Publishing Co.: Reston, Va. 1981.

Stenner, Oscar H. "Our Housing Jungle, and Your Pocketbook—How to Turn Our Growing Slums into Assets," University Publishers Inc.: New York, 1960.

Stratton, Jim. "Pioneering in the Urban Wilderness," Urizen Books: New York, 1978.

Teckemeyer, Earl B. "How To Value Real Estate," Prentice-Hall Inc.: Englewood Cliffs, N.J., 1956.

Temple, Douglas M. "Making Money in Real Estate," Contemporary Books Inc.: Chicago, 1976.

Weir, Mary. "Housing Recycling, The Best Real Estate Opportunity for the '80s," Contemporary Books Inc.: Chicago, 1982.

"How To Make Money in Real Estate with Government Loans and Programs," Simon & Schuster: New York, 1985.

## APARTMENTS

### Periodicals

"Community, Residents, Owners Benefit from Turnaround of Distressed Apartment Complexes," *Mortgage Banking*, February 1978.

"Effective: The New Bankruptcy Code on Apartment Owners and Managers," *Unit National Apartment Association*, Summer of 1980.

"Apartment Investment," *Mortgage Banking*, February 1982.

"Major Changes," *Mortgage Banking*, March 1982.

"Location? Location? Location? Location? Location? Location?" *Multi-Housing News*, December 1982.

"Investing in Real Estate in Unsettling Times," *Board Room Reports*, 1 January 1983.

"Where World Rents are Highest—and Lowest," *Business Facilities*, May 1983.

"A Drop in Apartment Value Slows Down in Late '86," *Multi-Housing News*, June 1987.

"Rental High-Rise in Default Sold to Real Estate Firm," *Multi-Housing News*, June 1987.

"Life Outside of the Apartment Walls," *Christian Science Monitor*, 20 August 1987.

"Analyzing Performance, The Return on Equity Way," *American and Condominium News*, September/October, 1987.

"Discrimination: Rental Housing's Black Eye," *American and Condominium News*, September/October, 1987.

"Goal Recordkeeping," *American and Condominium News*, September/October, 1987.

"Financing Options for Energy Improvements, Energy Savings for Low Income Residents," *Journal of Property Management*, September/October 1987.

"Tax Laws, Increasing Competitiveness and the Need to Lower Expenses are Pushing Renovation to the Top of Property Management Slate Priorities," *Journal of Property Management*, September/October 1987.

"The Rehabilitation of Lake Park Apartments," *Journal of Property Management*, September/October 1987.

"The Use of Demographics In Modernizing Residential Assets," *Journal of Property Management*, September/October 1987.

"Buying to Rent," *Black Enterprise*, October 1987.

"Developments Hold Change for Near South," *Crain's Chicago Business*, 19 October 1987.

"Rent Control Battle Brewing," *Crain's New York Magazine*, 26 October 1987.

"Tenants Should Buy Chicago Project, Report Said," *City and State Magazine*, November 1987.

"The Homeless," *Fortune Magazine*, 23 November 1987.

### Newspapers

"Rents Go Up As Fall Comes Along," *Chicago Sun-Times*, 20 September 1987.

"Publisher Drills Landlord and Management Survival," *Chicago Sun-Times*, 27 September 1987.

"New Tenant Law Puts Fixed Arm on Landlord," *Chicago Sun-Times*, 30 September 1987.

"City Planners Keep Eye on Chicago River," *Chicago Tribune*, 4 October 1987.

"City Front Center: New Neighborhood on Lake Front," *Chicago Sun-Times*, 11 October 1987.

"Land Lunancy is Choking Japanese Cities," *Wall Street Journal*, 16 October 1987.

"Positive Signs for Real Estate," *New York Times*, 17 October 1987.

"Land of Opportunity," *New City South Loop Paper*, 21 October 1987.

"Housing Starts Rise 4.4% in Month," *Wall Street Journal*, 21 October 1987.

"Rebound: Center City Neighborhoods On the Way Back," *Philadelphia Enquirer*, 21 October 1987.

"Real Estate May Gain from Market Upheaval," *Chicago Sun-Times*, 23 October 1987.

"Allow Projects Outward Bound," *Chicago Tribune*, 26 October 1987.

"Tenants React to Uptown Goes Upscale," *Chicago Sun-Times*, 1 November 1987.

"Exchange Giving Chicago a Lift Too," *New York Times*, 5 November 1987.

"Multifamily Housing Offer Buys More Living Space at Reduced Cost," *Chicago Tribune*, 7 November 1987.

### Real Estate Newsletters

"Becoming a Landlord May Be Your Retirement Answer," *Real Estate Investment Planning*, August 1983.

"Apartment Building Buyers Can Protect Themselves Against Hidden Rent Confessions," *Real Estate Investment Planning*, July 1984.

"Ways to Get Income from Vacant Land," *Real Estate Investment Planning*, January 1986.

"A Tax Tip in Selling Income Property," *Real Estate Investment Planning*, November 1986.


## AUCTIONS

### Periodicals

"Auctions are the Answer to Rochester City Held Property Inventory. Do They Work?," *Housing*, May 1977.

"Getting Bargain Houses," *Money*, March 1982.

"Deep Discounts at Condo Auction," *Barron's*, 10 May 1982.

"Real Estate Auctions Marketing Route," *Mortgage Banking*, October 1982.

"Home Buying at Auction," *Parent's*, January 1984.

"Neighborhood Changes in New York City," *American Demographics*, October 1984.

"Hammering Down an Auction Bargain," *Money*, April 1986.

"Own a Piece of the City," *Black Enterprise*, October 1986.

### Real Estate Newsletters

"Buying and Selling at Auctions: Real Estate's New Market," *Real Estate Intelligence Report*, September 1980.

"Auctions: Auctioneer's Errors Cost Bidder a Bargain," *Real Estate Law Report*, 22 December 1980.

"The Benefit of Auction Property," *Real Estate Investment Planning*, February 1983.

"How Real Estate Auctions Work to Benefit You," *Real Estate Investment Planning*, February 1984.

"Bargain Priced Properties for Sale," *Real Estate Investment Planning*, February 1986.

"Shockingly Low Price Wasn't Enough to Avoid Foreclosure Sale," *Real Estate Investment Planning*, February 1986.

"Auction: What's in it for You?" *Real Estate Today*, January/February 1987.

"Auctioning the Single-Family Home," *Real Estate Today*, January/February 1987.

"How You Can Profit From Real Estate Auctions," *Real Estate Investment Planning*.

### Newspapers

"Tax Delinquent Realty Group Buys More Property at Municipal Auction, Though Law Bars The Sales," *New York Times*, 2 March 1978.

"Condo Auctions May Be A First," *Real Estate Advertising*, 19 February 1980.

"The Auction Process Puts the Price Too High," *New York Times*, 18 March 1985.

"Auction Speeds Real Estate Transfer," Chicago Title Insurance Co., January/February 1987.

"Auctioneer to Sell Big Country Ranch," *Las Vegas Review*, 30 August 1987.

"Low Cost Housing Besieged," *New York Times*, 13 September 1987.

"Mixed Record Emerges from Auction Sales of City Houses," *New York Times*, 13 September 1987.

"Idaho Town's Last Hurrah is an Auction," *Chicago Tribune*, 4 October 1987.

"Auction of a Bank's Assets in Austin Marks the End of High Flying Texas-Style," *Wall Street Journal*, 6 November 1987.

"Judge Blocks Sales of Targeted Land," *Chicago Tribune*, 6 November 1987.

## BUYING REAL ESTATE

### Newspapers

"Real Estate Forum on Various Topics," *Washington Post*, 20 November 1975.

"Overlook the Idea for Downpayment," *Chicago Sun-Times*, 30 November 1975.

"When to Buy? When to Wait? The Answer Hasn't Changed," *Savings and Loan Newsletter*, August 1978.

"Tips for Selling Your Home," *The Real Estate Digest Newsletter*, August 1983.

"Ex-Schoolteacher Creates Giant in Real Estate," *Chicago Sun-Times*, 22 July 1984.

"Home Selling Tactics," *Real Estate Letter*, 7 February 1985.

"What Drives Younger First Time Buyers," *Real Estate Insider Newsletter*, 1 April 1985.

"Get Rich Quick Tale Ends at Chapter 7," *Chicago Sun-Times*, 4 June 1987.

"Buy The Worst House on the Street," *Chicago Tribune*, 6 June 1987.

"Hyde Park Rehabs Add Sparkle to Dollars," *Chicago Tribune*, 21 June 1987.

"Justice Department Sues Atrium Village; Sites Biased to Blacks," *Chicago Tribune*, 24 July 1987.

"U.S. Sues Integrated Housing Complex in Chicago on Use of Quotas," *New York Times*, 24 July 1987.

"For Sale Fight Boils Again," *Chicago Sun-Times*, 25 July 1987.

"Short of Cash, You Can Still Purchase A Home," *Chicago Tribune*, 1 August 1987.

"Uncovering House Defects," *Cincinnati Enquirer*, 1 August 1987.

" 'Locking Up' Assets in Home has Pros and Cons," *Chicago Tribune*, 2 August 1987.

"Uncle Sam Slows Down on Home Loans," *Chicago Sun-Times*, 7 August 1987.

"The Question of Housing," *Washington Post*, 8 August 1987.

"Developers Using Incentives to Lure Renters," *Chicago Tribune*, 14 August 1987.

"A Pre-Purchase Home Inspection Can Prevent Nasty Surprises Later," *Chicago Tribune*, 15 August 1987.

"Builders Increasingly Cater to Trade-Up Market," *Dallas Morning News*, 20 August 1987.

"Terminology Brings it All Home," *Chicago Sun-Times*, 21 August 1987.

"Words To Shop by in Today's Housing Market," *Chicago Tribune*, 22 August 1987.

"Ten Ways to Buy a House Even if You're Short of Cash," *Chicago Tribune*, 29 August 1987.

"Pricing Your Home Realistically," *Cincinnati Enquirer*, 1 September 1987.

"New Fixed Rate Loan Helps Homebuyers," *Chicago Tribune*, 4 September 1987.

"Bug the Lender to Get Fast Results on Home Mortgages," *Chicago Tribune*, 5 September 1987.

"Home Sellers, Beware of Escape Clauses," *Chicago Tribune*, 5 September 1987.

"When to Accelerate Principal Payments on Home Mortgages," *Chicago Tribune*, 5 September 1987.

"Paying Loan Ahead Totes Up Big Savings," *Chicago Sun-Times*, 6 September 1987.

"Goofs Nip Home Sales in the Bud," *Chicago Tribune*, 9 September 1987.

"Most Rich Americans Invest in Realty—Poll," *Chicago Sun-Times*, 11 September 1987.

"Finding A Ready Market," *New York Times*, 12 September 1987.

"In Bronx, New Twist on Old Swindle," *New York Times*, 12 September 1987.

"Owning a Home Recedes as An Achievable Dream," *New York Times*, 13 September 1987.

"Why Developer-Tenant Joint Ventures Make Sense," *Morgage and Real Estate Executive Report*, 15 September 1987.

"FHA Charges More Than It Needs—Study," *Chicago Sun-Times*, 18 September 1987.

"Growth of Service Economy Creates a Crisis for Workers," *Chicago Sun-Times*, 20 September 1987.

"Predict 128% Jump in Home Prices by the Year 2000," *Chicago Defender*, 23 September 1987.

"Homeownership Allows Freedom To Decorate," *Chicago Defender*, 26 September 1987.

"New Homebuyers Could Be Buying Trouble by Selling Inspections, Fix-up Rights for Cash," *Chicago Tribune*, 27 September 1987.

"Ownership Style Changes with Times," *Chicago Tribune*, 27 September 1987.

"Repairs Increase Final Price of Home," *Chicago Sun-Times*, 27 September 1987.

"New House Sales Rise 2.7 Percent," *Chicago Tribune*, 1 October 1987.

"A Community Going to Court Over 'Poisoned' Property Values," *Chicago Tribune*, 1 October 1987.

"Brick Thieves Building Nest Eggs on Yuppie Fad," *Chicago Sun-Times*, 4 October 1987.

"Suburbs Becoming One Big Traffic Jam," *Chicago Sun-Times*, 8 October 1987.

"Court Decision Takes Some Risks Out of Buying a House As Is," *Chicago Tribune*, 10 October 1987.

"Tips on Avoiding the Top Home Buying Traps," *Chicago Tribune*, 10 October 1987.

"Lots of Lots, But City Has Little for Development," *New York Times*, 11 October 1987.

"Levittown Turns 40," *Chicago Tribune*, 11 October 1987.

"Housing Issue to Test Foundation of '88 Presidential Campaign," *Chicago Tribune*, 18 October 1987.

"Defects Found During Inspection are Just Cause for Deposit Refund," *Chicago Tribune*, 22 October 1987.

"Don't Let Wall Spook House Plans," *Chicago Sun-Times*, 30 October 1987.

"Simon Shapes '30s To Fit Problems of 80s," *New York Times*, 30 October 1987.

"Home Prices Skyrocket in Western Suburbs," *Chicago Sun-Times*, 30 October 1987.

"Interest Jitters Fail to Deter Buyers," *Chicago Tribune*, 1 November 1987.

"Northwest Side Hits Record for Resale Prices," *Chicago Sun-Times*, 6 November 1987.

"What to Expect When Buying a New House," *Chicago Sun-Times*, 6 November 1987.

"Single-family Housing Starts Booming," *Chicago Sun-Times*, 6 November 1987.

"Dream House a Nightmare," *Chicago Tribune*, 8 November 1987.

"How Sellers Avoid Flaky Buyers," *Chicago Tribune*, 8 November 1987.

"Property Swaps Would Lose Luster Under House Proposal," *Wall Street Journal*, 11 November 1987.

"How A Florida Builder Eliminated Interest as a Reason not to Buy," *Real Estate Insider Newsletter*, 16 November 1987.

## Periodicals

"Learn to Spot What's Wrong with a House," *Changing Times*, February 1970.

"What It's Like on a Street Where You Live," *Money*, March 1973.

"Buying a Home This Summer," *Money*, June 1976.

"How to Become A Millionaire: Never Buy Other People's Paint," *Ebony*, November 1976.

"Who Buys Houses? All Kinds of People," *Savings and Loan Magazine*, May 1978.

"Profile of a New Homebuyer," *Builder's Magazine*, 5 June 1978.

"How Whites are Taking Back Black Neighborhoods," *Ebony*, September 1978.

"A Home-Buyer Preference in Mid-Western Area," *The Appraisal Journal*, April 1979.

"Angles to Know When you Buy or Sell A Home," *Changing Times*, December 1979.

"The Home Buying and Selling Process," the National Association of Realtors Economic and Research Division, February 1980.

"What to Look for When you Buy a Home," *Texas Realtor*, October 1980.

"Conversions Remain Strong," *Real Estate Today*, June 1981.

"Who's Buying Washington's Expensive Housing," *Washington Monthly*, June 1981.

"Buy Now or Wait," *Changing Times*, November 1981.

"Buyer's Preference 1982," *Housing Magazine*, December 1981.

"Buying Your First House," *Creative Real Estate*, January 1982.

"Homebuying: Is An Emotional Decision," *Real Estate Today*, February 1982.

"Interest Rate Pressure on a First Time Homebuyer: The Affordable Question," *Mortgage Bankers Magazine*, May 1982.

"The 1982 Homebuyers' Survey," *Guarantor Magazine*, January/February 1983.

"Some Rays of Sunshine for Housing Industry," *U.S. News & World Report*, 7 February 1983.

"Why and How is a Good Time to Buy a House," *U.S. News and World Report*, 30 May 1983.

"Today's Homebuyers and Sellers Revert to Familiar Pattern," *Savings Institution*, May 1984.

"Shopping the New Mortgage Mart," *Real Estate Investment Ideas*, August 1984.

"How to Buy Real Estate," *Money*, September 1984.

"The Best Buy You Will Ever Make," *Money*, September 1984.

"Househunting in Winter: Tips for Savvy Buyers," *Home*, November 1984.

"Homebuyer's Pattern for Repeat Buyers," *Real Estate Quarterly*, Winter 1985.

"The Homebuyer's Process Searching for A Home," *Real Estate Quarterly*, Winter 1985.

"When is the Right Time to Buy a Home," *Texas Realty Magazine*, February 1985.

"What's Keeping Homeowners Out in the Cold," *Homebuyer's Magazine*, 4 February 1985.

"Builders 1985 Homebuyer's Survey," *Builder's Magazine*, April 1985.

"Investing in Rundown Houses," *Real Estate Newsletter*, July 1985.

"The Profile of a Mad Homebuyer—Summer 1985," *Real Estate Quarterly*, Fall 1985.

"Digging Up the Down Payment," *Money*, April 1986.

"Buy A House That Needs Paint," *Money*, April 1986.

"The Low Down on No Down," *Changing Times*, June 1986.

"Leverage, A Competitive Edge," *Real Estate Review*, Fall 1986.

"How to Become a Millionaire Through Real Estate," *Real Estate Review*, Fall 1986.

"Supply and Demand will have More Effect on the Value of Your Home than Tax Reform Will," *Changing Times Magazine*, January 1987.

"Looking Beyond the Obvious," *Real Estate Today*, January/February 1987.

"Don't Forget Seller Financing," *Real Estate Today*, May 1987.

"New Homes Vs. Resales," *Real Estate Today*, May 1987.

"Working with First Time Homebuyers," *Real Estate Today*, May 1987.

"House Savings and Home Ownership," *Illinois Business Review*, June 1987.

"Home Sales: Existing in New Single Family, Apartment Condos and Co-ops," National Association of Realtors, July 1987.

"What To Do To Save Troubled Properties," *Crain's Chicago Business*, 24 August 1987.

"Improvements that Add Value to Your Home," *Changing Times*, September 1987.

"Size of Houses to Increase with the Price," *Secondary Marketing Executive*, September 1987.

"The New Vise On the Middle Class," *Money*, September 1987.

"Signs of Revival: Finding the Next Hot Neighborhood," *Chicago*, October 1987.

"HUD Announces $100 Million in Housing Development Grants," U.S. Dept. of Housing and Urban Development Release, 1 October 1987.

"Syndicators Hope Stock Woes Will Spark New Interest in Real Estate," *Investors Daily*, 30 October 1987.

"Housing Experts See Only Slight Slump Despite Wall Street Troubles," *Investors Daily*, 30 October 1987.

"Housing Hot Spots," *Changing Times*, November 1987.

"Your Home: Best Bets for Housing," *Changing Times*, November 1987.

"Suburbia Through the Centuries," *Insight Magazine*, 2 November 1987.

"Home Purchasers Guide Booklet," Department of Housing, City of Chicago, 1987.


## SELLING REAL ESTATE

### Newspapers

"This Checklist of Homebuyer's Gripes Can Help You Sell More Older Homes," *Real Estate Opportunity Newsletter*, 5 August 1976.

"Mother Lode of Real Estate is Fool's Gold," *Chicago Tribune*, 6 December 1981.

"Money Saving Ways to Buy or Sell a House Right Now," *Board Room Reports*, 1 February 1983.

"Did You Sell Your Residence in 1986?" *Chicago Defender*, 2 September 1987.

"Sense of Home is What Sells Buyers on a House," *Milwaukee Journal*, 20 September 1987.

"Higher Interest Rates to Hamper Home Sales," *Real Estate News*, 21 September 1987.

"Sellers Beware The Barracuda: Hold Brokers to Promises," *Chicago Sun-Times*, 27 September 1987.

"Americans State Housing Preference," *Chicago Sun-Times*, 2 October 1987.

"Forged Quit Claim Deed Leaves Man's Widow in Trouble," *Chicago Sun-Times*, 23 October 1987.

## Periodicals

"When Should Real Estate Be Sold," *Real Estate Issues*, Summer 1979.

"Condomania or Condofobia," *Real Estate Issues*, Summer 1980.

"Can't Sell It, Rent It," *Builder's Magazine*, December 1982.

"The Economics of Seller Financing," *The Ohio Realtor*, December 1982.

"How To Get More Money for Your Home," *Real Estate Investment Ideas*, April 1985.

"Out of the Old House and into the New," *Money*, May 1985.

"Tax Free Cash Without Moving or Refinancing," *The Hawaiian Realtor*, November 1985.

"Ten Tips on Getting Top Dollar," *Money*, April 1986.

"How to Help First Time Buyers Finance a Home," *Real Estate Today*, May 1987.

"Homebuying Behavior: An Empirical Study in Cross Cultural Buyer Behavior," *Journal of American Real Estate and Urban Economics*, Spring 1987.

"Time on the Market and Selling Price," *Journal of the American Real Estate and Urban Economics*, Summer 1987.

"When Should Real Estate Be Sold," *Real Estate Issues*, Summer 1987.

"The Risks and Rewards of Buying and Selling a Home," *Black Enterprise*, October 1987.

"The Quickest Way to Sell Real Estate," *Fortune*, 12 October 1987.

## RENOVATION AND REHABILITATION

### Newspapers

"South Side Rentals Lure Investors," *Chicago Sun-Times*, 1 February 1987.

"Landmark's Bill Linked to History: Preservation Effort to Move City to Front," *Chicago Sun-Times*, 8 May 1987.

"Apartments are Caught in Catch 22," *Chicago Tribune*, 19 June 1987.

"Dumps Become Arguments in Favor of Gentrification," *Chicago Tribune*, 16 August 1987.

"Safer, Cheaper to Remodel Than Construct New Building," *Chicago Tribune*, 29 August 1987.

"Tax Law Change Didn't Demolish Rehab Potential," *Realtor News*, 31 August 1987.

"Rehab Theaters Deserve A Break," *Chicago Tribune*, 16 September 1987.

"Manufacturers Resist Rehab Conversion of Chicago's Industrial Space," *Real Estate Times*, 16 September 1987.

"Can Land Trust Plans Save Homes for Poor?" *Chicago Tribune*, 20 September 1987.

"Cancel Rebuilding of LaSalle Street Station, METRA is urged," *Chicago Sun-Times*, 7 October 1987.

"Study Pushes Tenants' Ownership of Cabrini-Green," *Chicago Tribune*, 8 October 1987.

"Preservation Incentives Expected in Zoning Overhaul," *Real Estate Times*, 16 October 1987.

"Home Improvements, Preparing for Winter," *New York Times*, 22 October 1987.

"Ghetto is Headed Off at the Gap," *Chicago Tribune*, 25 October 1987.

"Rehabbing Can Be a Smart Investment," *Chicago Sun-Times*, 30 October 1987.

"Real Estate Revamping an 1800's Community," *New York Times*, 8 November 1987.

### Periodicals

"Sandburg Village Converter Sees Condo Market Transition," *Crain's Chicago Business*, 22 February 1982.

"Long Dormant South Loop Set to Bloom," *Crain's Chicago Business*, 3 January 1983.

"Chicago Area Rehab Market is a Busy One," *Realty and Building*, 24 April 1982.

"Rehabbing and the People's Priority," *Mortgage Banking*, September 1983.

"Secret to Finding 'Hot Spots'," *Real Estate Advisor*, March/April 1986.

"Neighborhood Housing Service of Chicago Revitalizes Chicago's Neighborhoods," *REM*, 13 April 1986.

"Variety of Financing Alternatives Available to Rehab Developers," *REM*, 13 June 1986.

"Condition Surveys: Prerequisite to Successful Rehabs," *Realty and Building*, 25 April 1987.

"Rehabilitation, Tax Programs Breathe New Life into Inner City," *Realty and Building*, 25 April 1987.

"Rehab Under Tax Reform: Is It Still Worth It?" *Realty and Building*, 25 April 1987.

"Developers Must Examine Zoning Building Codes Before Rehabbing," *Realty and Building*, 25 April 1987.

"Rehabbers Begin to Feel Tax Reform Impact," *Metro Chicago Real Estate*, 10 July 1987.

"Chicago Rehab Directory," *Metro Chicago Real Estate*, 10 July 1987.

"Rehabbing Chicago's West Side," *Equity Magazine*, Fall 1987.

"What's Happening to Rehab Today," *Real Estate Today*, October 1987.

"Houston Pushes HUD to Return Federal Construction Grant," *City and State Magazine*, November 1987.

## CONDOS

### Periodicals

"The Condo Option," *Changing Times*, April 1980.

"The Condo Home," *Real Estate Today*, February 1981.

"Housing Yourself in the 1980s, What About A Condo or Co-op," *Consumer Report*, July 1981.

"Why A Condo? The Buyer's Standpoint," *Delaware County Realtors*, April 1982.

"Profile of a Condo Project Gone Sour," *Crain's Chicago Business*, 6 December 1982.

"First Time Buyers Favor Condos," *Builder's Magazine*, October 1983.

### Newspapers

"Condominiums: A Consumer Guide," *Real Estate Investment Newsletter*, August 1984.

"How To Avoid Condominium Unhappiness," *Board Room Report*, 1 December 1984.

"D.C. Council Considers Two Condominium Measures; Limits in Liability of Volunteers Sought," *Washington Post*, 9 May 1987.

"Run Your Own Condo," *Washington Post*, 9 May 1987.

"Maryland is Wavering on Loan Rule Change," *Washington Post*, 9 May 1987.

"Arlington Village Co-op Marks 6th Year," *Washington Post*, 16 May 1987.

"Warranty Programs for Condos are Acceptable to HUD Officials," *Honolulu Sunday Star Bulletin and Advertiser*, 9 August 1987.

"Association By-Laws Do Not Overrule Illinois Statute," *Chicago Tribune*, 25 September 1987.

"Evidence Builds on Rebounding Condo Sales," *Chicago Tribune*, 27 September 1987.

"Seminar Lets Condo Members Quiz Attorney," *Chicago Tribune*, 27 September 1987.

"Why Some Manhattan Condos Flounder," *New York Times*, 4 October 1987.

"Auction Bid for Condo Buyers," *Chicago Sun-Times*, 4 October 1987.

"Fannie Trims Conversion Costs," *Chicago Tribune*, 4 October 1987.

"Study Pushes Tenant Ownership of Cabrini-Green," *Chicago Tribune*, 8 October 1987.

"Condominium Board Knows Things are Going Well," *Chicago Sun-Times*, 16 October 1987.

"Condominium Needs Funds to Pay for Future Repairs," *Chicago Sun-Times*, 6 November 1987.

## MORTGAGES AND FORECLOSURES

### Periodicals

"Property Problems," *Real Estate Forum*, October 1973.

"Lenders Wrestle with Troubled Real Estate," *National Real Estate Investment Magazine*, January 1977.

"Default Property, Unseen Housing," *Journal of Property Management*, March/April 1977.

"Creative Financing Comes A Cropper," *Dun's Magazine*, July 1982.

"Buying Foreclosures: Pitfalls and Protective Measures," *Appraisal Review Journal*, Summer 1982.

"What is A House Really Worth?" *Mortgage Banking*, October 1982.

"Consumer's Opinion on Mortgages and Housing," *Mortgage Banking*, November 1982.

"Bank Owned Real Estate Presents Valuation Problems," *Business Facilities*, March 1983.

"A Word About Mortgage Security," *Business Facilities*, May 1983.

"Down to Earth Look at the Balloons," *Real Estate Today*, July/August 1983.

"It's Time to Refinance," *Real Estate Today*, July/August 1983.

"Residential Mortgage Delinquencies and Foreclosures: Improvement Underway," *Economic Review by the Federal Reserve Bank of Atlanta*, December 1983.

"Interest Rates Begin to Bite," *Business Week*, 26 March 1984.

"Sample Distressed Properties," *Real Estate Today*, May 1984.

"The Economics of Assumable Mortgages," *Real Estate Today*, June 1984.

"Workouts for Problem Properties," *Mortgage Banking*, July 1984.

"All About Reverse Mortgages," *Board Room Report*, 1 December 1984.

"Delinquency Hits Highs—But Portfolio Lenders Fair Best," *Savings Institution*, April 1985.

"The Yuppie Mortgage," *Mortgage Estate Today*, August 1985.

"Foreclosures: A Forgotten Market," *Real Estate Today*, November/December 1985.

"Nail Down What That House is Really Worth," *Changing Times*, March 1986.

" 'Grave Dancing' on Lost Homes," *Newsweek*, 6 March 1986.

"Mortgage, Where is Thy Sting?" *Money*, April 1986.

"Extracting Cash From Your House," *Money*, April 1986.

"It's the Last Roundup for Texas Real Estate Tycoon," *Business Week*, 15 December 1986.

"Mortgage Rates: Catch the Best Deal," *Changing Times*, September 1987.

"High Interest Rate Perils for Borrowers, Gains for Savers," *Christian Science Monitor*, 14 September 1987.

"Is Your Bank Account Safe," *Parade Magazine*, 20 September 1987.

"Illinois Mortgage Foreclosure Law," *Illinois Bar Journal*, October 1987.

"Trade Down Without Tripping Up," *Changing Times*, October 1987.

"Second Thoughts on Second Mortgages," *Forbes*, 5 October 1987.

"Brokerage Cut Raises Fears of Recession," *Crain's New York Magazine*, 26 October 1987.

"For Real Estate Brokers: Silent Phones," *Crain's New York Magazine*, 26 October 1987.

"Money-Saving Mortgage Math," *Changing Times*, November 1987.

## Newspapers

"Illinois Leads the Country in Delinquent Mortgages," *Chicago Tribune*, 6 March 1981.

"Tardy Mortgage Payments Add to Housing Woes," *Chicago Tribune*, 7 November 1981.

"Bankruptcy May Skirt Foreclosure," *Chicago Tribune*, 20 June 1982.

"Even after Foreclosure, the Owner Can Recover," *Chicago Tribune*, February 1983.

"Qualifying for a Home Mortgage," *Real Estate Investment Planning Newsletter*, January 1984.

"Leavitt Fortune Dwindles, Developer's Empire is in Shambles," *Washington Post*, 16 May 1986.

"Consumer Groups Say Equity Loans Unfair," *Washington Post*, 16 May 1986.

"Homebuyers Re-Arm as Fixed-Term Rise," *Washington Post*, 16 May 1986.

"Unwise for Amateur Investors to Borrow on Home Equity," *Boston Globe*, 22 June 1986.

"VA Foreclosures, 'No Bid' Vary Widely by Region," *Real Estate Finance Today Newsletter*, 4 July 1986.

"How To Become A Millionaire Through Real Estate," *Real Estate Review*, Fall 1986.

"Analysis of Home Mortgage Delinquency Rates," *The Appraisal Journal*, October 1986.

"Refinancing is Now More Costly," *Real Estate Investment Planning Newsletter*, November 1986.

"Codes of Federal Regulations," Housing and Urban Development: Washington, D.C., Revised April 1, 1987.

"Senate Begins Work on Mortgage Commitment Bill," *Washington Post*, May 1987.

"Foreclosure Sales Will Not be Deferred," *Chicago Board of Realtors Newsletter*, June 1987.

"Broker Says Lower Mortgage Rates are Not All Bait and Switch Tactics," *Chicago Tribune*, 13 June 1987.

"Deducting Your Mortgage Interest Might Prove to be Tricky Business," *Chicago Sun-Times*, 3 July 1987.

"Precasting An Image for Commercial Property," *Metro Chicago Real Estate*, 10 July 1987.

"Adjustable Rates Get Some Respect," *Chicago Tribune*, 13 July 1987.

"State New Foreclosure Law Shortens Redemption Period," *Chicago Sun-Times*, 31 July 1987.

"Real Estate Woes Force Connally Bankruptcy," *New York Times*, 1 August 1987.

"Explosive and Talented Director Turns Houston's Housing Agency Around," *Houston Chronicle*, 4 August 1987.

"Critics Take Second Look At Home Equity Loans," *Chicago Tribune*, 6 August 1987.

"Ex-Husband Bill Led to Lien," *Chicago Sun-Times*, 7 August 1987.

"Second Mortgage Shouldn't Depend on Residency," *Chicago Sun-Times*, 7 August 1987.

"Mortgage Payments Can Be Taxing Matter," *Chicago Sun-Times*, 14 August 1987.

"Here's How to Speed Up Approval of Your Mortgage Loan Application," *Chicago Tribune*, 22 August 1987.

"Benjamin Franklin Savings Files Lawsuits in 48 Foreclosure Cases," *Houston Chronicle*, 24 August 1987.

"Survey of Mortgage Lending Activity in May 1987," *U.S. Department of Housing and Urban Development News Release*, 26 August 1987.

"Texas Farm Forecloses on 422,000 Acres," *Houston Chronicle*, 27 August 1987.

"Sanitary Tax Will Double in 1988 for Gary Property Owners," *Gary Post-Tribune*, 27 August 1987.

"Sky the Limit for Home Equity Loans," *Chicago Sun-Times*, 28 August 1987.

"Taxpayers Can Show Creativity on New Form," *Chicago Sun-Times*, 28 August 1987.

"Experts Expect A Rising Tide of Foreclosures," *Dallas Morning News*, 28 August 1987.

"Study Says FHA Should Lower Mortgage Insurance Premiums," *Dallas Times*, 29 August 1987.

"Take Advantage of Creative Mortgages, Says Realtor," *Star Ledger* (Newark, N.J.), 30 August 1987.

"More Options Are Available Today in a Home Mortgage," *Star Ledger* (Newark, N.J.), 30 August 1987.

"Bankruptcy, Thousands of Houstonians are Battling Back from the Brink of Financial Disaster," *Houston Chronicle*, 1 September 1987.

"New Law Protects People from Credit Repair Abuse," *Houston Chronicle*, 1 September 1987.

"Decrease in Foreclosure Breaks Trend," *Houston Chronicle*, 3 September 1987.

"Connally Lists $93 Million Debts," *Houston Chronicle*, 3 September 1987.

"Connally Says He Will Bounce Back From Bankruptcy," *Houston Chronicle*, 4 September 1987.

"City Buying Foreclosed Apartments for Use in Co-op Housing Program," *Houston Chronicle*, 4 September 1987.

"Home Equity Loan Has Its Costly Side," *Chicago Sun-Times*, 4 September 1987.

"Mortgage Rates Soar," *Chicago Sun-Times*, 4 September 1987.

"New Breed of Loan Types," *The Oregonian*, 5 September 1987.

"Home Sales in Oregon Roll Along at Steady Pace," *The Oregonian*, 5 September 1987.

"Connally Blames Tough Times in Texas for Financial Woes," *Chicago Tribune*, 5 September 1987.

"Connally Files Plan for Reorganization," *Houston Chronicle*, 5 September 1987.

"Aging Baby Boomer Generation Will Put New Strains on Houses," *Star Ledger* (Newark, N.J.), 6 September 1987.

"Mortgages Won't Cost An Arm," *Cincinnati Enquirer*, 6 September 1987.

"Chase Mixes Fixed Rate, Adjustable," *Cincinnati Enquirer*, 6 September 1987.

"Regulations Coming For Appraisals," *Cincinnati Enquirer*, 6 September 1987.

"Mortgage Rates Here Top 11 Percent," *Houston Chronicle*, 9 September 1987.

"Local Mortgage Rates Closing in on 11 Percent Barrier," *Chicago Tribune*, 10 September 1987.

"Texas Bank Finds Rescuer in Aboud," *Chicago Sun-Times*, 10 September 1987.

"Do All in Your Power to Avoid Foreclosure," *Chicago Sun-Times*, 11 September 1987.

"Texas Deals Gives FDIC Breathing Room," *Chicago Tribune*, 13 September 1987.

"Don't Bank on Just Any Home Equity Loan," *Chicago Tribune*, 20 September 1987.

"New Home Equity Plan Aids Elderly," *Milwaukee Journal*, 20 September 1987.

"Why Do Loan Rates Change? It's Complex," *Milwaukee Journal*, 20 September 1987.

"Adjustable Rate Loans Growing More Popular," *Seattle Times*, 20 September 1987.

"New Line of Credit Plan Can Aid Seniors," *Seattle Times*, 20 September 1987.

"Balcour Fires 60, Blames Plunge in Syndication," *Chicago Sun-Times*, 23 September 1987.

"How To Make End Run Around Interest Rates," *Chicago Sun-Times*, 25 September 1987.

"More Mortgage Lenders Face Indictments," *Chicago Sun-Times*, 25 September 1987.

"Clamp Down on Lender to Secure Locked-In Rate," *Chicago Sun-Times*, 27 September 1987.

"August 1987 New Private Mortgage Insurance Activity," U.S. Department of Housing and Urban Report, 29 September 1987.

"Mortgage Cause Provisions Must Be Disclosed," *Mortgage and Real Estate Executive Report*, 1 October 1987.

"Commercial Equity Loans Hit Market," *Mortgage and Real Estate Executive Report*, 1 October 1987.

"Projecting Real Estate Returns," *Mortgage and Real Estate Executive Report*, 1 October 1987.

"Mortgage Rate Cap Set by VA," *Chicago Sun-Times*, 5 October 1987.

"Fed May Seek Loan Information," *Chicago Sun-Times*, 7 October 1987.

"Feds Eye Home Loan Disclosures," *Chicago Tribune*, 7 October 1987.

"Big Banks Raise Prime Rate to 9.25%," *Chicago Tribune*, 8 October 1987.

"Withdrawal Exceeds Deposits at S&Ls in August," *Chicago Tribune*, 8 October 1987.

"Borrowers: Be Aware of Bad Guy Convertibles," *Chicago Tribune*, 11 October 1987.

"Sweet Dreams of A Home and the Sour Awakening," *New York Times*, 15 October 1987.

"Interest is One Item Lifting Cost of Housing," *Chicago Sun-Times*, 16 October 1987.

"Buying Options When Buying Housing Can Save," *Chicago Sun-Times*, 16 October 1987.

"Rule Changes May be on the Way for Home-Equity Loans," *Chicago Sun-Times*, 16 October 1987.

"Lock-in Controversy Angers Lenders," *Chicago Sun-Times*, 16 October 1987.

"First Time Buyers Often Wait Too Long," *Chicago Sun-Times*, 16 October 1987.

"9.75% Mortgage Program Starts Monday," *Chicago Sun-Times*, 16 October 1987.

"Home Sellers Get Easy Out From Caldwell," *Chicago Tribune*, 18 October 1987.

" 'Mortgage First' Deal Offered Citicorp," *Chicago Tribune*, 18 October 1987.

"A New Order of Farm Ownership," *Philadelphia Enquirer*, 19 October 1987.

"Feds Go: A Common Effect," *New York Times*, 29 October 1987.

"Market Jitters Cause Consumers to Reassess Their Spending Plans," *Wall Street Journal*, 21 October 1987.

"FDIC, FSLIC Face Threat of Costly Blow if Stock Drop Slows Buying of Failed Banks," *Wall Street Journal*, 21 October 1987.

"Mortgage Rates are Home-Wreckers," *New York Daily News*, 22 October 1987.

"Another Change in Work for Mortgage Write-Offs," *Chicago Sun-Times*, 23 October 1987.

"Adjustable Rate Loans Appealing to More," *Chicago Sun-Times*, 23 October 1987.

"Deterrents Keep Vets from Getting Loans," *Chicago Sun-Times*, 23 October 1987.

"Slayings Linked to Mortgage Crash," *Chicago Tribune*, 27 October 1987.

"Margin Called at Center Astound," *Chicago Tribune*, 27 October 1987.

"Mortgage Rates Drop by a Full Point to 11%," *Chicago Tribune*, 27 October 1987.

"Treasury Bond Prices Rise as Investors Run for Cover," *Chicago Tribune*, 27 October 1987.

"Feds Pushing Interest Rates Down," *Chicago Sun-Times*, 27 October 1987.

"Mortgage Rates Here Dip: Fixed Loans Down to 11% or Less," *Chicago Sun-Times*, 27 October 1987.

"Mortgage Rates Go for Rollercoaster Ride," *Chicago Sun-Times*, 30 October 1987.

"Stock Fall Rattles Real Estate Market," *New York Times*, 30 October 1987.

"Coming: Caps on Home Equity Rates," *Changing Times Magazine*, November 1987.

"Those Poised at Exit Door Came Out of Market Ahead," *Chicago Sun-Times*, 1 November 1987.

"Juice Loans Flow into Stock Gap," *Chicago Sun-Times*, 1 November 1987.

"Average Purchase Price of New Home Reaches $143,900," *Wall Street Journal*, 6 November 1987.

"FHA Buy Now Can Be As 3-2-1," *Chicago Sun-Times*, 6 November 1987.

"Market Seesaw Has Mortgage on Slide," *Chicago Sun-Times*, 6 November 1987.

"Lenders Get Caught in Lock In Shock," *Chicago Sun-Times*, 6 November 1987.

"ARMS are Gaining Acceptance Among Move-Up Buyers," *Chicago Sun-Times*, 6 November 1987.

"Interest Rates Increase a Bit," *New York Times*, 7 November 1987.

"Trump Casino Designed for New Atlantic City Housing Gains, *New York Times*, 7 November 1987.

"Owning A Home Still a Benefit," *Chicago Tribune*, 7 November 1987.

"Illinois Set Aside $9 Million for First Time Home Buyers," *Chicago Defender*, 7 November 1987.

"Lenders Lock In Interest Rates Before Mortgage Loan is Approved," *Chicago Tribune*, 7 November 1987.

"Home Sales Dip as Mortgage Rates Rise," *Chicago Tribune*, 7 November 1987.

"Even With Bad Credit Reports You Can Purchase a Home," *Chicago Tribune*, 7 November 1987.

"Dual Mortgage to Assist Buyers on Income," *Chicago Sun-Times*, 8 November 1987.

"Home Equity Plan Not What it Seems," *Chicago Tribune*, 8 November 1987.

"Buyers of Expensive Homes Adjust to 1980," *Chicago Tribune*, 9 November 1987.

"Citicorp Prepares Bid for Branch System of Financial Corp of America," *Wall Street Journal*, 9 November 1987.

"Study Hits Lending Trend," *Chicago Sun-Times*, 9 November 1987.

"Bank Board Hopes to Solve Major Thrift Woes Soon and to Arrange 16 Takeovers," *Wall Street Journal*, 11 November 1987.

## REAL ESTATE TAX SHELTERS

### Periodicals

"Gimme Shelter Too," *Gentleman's Quarterly*, June 1984.

"Tax Shelter Architect Who's on Shaky Ground," *Business Week*, 24 March 1986.

"Domesticating the Home Equity Loan: Don't Let Tax Reform Tempt You to Turn Your House into a Credit Card," *Money*, December 1986.

"Tax Highlights," *Changing Times*, January 1987.

"Any Pay Dirt Left in Real Estate," *Changing Times*, January 1987.

"Tough New Rules for Rental Real Estate," *Money*, April 1987.

"Low Income Housing Deals Still Offering Some Tax Breaks," *Financial Products News*, September 1987.

### Newspapers

"How To Win in the New Real Estate Game," *Board Room Reports*, 15 February 1987.

"Real Estate Items Remain on List of Revenue Targets," *Chicago Sun-Times*, 7 August 1987.

"Failure to Charge A Fair Rent is Costly," *Chicago Tribune*, 27 August 1987.

"Heard the Promise of Simpler Taxes? Well, Meet the Reality," *Chicago Sun-Times*, 6 September 1987.

"Balcour Fires 60: Blames Plunge in Syndication," *Chicago Sun-Times*, 23 September 1987.

"A Crucial Trial for Tax Shelters," *New York Times*, 8 October 1987.

## TAX SALES

### Newspapers

"Tax Buyer Wins, Homeowner Loses," *Chicago Defender*, 13 August 1987.

"Buy a House for Only $50," *Chicago Sun-Times*, 30 August 1987.

"Standing Room Only as Tax Delinquent Sites Here Go on Sale," *Chicago Sun-Times*, 6 October 1987.

"73 Tax Sale Bidders Told to Hit the Road," *Chicago Tribune*, 7 October 1987.

## TAXES

### Periodicals

"The President's Tax Proposal, What it Means for Rental Housing," *The Units Magazine*, Summer 1985.

"The Silver Lining in the Wrap Around Mortgage Rule-Free Basis on Foreclosure Under Section 1038," *Tax Magazine*, August 1986.

"Is Syndication Dead?" *Real Estate Today*, February 1987.

"Property Tax Assessments," *Illinois Business Review*, April 1987.

"Tax Reform Act Affects Installment Sales," *Multi-Housing Magazine*, June 1987.

"Answers to Your Questions on the New Tax Law," *Money*, December 1986.

"Current Industries Don't Reflect Stable Real Estate Built-in Tax Advantage," *Real Estate Times*, 16 September 1987.

"Aggressive Anti-Growth Forces Fog San Francisco's Future," *Insight Magazine*, 5 October 1987.

### Newspapers

"City Tax Wallop on a Time Delay," *Chicago Tribune*, 16 May 1986.

"Property Tax Increase Passes," *Chicago Tribune*, 20 September 1986.

"City Not Only Culprit Driving Tax Bill Up," *Chicago Sun-Times*, 28 September 1986.

"Behind Scene of City Tax Fight," *Chicago Tribune*, 28 September 1986.

"Presidential Towers Assessment Hit," *Chicago Tribune*, 17 June 1987.

"Tax Bill Seen As Dark Cloud for Real Estate Buyers," *Boston Globe*, 26 June 1987.

"Scavenger Sale to Aid County Tax Districts," *Chicago Tribune*, 22 July 1987.

"Kusper Disputes Helping Real Estate Investors," *Chicago Defender*, 23 July 1987.

"Over 55 Years Seller a Tax Break," *Chicago Sun-Times*, 31 July 1987.

"Seven Percent City Realty Tax Hike Asked," *Chicago Sun-Times*, 4 August 1987.

"City Short $34.7 Million," *Chicago Defender*, 4 August 1987.

"City Budget Hits 16 1/2 Percent Leap in Tax on Property," *Chicago Sun-Times*, 5 August 1987.

"City Plans To Hold Line on Property Tax," *Chicago Tribune*, 5 August 1987.

"Tax Time in Suburbs as Big Bills Stun Owners," *Chicago Sun-Times*, 5 August 1987.

"Big Tax Hike Called a Snap From Mayor," *Chicago Sun-Times*, 6 August 1987.

"Tax Bills for Many Homes," *Chicago Sun-Times*, 7 August 1987.

"Fewer Multi-family Units Built So Far," *Chicago Sun-Times*, 7 August 1987.

"New Tax Law is Blamed for Drop in Rehabbing," *Chicago Tribune*, 9 August 1987.

"$1 Million Vacant Lot," *Chicago Sun-Times*, 10 August 1987.

"Zoning Board Chairman Resigns Over New City Ethics Code," *Chicago Tribune*, 11 August 1987.

"Probe of State's $1 Million Buy of Vacant Urged," *Chicago Sun-Times*, 11 August 1987.

"City Proposed Budget, Taxes Get Bounced Around in Public," *Chicago Tribune*, 26 August 1987.

"Homeowners Stew as Property Taxes Boil Over," *Chicago Sun-Times*, 28 August 1987.

"Most Tax Bidders Fail to Pay After Tax Sale," *Chicago Tribune*, 2 September 1987.

" '86 Tax Reform Act May Mean The End of Apartment Rehabs," *Chicago Sun-Times*, 4 September 1987.

" '86 Tax Reform Measures Favor Renters," *Atlanta Journal and Constitution*, 12 September 1987.

"Try to Avoid Paying Taxes on Sale Profit," *Atlanta Journal and Constitution*, 12 September 1987.

"Land Costs Keep Housing Souring," *Chicago Sun-Times*, 16 October 1987.

"It's SRO as Tax Delinquent Sites Here Go On Sale," *Chicago Sun-Times*, 6 October 1987.

"Tax Laws Prompt Scramble Among Land Partnerships," *Chicago Sun-Times*, 4 October 1987.

"Mayor Sets Sights on Additional Tax," *Chicago Tribune*, 16 October 1987.

"Real Estate Market Now Favorable Says IRS Top Official," *Chicago Defender*, 3 November 1987.

"Tax Spoil Forcing Family Outside," *Chicago Defender*, 4 November 1987.


## MANAGEMENT


"Special Commercial Real Estate Report, Hot Trends in Office Space," *Chicago Sun-Times*, Fall 1987.

"Real Estate is Big Corporate Asset," *Chicago Tribune*, 11 October 1987.

"Real Estate Men: You Get to Play God," *Fortune*, 12 October 1987.

"Chicago Still Most Segregated City," *Chicago Defender*, 29 October 1987.

"Real Estate Still a Hands-on Affair," *Changing Times*, November 1987.


## REAL ESTATE VS. STOCK MARKET

### Newspapers

"Real Estate Limits Set in Boston Downtown," *New York Times*, 4 November 1987.

"Some Firms' Share Buy Backs Could Hurt Them and Their Shareholders, Analysts Say," *Wall Street Journal*, 4 November 1987.

"Bonds Are Attracting Interest From Investors Seeking Hedge," *Wall Street Journal*, 4 November 1987.

"Racist Term for Wall Street Crash," *Chicago Defender*, 5 November 1987.

"Market Crash Isn't Worrying Realty Industry," *Chicago Tribune*, 5 November 1987.

"Mob Stock Tips: Stick to Cash," *Chicago Tribune*, 8 November 1987.

"Volcker on the Crash," *New York Times Magazine*, 8 November 1987.

"A Falling Dollar Can Only Help," *New York Times*, 8 November 1987.

"Stock Market Turmoil Scares Prospective Tenants," *New York Times*, 8 November 1987.

"What the Bears of Summer Sensed," *New York Times*, 8 November 1987.

"Rate Drop is Viewed as Cushion," *New York Times*, 9 November 1987.

"Survey Finds Sharp Drop in Confidence of Consumers After Stock Market Crash," *Wall Street Journal*, 9 November 1987.

"Crash Doesn't Deter New Stock Funds," *Wall Street Journal*, 9 November 1987.

"An Appraisal: Professionals Ponder Proper P.E. Ratio After the Crash," *Wall Street Journal*, 9 November 1987.

"Some Lenders See Fewer Home Buyers in Wake of Stock Market Crash," *Wall Street Journal*, 11 November 1987.

## Periodicals

"Why and How Real Estate Investments Have it All over Security," *Real Estate Investment Ideas*, 8 November 1966.

"Says RE Investments are Choice over Wall Street Stocks," *Real Estate Weekly*, 25 February 1971.

"Seven Advantages of Real Estate Investments Over Investments in Securities," *Real Estate and Investment Ideas*, March 1973.

"The Single-Family Residence as an Investment Vehicle," *Real Estate News Observer*, March 1974.

"Real Estate Vs. Common Stock is Inflation Hedge," *The Mortgage and Real Estate Executive Report*, 1 June 1977.

"Stocks are the Only Bargains Left," *Salomon Brothers Newsletter*, 7 July 1977.

"Stocks Vs. Tangible Investments," *Real Estate Investment Letter*, 22 August 1977.

"Shift From Real Estate to Stocks," *U.S. News and World Report*, 26 June 1978.

"Real Estate is an Investment in Comparison with Other Investments," *Business Week*, 30 April 1979.

"Basic Metals Vs Basic Shelter," *Creative Real Estate*, January 1980.

"Equity Yield," *Appraisal Journal*, January 1980.

"How to Win While Losing," *Investing in Real Estate Magazine*, 18 July 1980.

"Real Real Estate Equities, Or Higher Yielding Bonds," *Money and Real Estate Magazine*, November 1980.

"Realty Investments Outperform Securities," *Real Estate Forum*, February 1981.

"Bonds Still May Be the Only Bargain," *Salomon Brothers Newsletter*, 8 June 1982.

"How To Invest: Weigh Those Considerations," *Daily Commerce Investment Magazine*, 9 June 1987.

"Realty Investors Earn Easy Money Using Lease," *Daily Commerce Investment Magazine*, 23 June 1987.

"Stock Market Woes Trigger Peak Interest in Income Real Estate," *Real Estate Newsletter*, November 1987.

"Real Estate Vs. Wall Street," *Daily Commerce Investment Magazine*, November 1987.

"The Economy: Down Not Out," *Fortune*, 23 November 1987.

"1987 Need Not Become 1929," *Fortune*, 23 November 1987.

# INDEX

# V

# W

# Y

# Z